DANIEL DEFOE: A CRITICAL STUDY

Encyclopaedia of World Great Novelists Series

DANIEL DEFOE

A Critical Study

Edited by

Robert Hudson

Edwin Arnold

ANMOL PUBLICATIONS PVT. LTD.

NEW DELHI - 110 002 (INDIA)

ANMOL PUBLICATIONS PVT. LTD.
4374/4B, Ansari Road, Daryaganj
New Delhi - 110 002
Ph.: 23261597, 23278000
Visit us at: www.anmolpublications.com

Daniel Defoe: A Critical Study

First Published, 2005

ISBN 81-261-2058-4

PRINTED IN INDIA

Published by J.L. Kumar for Anmol Publications Pvt. Ltd., New Delhi - 110 002 and Printed at Mehra Offset Press, Delhi.

Contents

Preface

Daniel Defoe was born in London in 1660 received a very good education, as his father hoped he would become a minister, but Daniel wasn't interested. He was a very good student, and his teacher, the Reverend Mr. Norton himself, would later show up as a character in some of Daniel's fiction. Daniel graduated in 1679, and by then he'd pretty much decided against the ministry, though he wrote and spoke in favor of the Dissenters all his life.

In 1701, he wrote a poem called *The True-Born Englishman* which became the best-selling poem ever at that time. It was so well-known that he signed several of his later works as The True-Born Englishman, and everyone knew exactly what that meant. Still, it was only a pamphlet, which made Daniel the lowest form of writer as far as his contemporaries were concerned. He also started taking on a few "unofficial" government jobs, most notably an assignment to Scotland. There was at that time a movement to finally unify England and Scotland, a movement which was very misunderstood by the average Scotsman. So Daniel tried to explain things to them calmly.

The first volume of *Robinson Crusoe* was published on 25 April 1719, and it was a big hit, especially with the lower and middle classes. Since that one worked so well, Daniel published *Moll Flanders* in 1722. This novel got him the label of a social historian, much, much later, of course. The point was, the public ate up this kind of thing, and Daniel wrote lots of it. He also worked for a publisher named Mr. Applebee between 1720 and 1726, who liked to publish lives of condemned criminals. Daniel used to go to prison cells and even the scaffold to receive manuscripts for these lives from the criminals themselves. He sometimes goofed up on dates and numbers, but all of these lives are wonderful studies of character and society, though often a bit too heavy on the moral lessons by today's standards.

Daniel wrote on various economic issues of the day, as well as on the problems of long-term colonization and exploration, showing that he really was paying a lot of attention to everything. He even wrote a travel book, *A Tour Thro' the whole Island of Great Britain*, which was highly unusual for the time in that he'd actually travelled to the places he wrote about. He was really kind of a Renaissance man, I suppose, though he didn't quite live in the right time period for that. He died in Cripplegate on 24 April 1731, of a lethargy.

This book gives a vivid account of his life events and critique of his literary works by various commentators on him. Certainly this will be useful and informative for students, researchers and teachers besides the general readers.

—Editors

1

Daniel Defoe: An Overview

The whitest thing in Bunhill Fields, the old Dissenters' Burial-Ground off the City Road, London, is the granite obelisk erected in 1870 over the bones of Daniel Defoe, and newly cleaned in 1949. Nearby in that small and crowded plot opposite Wesley's Chapel lie John Bunyan the tinker and William Blake the hosier's son, and the parents of Oliver Cromwell, and Isaac Watts who wrote hymns, and Thomas Stothard who illustrated *Robinson Crusoe*. It is also, this monument to Defoe, very nearly the tallest thing standing, in 1952, between Bunhill Fields and the gaunt and scaffolded tower of St. Giles-in-Cripplegate, nearly half a mile to the south. Were it not for a projecting wing of the artillery barracks, one could stand beside Defoe's grave today and look almost to Guildhall over the flat wilderness left by the German bombers in the parish of St. Giles, where nearly three centuries earlier the Plague began and the Fire stopped. Spared by that famous conflagration that Defoe perhaps remembered and certainly recorded, all that area he knew so well lies now like a map, with the ragwort and the fireweed growing over it and low walls and fences to mark the streets: Bunhill Row where Milton came to live in his old age, Ropemaker Street where Defoe himself died almost secretly, Milton Street that was once Grub Street of the hacks and booksellers, and so down to Fore Street where Defoe's father man who will be mentioned more than once in these pages. How could one thus succinctly catalogue the other remarkable Englishman who is their subject? Daniel Defoe, Tradesman and Novelist? Turncoat and Topographer? Hosier and Journalist? Pamphleteer and Spy? Dissenter and Public Relations Officer? He was, or has been called, all these things by turn or together. He has also been described (by Professor W.B. Trent) as 'the greatest of plebeian geniuses,' and as the man who established English realistic fiction (says Professor Ernest Baker) 'on granite foundations.'

But there is no portrait of Daniel Defoe in the National Portrait Gallery. There is no original portrait of him known to exist, and it is hard to know how far to trust the few engravings. It has become natural to speak of Defoe's England as we speak of Shakespeare's England or Chaucer's England. But England's Defoe must be conjured up, in his physical aspect, from a verbal description:

> 'He is a middle-sized, spare man, about fifty years old, of a brown complexion, and dark-brown coloured hair, but wears a wig; a hooked nose, a sharp chin, grey eyes, and a large mole near his mouth: was born in London, and for many years was a hose-factor in Freeman's Yard in Cornhill, and now is the owner of the brick and pantile works near Tilbury Fort in Essex.'

Among pen-pictures of the great writers this is certainly of the oddest. It reads like a criminal *dossier,* which is what it is. Defoe was wanted for seditious libel when that description was issued, in 1703, with the offer of a reward for his discovery. And his subsequent appearance in the pillory is probably, next to his authorship of *Robinson Crusoe*, the most readily remembered fact of his existence on this earth. By Dr. Jonathan Swift, indeed, the creator of *Robinson Crusoe*—a resounding success when *Gulliver* was taking shape as an idea-could be pointedly ignored: 'The fellow that was pilloried, I have forgot his name.'

It is still *Robinson Crusoe* that sends us in search of Daniel Defoe, and then in his elusive company in search of his times; a voyage of discovery in reverse, from the Island at the mouth of the Orinoco to the England of James II, William and Mary, Anne and the first two Georges. The *Life and Strange Surprizing Adventures of Robinson Crusoe* was written 'by himself,' the *Journal of the Plague Year* by 'A Citizen.' The name on a title-page may be ' Andrew Moreton' or 'A Gentleman,' 'The Author of *The True-Born Englishman*' or 'An Officer.' It may be D.D. or D.F. or nothing at all. To Defoe's contemporaries the concealment must often have been no thicker than that of calling a rogue a 'r—e' or the victor of Blenheim 'the D—of M—gh.' But if he had advertised his own name—Daniel Foe, later altered to Daniel De Foe—more freely among the three hundred and seventy-five separate works he is authoritatively presumed to have published,[1] there would not have been so open a field for the 'probable ascription' of upwards of three hundred more to the hand whose versatile industry relaxed at length in a lethargy abundantly earned.

From this prodigious journalism sprang *Robinson Crusoe*. When Macaulay in an echoing phrase declared that every schoolboy knew who imprisoned Montezuma and who strangled Atahualpa he may have been flattering his young contemporaries. But he intended the contrary. He was contrasting outlandish and unnecessary knowledge with the general ignorance of more relevant historical matters. With a similar asperity those who would speak at length of Daniel Defoe commonly begin by assuming that every schoolboy knows who found a footprint in the sand and who saw the goat's eyes shining in the inky darkness of the cave. They may be right. Despite the rivals for juvenile attention which magistrates now and then deplore, *Robinson Crusoe* still finds new editions year by year. Pantomime has remained incongruously faithful since David Garrick played Crusoe, with Pantaloon, Columbine, and Harlequin Friday thrown in, in Sheridan's three-part version of 1781. Even the American 'Funnies' have adopted, beside the extravagancies of Superman, this pioneer of courageous commonsense.

That is one aspect of this extraordinary creation. For some of us a juvenile version of *Robinson Crusoe* was the very first book in which we learned to read our own language, half aloud, a finger following the line and pausing in memorable perplexity at the name Xury or the word pallisade. In its other aspect *Robinson Crusoe* is what the Germans call a *Weltbuch*. Its literary ancestry is still debated. Its literary progeny still populates the world's libraries. Its hero is part of our human signlanguage, one of a handful of universally recognised figures that can as easily turn up in a Russian political cartoon or a South American advertisement as in an English pantomime. And it contains a central incident which Robert Louis Stevenson rightly placed in the best company:

> 'Crusoe recoiling from the footprint; Achilles shouting over against the Trojans; Ulysses bending the great bow; Christian running with his fingers in his ears . . . each has been printed on the mind's eye for ever.'

It is almost unnecessary to add that neither of these aspects—the juvenile and the classical—can have lain within Defoe's conception, when in about his sixtieth year, after so many shifts of fortune, he found himself, in Paul Dottin's words, 'peacefully settled at Stoke Newington with but one problem, the necessity of furnishing the booksellers with enough copy to supply himself with an adequate income.' Where he collected the bones of his story will be considered in the proper place, but what he made out of them is something to be clear about at the outset. For *The Life and Strange Surprizing Adventures of Robinson Crusoe, of York, Mariner*, is still the first and best reason—despite the later fiction, despite the remarkable one-man paper *The Review*, despite the *Tour* and the *Plague Year* and the excellent best of the pamphlets—for tracing at this day the life and strange surprising adventures of Daniel Defoe.

The right place to begin is not therefore in the Northamptonshire village of Grandfather Foe, but on the first page of *Robinson Crusoe*: which first page, in any edition, does not carry us very far into the narrative so sensationally promised in the title of a mariner of York *'Who Lived Eight and Twety Years, all alone in an uninhabited Island on the Coast of America, near the Mouth of the great River of Oroonoque; Having been cast on Shore by Shipwreck, wherein all the Men perished but himself. With an Account how he was at last strangely deliver'd by Pyrates.'* We are presented, briefly and convincingly, with the necessary details of birth, parentage and name. We are apprised of the rambling thoughts that early filled young Crusoe's head. After a thousand words or so the boy born in the first sentence has got upon a London-bound vessel at Hull and is running into the terror and sickness of a storm. But it is not the storm that will cast him on the Island for twenty-eight years. We need fifty odd pages of circumstantial narrative before we are ready for the heart of the matter.

Compare this method with another, that of Swift, whose *Voyage to Lilliput* appeared seven years later, in 1726. Lemuel Gulliver reaches maturity and his first ship on page one, starts the voyage that makes the story on page two, is wrecked on page three and already tied down by the Lilliputians on page four. This beautifully athletic approach is one of the delights of Swift's style, and for two reasons appropriate to his purpose. The first reason is that Lemuel Gulliver, unlike Robinson Crusoe, is to be less a character than a literary contrivance for provoking the opportunities of satire. The sooner he is in Lilliput the better. The second reason is that Gulliver's adventures are to be frankly impossible while those of Crusoe, however unlikely, are to be made not only credible but vividly real.

So we are given the warming-up pages, establishing our belief in Crusoe's identity, leading us to a natural and effortless acquaintance with him, introducing us to the reasonable business that took men abroad in his days and gently persuading us—what with storms, Moorish slavers and the beasts and men of the West African coast—that strange things can happen to those who go voyaging. Those first fifty pages are often mutilated in abbreviations of the book, but they are not tedious. Perhaps we come to them now with a respect exaggerated by the consciousness that we are reading the first fifty pages of English realistic fiction. It is what Defoe himself called, with assumed modesty, 'homely plain writing', and critics have exhausted themselves in the attempt to determine where artlessness ends and art begins. It is an easy, enjoyable, picturesque flow of prose that is neither Elizabethan nor Augustan, avoiding exuberance and pretending to no refinement. The homely plain writing in the event found a homely plain audience: a new audience, many think, and surely a wider one than either Defoe or his bookseller expected. A public of porters and oyster-wenches and old women, said the town Wits, who were as fearful as a modern highbrow might be to be caught reading a best-seller. If we call it, less contemptuously, a middle-class public, we shall at once enter upon one of the peculiar fascinations of the life and writings of Daniel Defoe. We seem to be in at the birth of a style and a literary form. Are we also witnessing the emergence of a social class?

Robinson Crusoe's father encourages us to think so. His brief appearance at the beginning of the book fulfils a stock purpose. The wiseacre vainly attempting to restrain the roving ambitions of youth is not uncommon in the picaresque tradition. But what is it that Crusoe senior recommends, and that Crusoe junior keeps remembering though he disobeys the advice? Not merely prudence and *terra firma,* but a precise and positive place in society: the Middle Station of Life, defined as a mean between 'the mechanick part of mankind' and the great and wealthy with their warring passions and anxieties. The middle classes of our own day would hardly recognise themselves in the old man's picture of an existence 'not embarras'd with the labours of the hands or the head, not sold to the life of slavery for daily bread, or harrast with perplex'd circumstances, which rob the soul of peace, and the body of rest.' Even for Defoe's day the delineation is doubtless brightened for the occasion. Crusoe the younger, at any rate, does not altogether forget this sober advice. The restless adventurer in him is at war with the resourceful citizen, and those who have acclaimed him as a typical Englishman have the nation of shopkeepers in mind as well as the voyagers to the world's ends. Finally it is the citizen who survives the conflict, even on an uninhabited island. Is it Defoe's own conflict, his own repentance of the ventures that went wrong in his career, of the bold voyages in political society that came to wreck through a change in the weather or an error in navigation? Nearing sixty, after hazards and calamities and humiliations, does he long above all things for the anonymous security of 'the middle state, or upper station of low life? The author himself gave colour, in his Third Part of *Robinson Crusoe,* to an interpretation of the tale as personal allegory; and the gaps and doubts in our information about him have stimulated the search for such internal evidence. Some of the surmises that have been made are indeed extravagant; but it is not altogether fanciful to feel, as one reads the book, that by the time that Defoe had case his hero on the

Island he was beginning to identify himself with him. The skill of the circumstantial manner beguiles us up to that point. But when once Crusoe is alone, so utterly alone that the narrative *must* either be autobiography or invention, it is Defoe for whom we look in that costume of goat-skins. With the imaginative act of identification which the author was bound to make, if he had not made it before, when Crusoe's companions perished in the sea, the temperature of the work rises to that at which a masterpiece can be precipitated (a masterpiece to some so unaccountable that they have even found a Bacon for Defoe and attributed *Robinson Crusoe*, without evidence or ado, to his political patron Robert Harley, Earl of Oxford). 'An employment quite remote to my genius,' Crusoe has remarked of his tobacco-planting business in Brazil, which seemed to be tempting him to settle down to middle-class felicity. The Island at the mouth of the Orinoco awaits his genius.

It is a testing-ground in which the specimen is to be isolated. In the experiment that has become immortal, the ingredients of Defoe's best-seller combine perfectly. Sermons and narratives of exploration were already, to judge by the lists, the safest money-spinners for the booksellers. On Crusoe's Island we have both. We have also the opportunity to enjoy the inquisitive intelligence that produced one of the earlier of Defoe's works, the enterprising and still very readable *Essay Upon Projects*. The grass-roots of political economy may be revealed under the tropical sunlight of an island virgin to the colonist, where the tools must be contrived before the work can be done; where salvage from the wreck, beloved of every boy, is also the capital for a one-man company; where a device as ancient as the wheel will have to be produced afresh, and where the cultivation of food-grains will be reached, as doubtless it was reached in human beginnings, by observation out of accident. Whatever is sincere in the tremendous verbosity of Defoe's Protestantism will have to express itself in the thoughts of a man alone with God, a man hitherto content, as Crusoe confesses, with 'a certain stupidity of soul, without desire of good or conscience of evil.' And his relations with his fellow-beings must leave some trace, surely, upon Crusoe's solitude, as well as upon the deliverance from solitude through Friday, then through Friday's father and the Spaniard, and finally in the return to civilisation. If Defoe, tossed and battered by the world, had had a touch of Swift's misanthropy, we should know it after reading *Robinson Crusoe.* The fellow that was pilloried could make enemies, but he was no foe of mankind.

Whatever detail or idea was gleamed from Alexander Selkirk's narrative or Dampier's voyages or Knox's *Historical Relation of Ceylon*, or any other Crusoe sourcebook, Friday was Defoe's delightful invention. It may be that Friday was created partly for the literary purpose of introducing dialogue into an account that had to cover twenty-eight years. The need of this device of dialogue strikes one in the debates, occasionally aloud, which the solitary Crusoe holds with himself, considering first one view and then another; and in the voices which speak to him in dreams; even in the squawking of that 'honest, sociable creature,' his parrot. Yet Friday, so inseparable from Crusoe in our own mental picture, is almost an afterthought. He is ignored in the title-page presenting the castaway 'who lived all alone in an uninhabited Island.' Nor does Defoe seem in any sort of hurry to produce this second character. The time-scale of the narrative, so often telescoped by abridgments or in the reader's memory, is noteworthy. Crusoe is fifteen years on the Island before he sees the terrifying footprint on the shore and goes tearing back to what he ever after refers to as his 'castle'—a most veracious touch. He spends two years more in 'the constant snare of the fear of man,' securing himself and his belongings, before he first sees the gruesome remains of a cannibal feast at the south-west point. It is in his twenty-third year of residence, being now well prepared, that he observes the savages themselves, on his own side of the Island; and in his twenty-fifth year, that is ten years after the footprint incident, Friday is discovered and rescued. Only three years afterwards Crusoe finds the means of leaving the Island, having been upon it twenty-eight years, two months and nineteen days. The exact reckoning is characteristic, and so is the coincidence of Crusoe's deliverance 'from this second captivity, the same day of the month that I first made my escape in the *barco-longo* from among the Moors of Sallee.' To match those early adventures there is a kind of epilogue to the First Part of *Robinson Crusoe* in the journey with Friday from England to Spain and back across the Pyrennees in winter, with wolves and bears for good measure of excitement. And already, in the concluding paragraphs, a further volume is foreshadowed.

The Second Part of *Robinson Crusoe* is little read now, and the Third not at all. But we learn something of Defoe's market, as of his literary fertility, by noticing that Part II was issued in August 1719, only four months after Part I, of which four editions were already in print (as a mere operation of publishing this could not be approached today). Early in October of the same year the first serial edition began its run in the tri-weekly *Heathcote's Intelligence*, and Part III was on sale by August of the following year. The comparative failure of this Third Part, the *Serious Reflections of Robinson Crusoe*, can only be called deserved. But the Second Part, containing Crusoe's return visit to his Island, now colonized by Spaniards and Indians, his travels to the Orient and back overland through Siberia and Russia, seems on its first printing to have sold even better than Part I. Even if we attribute some of this popularity to the interest already created by the first appearance of Crusoe, we must still conclude that it was the lively reporting of travel and adventure that made the strongest appeal to Defoe's public.

That element remains, even though the earth be shrunken to a pattern of tarmac runways. And there is the sea, which we are in danger of forgetting in the fascination of Crusoe's island-life. 'I had read *Robinson Crusoe* many times over and longed to be at sea,' is the simple testimony of a seaman (John Nicol) of Nelson's day; and the sailor is bracketed by Charles Lamb with the serving-maid in his relegation of Defoe's fiction to 'kitchen-reading.' Before Crusoe and the tales and histories of Defoe's last decade there is not much evidence of his intense interest in geography and travels, which must have been based on wide and thorough study: but in *Captain Singleton*, which followed close upon *Crusoe*, he not only made surmises of the route across Africa which were confirmed long afterwards, but also 'discovered' the strait called Bass's Strait, between Southern Australia and Van Diemen's Land (Tasmania), seventy-eight years before Bass went there. In his earlier writings the masts and rigging are to be descried, if at all, over his shoulder. He was not much of a sailor himself. There is a probability of one or more mercantile voyages to Spain and Portugal in his young days, but when he was urged to make a venture to Cadiz to recover from his bankruptcy in 1692 he found 'a secret aversion to quitting England.'

A Londoner and a tradesman need not quit England to write of ships and the sea, at all events not if he is a Daniel Defoe. Pondering one of his 'projects' he examined the guns on the *Royal Charles* with an interest worthy of Pepys. The forest of shipping in the Port of London fascinated him: he knew the cargoes and the prices and dues upon them, whither and whence they were bound, and all the language of weather and manoeuvre. One of his enterprises, the Tilbury tilefactory, kept him in sight of the Thames traffic, and he stored up much to say of these matters in the later *Tour Through Great Britain*. Indeed a special feature of the *Tour* is the attention paid to coastal matters of every kind, from the trading-fleets of

Hull to a fight between French men-of-war and an English convoy which he watched from the Lizard. Like his own Colonel Jack, Defoe was 'always upon the inquiry, asking questions of things done in publick, as well as in private,' and happy especially in talking with 'old soldiers and tars.' Crusoe's voyages, the storms, the changes of wind and current, are given us with convincing detail. The impressionism of a later literary fashion is not to be looked for, but there are unforgettable touches—in the *Tour* it is the fury of the sea on the Cornish coast: 'How high the waves come rowling forward, storming on the neck of one another;' in *Robinson Crusoe* a few words, from a pen so prolific of them, give suddenly to the imagination a Van de Velde seascape: 'Our ship making her course towards the Canary Islands, or rather between those Islands and the African shore, was surprised in the grey of the morning by a Turkish rover of Sallee, who gave chase to us with all the sail she could make.'

It seems to have been to some extent due to Rousseau that Defoe's masterpiece, or the First Part of it, came to find that place in juvenile literature which it has ever since retained—not entirely to its just advantage. The book had been known and talked about, translated and imitated across the Channel during the forty years before Rousseau *Emile* appeared in print. *Emile* is a text-book of educational and philosophical theory under the thin disguise of fiction, and the author's own text-book, he tells us, was *Robinson Crusoe*. Henceforward, among the translations and *Robinsonades* in many literatures, more or less pedagogic versions abound. For here was instruction in natural piety and natural science, in self-help as well as submission to Providence, uniquely combined with every innocent excitement. To judge of the pleasure with which a late eighteenth-century father could put such a book into the hands of his son, or a schoolmaster prepare a series of lessons upon it, one has only to conceive of a time when *Robinson Crusoe* did not exist, indeed when there were no 'children's books' at all: for on that shelf *Crusoe* is the first as well as the greatest.

If Rousseau helped to give *Robinson Crusoe* to the young, he certainly recommended it to the European Romantics. From Werther and the Byronic hero and the 'Man of Feeling' Crusoe appears unsentimentally remote. By his very solidity he survives them. Yet the idea of Defoe's book, the central situation and its philosophical consequences, were such as Rousseau could fasten upon with his almost lunatic passion for primitive virtue, strangely and powerfully combined with rational enquiry into the social contract. Through his great influence, as well as through its own, the story of a man preserving himself alone upon an island was to provide morals for misfits. Crusoe's own serious reflections, as a commercial sequel, might remain unread; but a later generation of young men escaped in imagination to his Island and there nourished their spleen against society. With no machinery of government to control him and no church to admonish him, Crusoe was recognizably good. He exalted the stature of man, and by implication placed upon the social system the onus of its justification. Political revolution and literary romanticism both called him brother, while Friday, not to be overlooked, was cast for the role of The Noble Savage.

It would be possible to show, with copious and sometimes diverting illustrations, that all this was very proper. With his Island (not, as is so often said, a *desert* island), Defoe does broadly infer a criticism of a society which had not continuously treated him well; and in Part Two, in Siberia, he gives Crusoe a memorable interview with an exiled Russian aristocrat who philosophically declines the chance to return to court. Crusoe, save for his monumental indifference to sex, is a very human individual (too human, some critics have complained, in the face of dehumanizing circumstances). He does not, like his distant literary progeny, weep aloud in a wild ecstasy on the smallest provocation, but he lets us know for a fact that in an emotional crisis his teeth 'would strike together, and set one against the other, so strong, that for some time I could not part them again.' He knows fear and anger and compassion, remorse and magnanimity, much doubt and searching of himself and going about with God. Before his eyes, after long years alone, an approaching vessel goes to pieces with all hands lost, and he can touch the heart and nerves with a cry: 'That but one man had been sav'd! O that it had been but one!' The sequence of emotions upon the disturbing discovery of the footprint can still attach readers weaned on the psychological novel, though the conflict be played out over months and years instead of in the clouded crystal of a moment of time which has engrossed some of Defoe's successors.

As for Friday, he owes his claim to the title of Noble Savage, as he owes everything else, to his master. If Robinson Crusoe were not a popular hero, a practical Protestant hero to replace the discredited mediaeval hagiology, his servant would no more live in the mind's eye than Ariel without Prospero or Hanuman without Rama. He *is,* after all, a servant, utterly at Crusoe's command. The project of obtaining such a servant had begun to grow in Crusoe's mind as soon as he realized that Caribs from another island occasionally visited his own. In the event Friday responds completely to kindness, as Defoe suggested in more than one of his books that slaves would respond—an idea of some novelty, no doubt, but springing from the desire of getting better service as much as from humanity or religion. In religious as well as in practical matters Friday proves instructible; posing in the process, with a childish and heathen logic, some difficult questions of theology such as suited Defoe's enquiring and somewhat paradoxical temper. He shows courage, and devotion, and filial piety. But he is also a comic—in his daring game with the bear in the Pyrennees, and on the

Island in the drolleries of his conduct and his speech (Defoe was seriously interested in variants of English pronunciation). It is plain that Defoe's Friday cannot be acquitted of complicity in the pantomime and music-hall tradition of a far from noble savage. If we seek the literary roots of the Noble Savage theme we must probably go back before *Robinson Crusoe*, at least to Aphra Behn *Oroonoko, or the Royal Slave*, of 1688, with its superior African hero and heroine, victims of the slave-trade. And for any practical mobilization of opinion against slavery as such we have to wait for the Quaker petition to Parliament of 1783, more than fifty years after Defoe's death—although some lines in Defoe *Reformation of Manners* (1702) have been picked out as a denunciation of the Trade.

Backwards and forwards the bookworms have burrowed, until *Robinson Crusoe* itself is perforated almost to illegibility: back to find a negro hero in Aphra Behn, goats and cats in Selkirk's narrative, the Island itself in *Krinke Kesmes*; forward not only to the *Swiss Family Robinson* and the like, but towards Rousseau, towards the French Revolution, towards the Emancipation of Slaves. Some comment on Crusoe's ancestry and influence is not to be avoided in a book on Daniel Defoe. But there is a question that is more important than his share of responsibility for social upheaval in Europe. As a text-book for Rousseau, as the hero in our own day of a Soviet film, it must be admitted that the endearing figure in the goatskin cap, with his parrot and his Carib servant and his ingenious umbrella, looks more than a little out of place. But as an Englishman of the early eighteenth century, as the Englishman, the trueborn Englishman, as Defoe himself translated from Stoke Newington, and moreover as the sort of Englishman who was in fact translated with momentous consequences to North America, Crusoe is as large as life. The historical perspective persuades us to look back from 1789 to see by what tides in the mind of

European man the pyramidal form of society was washed away. Instead we should be looking forward from 1689 to see why England*avoided* the French Revolution.

To Defoe, twenty-eight at the time and of respectable Dissenting stock, 1689 (or the previous year of William's landing) was an *annus mirabilis.* He became the defender and perhaps even the confidant of William III, trouncing his detractors and keeping his memory green through the hurly-burly politics of the reign of Anne. That he became 'Queen Anne's man' also, after pamphleteering himself into Newgate prison and the pillory, is chiefly the story of the mild Whig Daniel Defoe in alliance with the mild Tory Robert Harley (and then with Godolphin) —a notable story of moderation served by keen intelligence at a time when the country needed both. That story covers among other things the first formative development of British journalism, and here at least there can be no disputing Defoe's impressive share of parenthood. It covers many of Defoe's journeys through the whole kingdom which produced, besides material for the well-known *Tour*, the confidential reports on public and private opinion which have only been appreciated with the partial publication of the Harley MSS. It covers in history the peaceful Union with Scotland, which Defoe laboured to promote and then to consolidate. And it ends with the death of Queen Anne in 1714 and the accession of the first Hanoverian. With George I the extreme Whigs came into their own; and Defoe, who had served, and well served, ministries of moderate Whigs and even of High Tories under the check of Harley, extricated himself from danger by a manoeuvre which may have debased and constricted his journalism, but turned his best powers into a new and wonderful field. His Georgian age was the age of *Robinson Crusoe* and *Captain Singleton*, of *Moll Flanders* and *Roxana* and *Colonel Jack*, of the *Journal of the Plague Year* and the *Tour*, in fact of nearly everything for which he is now widely known. 'It is hard,' his friend John Dunton had said of him, 'to leave off when not only the itch and inclination, but the necessity of writing, lies so heavy upon a man.'

When that itch and that necessity pounced upon the idea of *Robinson Crusoe*, Defoe had a vast amount of work and experience behind him. He had been 'shipwrecked more often by land than by sea.' His voyaging in strange waters had been done (at any rate for the most part) in his library and his counting-house, in dockside conversations, in the reporter's calling which may or may not have brought him into contact with the ex-castaway Alexander Selkirk in Bristol. Defoe sat like Henry the Navigator on his cliff, looking out upon oceans where others adventured. But there was one island that he knew like the back of his hand, and that was Britain.

He saw Britain as it could not be seen from a villa at Twickenham or a vast new country seat, or even from Wills' Coffee-House and the Kit-Cat Club. He knew it, in the first place, as a business-man, a liveryman of a City Company, engaged successively in a variety of trading and manufacturing enterprises; a commercial traveller, also, over the atrocious roads that had for so long hindered economic progress and yielded only slowly, after the Act of 1706, to the turnpike-system. It was failure in business, it has sometimes been said, that made Defoe a writer, but this is a little misleading. It is true that the full flood of his publications can be dated from 1697, after his first bankruptcy and the closure of his hosefactor's business. But he had written before that, and he went into business again afterwards. It was writing that made him a writer, the itch first and then the necessity. But neither his political activities nor the later success of his popular tales could extinguish his absorbing interest in the subject of trade. Crusoe's cargoes and enterprises are enumerated; Roxana and Moll Flanders, quite apart from the mercantile character of their amours, know all about shipments and bills of exchange and capital stock. The *Tour* is rich in information of the internal trade of Britain, and in the *Compleat English Tradesman* Defoe gives us the costume of a countrywoman, garment by garment, and tells us where each was made. Writing about trade, he once affectionately confessed, was 'the whore I really doated upon and designed to have taken up with.' If nothing else had set him apart from the smart literary coteries to which as a young man he had seemed to aspire, this passion for the market-place would have done so.

Yet in the market-place England was becoming a world power. Learning from the Dutch, fighting them at sea, and then in alliance with them against the ambitions of Louis XIV, the English were building up their mercantile empire with the City of London as headquarters. The sixteen-nineties, following the 'Revolution Settlement' of William III, saw the establishment of the Bank of England, the first Fire Insurance Companies, the new East India Company, the proliferation of joint-stock undertakings. The 'middle part of mankind' that was, pushing forward in England as in the Netherlands had the character of an evolutionary force, intellectually adventurous but with a material stake in constitutionalism and stability. Of that middle class, and of the Dissenting community that formed so important a part of it, came Defoe, acutely conscious of the wealth and standing of the new business-gentry. In his writings can be studied, not only the play of economic and political forces which were slowly preparing Britain to become the greatest trading and industrial nation on earth; but also the curious growth of the 'double ethic' which we have since taken so much for granted that it is only now being examined historically —the development, that is, of a separate business code, a compendium of rules for economic behaviour quite independent of any philosophic or theological concept of man. Charles Lamb was so shocked by the conduct recommended by Defoe in *The Compleat English Tradesman* that he could only imagine the intention was satirical. But Defoe the Dissenter and Defoe the merchant are there in the middle of it all.

Defoe the writer has been called an excluded genius, and it is commonly assumed that it was his middle-class origin alone that kept him out of the charmed circle of Wits and Beaux. He was not even, as was Samuel Johnson a generation later, a down-at-heel University scholar. He was educated at a Dissenters' Academy, and it was Dissent more than birth which set a gulf between him and the intellectual aristocracy. This has been well pointed out by James Sutherland, who observes that Alexander Pope was the son of a London merchant and Matthew Prior's uncle kept a tavern. Even the last great poems of Milton had to await their reputation until his attitude to the Church by law established could be forgiven, or forgotten, along with his republicanism. Dryden went over to the Church of Rome yet kept his great place among men of letters, but there was a needle's eye for the Puritan camels who had made such a trampling among the theatres and the bookshops and the poets' taverns. The eclipse of the greatest Puritan is referred to by Defoe in his poetic lampoon of 1702, *The Reformation of Manners*:

> Let this describe the Nation's character,
> One man reads Milton, forty Rochester.

And it was not alone, as Defoe pretended, the superior attractions of the lewd over the sublime that dictated the fashion.

Nor was it entirely a party matter, for the party system was only developing into an instrument of parliamentary government during the eighteenth century. Tories and Whigs, succeeding to Cavaliers and Roundheads, can be seen in an over-simplified view as supporters of the Church and the squirearchy on the one hand, and on the other the commercial and Dissenting interests. Yet whether

Whigs or Tories formed the Ministry, the landed classes and the Church were in fact in the dominant position, pre-eminent in society and setting the standards and fashions in literature and the arts. A Dissenter—even one with Defoe's capacity for teasing his fellow-Dissenters—could not be an Augustan. Whereever one might look for Daniel Defoe in his fifties (and like Colonel Jack's mother, he kept very good company), it would not be with Lord Burlington on the Grand Tour. The whole history of Puritanism and the reaction from it stood in his way.

That the social pattern found equilibrium under an agreed settlement of Crown, Parliament and Church was due, Carlyle thought, to the fact that the centre of gravity was sufficiently low for stability. The gulf between the aristocrat and the mob was not unbridgeable. The bourgeois who prepared revolution in France had other ways to satisfaction in England. Defoe, if he could not decorate the elegant summit of the structure, had some advantage in being near that centre of gravity. He never questioned class distinctions and he spent a deal of ink on the shortcomings of servants and workmen. But he certainly appreciated the phenomenon of fluidity in the social pattern. He delighted to watch the merchant-princes displaying their opulence and putting capital into the land (where it was needed) while the younger sons of the landed aristocracy turned their hands to trade. And the gibes about oyster-women had some substance. Defoe was *interested* in the lower orders. Aubrey had commented upon the widening literacy of the times, and if Defoe succeeded in giving common folk something to read besides the Bible and Foxe *Book of Martyrs* it was partly because he at least recognized their existence. In the years just before the accession of William and Mary he travelled much through the country, investigating, as he said, 'the common people, how they live, and what their employment.' In giving them their kitchen-reading—not only in tales of pirates and highwaymen, thieves and whores, but also in such improving works as the *Family Instructor*—he anticipated the sort of success achieved a little later by Hogarth with his popular engravings. If anyone should have painted Defoe's portrait it was Hogarth, who could conceivably have done so when he was young and Defoe was old. Hogarth in fact is Fielding's artist, not Defoe's; but Gin Lane was produced by the new cheap poison that Defoe condemned, and one cannot look at the Shrimp-Girl without feeling that Defoe knew her kind.

The England whose degree of freedom, toleration, and scientific progress drew such admiration from Voltaire and Montesquieu, visiting us in the 1720's, is still something of a marvel to the historian. It was not only the realm of Newton and Locke, developing that 'natural' approach to philosophy and politics which a terrible French logic was to carry to a bloody end. It was also a tight little island, proud of military and commercial success, conscious (from time to time) of being a leading European State. In the age that produced Arbuthnot *John Bull*, Arne *Rule, Britannia* and *The Roast Beef of Old England*, Defoe was using new and ringing terms: 'Great Britain,' 'Empire.' 'British Sovereignty at sea.' But with his *True-Born Englishman* he dealt racial snobbery so honest and resounding a thwack that two centuries later educated Indians were quoting it against us; and what is no less significant, it was received with popular delight in the England of his own day. In that England there were disease and dirt and yahoos and whipping at the cart's tail. But the general condition of the people, no less than their progressive institutions, astonished foreign visitors. The seal of the period, to a modern historian, is set by the Glorious Revolution of 1688—glorious because almost bloodless, observes G.M. Trevelyan, in distinction from 'the short, fierce, destructive blaze of *la gloire*.' And for forty-odd years thereafter, seeking Defoe in the crowd of betterknown Englishmen, we nearly always find him on the side of just those developments the history-books underline as contributing at the same time to our political liberties and to the enduring character of that constitutional settlement: parliamentary control of finance, for instance; electoral reform and measures against corruption; the subservience of the executive to the judiciary; the safeguarding of the Succession, the Union with Scotland; above all (and despite Defoe's occasional violence in argument) the broadest measure of tolerance consistent with security. Crusoe, when man came at last to his Island, did not contemplate a Utopia, a Soviet, or a Republic of the Saints. He thought of himself 'merrily' as a monarch by right of ownership of the territory:

> 'It was remarkable, too, we had but three subjects, and they were of three different religions. My man Friday was a Protestant, his father was a Pagan and a Cannibal, and the Spaniard was a Papist: however, I allow'd Liberty of Conscience throughout my Dominions.'

Liberty of conscience was a live idea, and the Settlement of Church and State in 1689 produced a climate in which religious toleration had a chance to develop. But the Settlement itself and all its fruits could be destroyed if Catholics could conspire with foreign foes or Nonconformists dispute the authority of the Established Church. Toleration, we know today in a political context, has always this problem and this limitation, and it was one which Defoe the Dissenter saw clearly. The Settlement, in which Whigs and Tories contrived to adjust their differences of outlook in a joint recognition of national necessities, has since been seen as the firm foundation of the constitution which has served us so well. But its permanence cannot have been so apparent to the men who made it and built upon it. It was an English (and Welsh) compromise. Scotland accepted William and Mary, but in a partisan spirit which postponed a peaceful settlement until 1707, or rather until the defeat of Jacobitism forty years later. Ireland, conquered for the new régime by the sword and exploited by Whig and Tory alike, is sundered to this day. The English people who disappointed the watchful Louis XIV by accepting William of Orange without another disastrous conflict, presumably did so because they were tired of civil war. But to be tired of conflict is not necessarily to be sure of freedom from disaster. From the excitements of Defoe's early boyhood—the Plague, the Fire, the Dutch in the Medway—he passed to manhood in a society nervous of fifth columns and aware that it had not yet balanced monarchical with parliamentary power. In the Glorious Revolution itself, swift as it was to accomplish mighty things, there were more chances and dangers than the winds that carried William's fleet to Devon instead of to the agreed assignment on the Yorkshire coast. And in the years that followed, the titles of many of Defoe's pamphlets offer a calendar of public concern: *An Argument Shewing that a Standing Army, With Consent of Parliament Is not Inconsistent with a Free Government (1698); The Danger of the Protestant Religion Consider'd, from the Present Prospect of a Religious War in Europe (1701); The Shortest Way with the Dissenters (1702); Advice to the Electors of Great Britain, occasion'd by the intended Invasion from France (1708); An Essay on the South Sea Trade (1711); Hannibal at the Gates (1712); And What if the Pretender Should Come? (1713); What if the Queen Should Die? (1713).*

That all these and many other writings from the hand of Defoe were directed in some measure against extremist agitation and panic remedies, only illustrates the fact that public passions had been aroused and required to be moderated. Defoe's method, very often, was to carry to absurd conclusions an argument which he aimed to demolish. The most celebrated example of this is *The Shortest Way with the Dissenters*, which suavely proposed measures so violent that the Dissenters were as disturbed at the possibility as the High-Church Party was wounded by the hoax. It is true that when the London mob at length grasped the nature of Defoe's rash jest they gave him a friendly reception in the pillory. But his tricks, and he played plenty of them, made him as many enemies as direct attack. For Swift, settled respectably in the bosom of the Church, the irony of which he was such a master was a safer weapon, worn as of privilege by gentlemen and wits. For the Dissenting tradesman it was always dangerous, yet always attractive; and the propensity to use it is not unconnected with an aspect of his reputation which demands some thought. William Minto called Defoe'a great, a truly great liar, perhaps the greatest liar in English literature,' and the phrase has been echoed again and again. What exactly does it mean?

In its way, of course, it is a tribute. To call Defoe, as a novelist, an accomplished liar is rather like calling David Garrick an accomplished hypocrite. But the theatre has long been accepted as the ground of make-believe. Literature, in Defoe's day, had nothing to correspond with our idea of fiction. There was respectable readingmatter—history, politics, the Classics, sermons and religious treatises and the Bible, voyages and travels, the new scientific essays stimulated by Charles II's patronage of the Royal Society. Beyond these there were the tediously artificial 'romances' notably by the feminine followers of Mrs. Behn, which Defoe despised as a sensible citizen. Fiction, in this latter dress, found serious approval neither with the intellectual aristocracy nor with the sober reading public. Fact was the recognized medium both of entertainment and instruction, and it was fact which Defoe's readers demanded. When it began to be rumoured of *Robinson Crusoe* that the whole thing was a work of imagination (not, be it noted, that it had been transcribed from Selkirk), the author's defence was to suggest that it was by way of being a personal allegory. Allegory might be accepted from Defoe as it had been from Bunyan: but not fiction.

There is thus no sharp dividing line between Defoe's accounts of the wars in Germany or the court of Sweden or a voyage round the globe (as accurate as his sources would allow and as vivid as the method of personal narrative could make them), and a book like *Moll Flanders* or *Robinson Crusoe*. Almost all that one can say is that in the latter the main interest is in the exploits and fortunes of a single individual, while in the former it lies in the events in which the narrator shares a part. To go further than that is to apply subsequent librarylabels that will not fit. Yet we cannot help trying to fit labels. We are content, no doubt, with the superb verisimilitude of the books we call his novels. But we want to know, when we take up the *Journal of the Plague Year* or the *Memoirs of a Cavalier*, whether we can rely on them as history. Objective research proves that we cannot altogether do so, and the notion of the 'great liar' begins to be extended from a judgment of craftsmanship to a judgment of character. A volume on English literature, published in 1950 in a "Teach Yourself" series, coolly declares that Defoe was 'constitutionally incapable of telling the truth.' Macaulay, who had his own turn of persuasive prose, was both tendentious and inaccurate; but nobody ever said that of him.

Defoe's reputation as a writer and a man (and the two are hard to separate) has had a curious and fluctuating history; but the extreme estimate of his unreliability is now much out of date. If the literary convention that demanded the appearance of truth is recognized, the skill and energy with which Defoe satisfied it can be praised. His art as a novelist, it is often said, was to make fiction as real as fact. Looked at another way, it was to translate fact into fiction. Investigation tends more and more to uncover the solid material, in something experienced or something read, with which he built and ornamented his narratives. In a busy and varied career he can have wasted little. A detail recaptured is as bright as new, and it sparkles still for us. For that very reason, perhaps, we judge his occasional lapses from historical or autobiographical truth more severely. The inaccuracies and inventions in the *Journal of the Plague Year* may affront our ideas of historical method. But consider that remarkable work—one of several in which Defoe treated of the supernatural—the *True Relation of the Apparition of Mrs. Veal*. This was celebrated by Sir Walter Scott and other as a work of fiction put out as fact, a brilliant device to serve as a puff for a fellowwriter. It has since been proved to have been indeed a true relation of evidence, a straightforward piece of reporting on a matter of topical and popular interest.

What, then, of those works of Defoe which are often indexed under the general head of 'hoaxes'? *The Shortest Way With the Dissenters* sometimes figures as one.

Another, credibly attributed to Defoe although he disavowed it, is the *Minutes of the Negotiations of M. Mesnager*, which purported to reveal the preliminaries to the Peace of Utrecht, and did so in a light favourable to Defoe's former patron, Robert Harley, Earl of Oxford. They were published—this is the point that nobody missed-at the very moment in 1714 when the fallen Minister was about to stand his trial on a charge of high treason.

Literary or political forgery clearly comes under a different head from the conventional disguise of fiction as fact. If Defoe sinned in this respect, he did so in good company. To take only one example, Swift faked an account of Prior's mission to Paris, purporting to come from a French valet. Subterfuges, hoaxes, deceptions litter the annals of the time. It was said that Pope could not take tea without a stratagem. Perhaps Titus Oates's enormous exploitation of popular prejudices in the reign of Charles II (and of fears that were not unjustified) was too dire in its effects to be classed with the practical jokes for which the Wits and the Beaux held something like a licence. Defoe may have witnessed the dreadful punishment of the author of the Popish Plot, a sight to frighten any political journalist whose manoeuvres might fall foul of authority. He also knew of the elaborate tricks and mystifications—'bites' as they were called[2]—which later kept the clubs and coffee-houses happy: the hounding of the fortune-teller Partridge with reports of his own death was one of the more notorious of these. It was in the seventeen-fifties, after Defoe's day, that wholesale hoodwinking became fashionable, as in the carefully fostered rumours of an earthquake that sent seven hundred coaches rolling out of London to the West. But Defoe may be allowed a 'bite' to challenge the inner circle of the men-about-town in his account of the disappearance of the Island of St. Vincent in a volcanic eruption, contributed to *Mist's Journal* in 1718. The original report, received in a letter from Barbados, proved to have been greatly exaggerated, but Defoe's sensational description had sold out the paper. Assailed by rival journalists he replied pleasantly in the same sheet that St. Vincent was now reported to have been found again: 'but we must acknowledge, we do not believe one word of it.'

That example, as it happens, is from the latter and darker days of Defoe's periodical journalism. His own famous *Review* was by then dead. He was anonymously increasing the popular circulation of *Mist's* and *Applebee's* and other papers, and at the same time carrying out the service to George I's government which has been found so equivocal—secretly directing Tory journals in such a way as to remove their sting. There is a sentence which well suggests the character of journalism in Defoe's time and his own contributions to it. It is on the first page of the *Journal of the Plague Year*, where he makes his saddler-chronicler remark: 'We had no such thing as printed newspapers in those days to spread rumours and reports of things, and to improve them by the invention of men, as I have lived to see practised since.' That might not have satisfied C.P. Scott as a definition of the function of newspapers, but it was not said in irony. The demand for readable matter grew quickly greater in Defoe's day than the ready supply of news; improvements by the invention of men were demanded and provided in the quest for what Fleet Street now calls 'readership' and pursues with at least equal zeal. The Review, of which for nine years the entire contents came almost certainly from Defoe's own hand, stands out from all its rivals: not only for the technique of presentation, enlivened by anecdote, reminiscence, snatches of character and conversation, fictitious correspondence; but because his policy and attitude were those of moderation rather than prejudice. 'The first that deservedly leads the way is Daniel De Foe,' wrote John Dunton in 1706 in his *Secret History of the Weekly Writers*. Dunton had been his friend and schoolfellow; but he felt himself to have been injured by Defoe in the writing business and he need not have been generous in tribute to a man with many enemies.

The testimony of those enemies for long held considerable weight. Needy, greedy Dan, the viper, the toady, the man with a pen for sale, confronts us in the broadsheets of his time. The hooked nose and the large mole itemized in the order for his apprehension were as fair game as Pope's dwarfish body for the hostile pamphleteer.

With a long nose and mouth as wide; With blobber lips and lockram jaws, Warts, wrinkles, wens and other flaws, With nitty beard, and neck that's scabby And in a dress that's very shabby. Who this should be I do not know Unless a Whig? I guess he's so-If I am right, pray take a throw!

That, of course, was a High Tory invitation to those who gathered at the pillory at Temple Bar. But it was not long before Whigs also were throwing curses instead of flowers, when they began to suspect that Defoe's pen was sold to their political opponents. The hunt seems often to have run the other way, and the impression grows that Defoe himself was feared, the more so as his journalism became more clandestine. Never quite sure behind which bush he was lurking, his enemies struck out whenever he appeared in the open, and when he did not they prodded the undergrowth with a nervous ferocity.

Not all the attacks on Defoe were undeserved. But in an age when mud was flung so indiscriminately it is right to ask why more should have stuck upon him than upon others. The commonest aspersion, that of political turncoat, has been taken a great deal too seriously. In an age of trimmers and Vicars of Bray it is clear that Defoe was on the whole truer to his political and religious principles than most public men. He spoke of Dryden (in the *Consolidator*) as 'having his extraordinary genius flung and pitched upon a swivel . . . every day to change his principle, change his religion, change his coat, change his master, and yet never change his nature.' Had Defoe been content to quote the temper of his times in defence of such shifts as he made he could have justified himself as fully as he tried to do in his *Appeal to Honour and Justice* of 1715. But he loved to cover his tracks. The money that he took from Ministers was earned honestly and for the most part without sacrifice of principle. His mistake, for the sake of his subsequent reputation, was to deny that he took money at all. Few preachers are entirely consistent in their practice. Defoe preached a great deal, and often movingly. Lapses about which a different character might hardly have troubled disturbed his conscience and were argued out of it in public. The labyrinth in which he thus found himself assorted ill, when opened by later research, with the candour of his prose. The Victorians lost something of an idol, a martyr to freedom of speech and worship, when William Lee (himself an ardent admirer) uncovered among other things the correspondence with Lord Stanhope, Secretary of State in the fourth year of George I's reign. The fallen idol, exasperating biographers by the necessity of checking his own statements, became for some the man 'constitutionally incapable of telling the truth.' More recent studies have rescued him from this absurd charge and have come to rest somewhere between the extremes. There are no sure grounds for concluding, as has been done in some cases, that Defoe's own story is that of a constant and painful conflict between his fundamentalist upbringing and his worldly commonsense. The further one reads in and about him (even with a consciousness of his shifts of mood and circumstance) the more of a piece does he seem: neither scoundrel nor saint, but with a fair human measure of vanity, honesty, charity, folly, foresight, greed, altruism, magnanimity and pettiness; and with a more than human measure of industry and vitality.

The results of that industry, too formidable in bulk for any editor who has so far ventured his hand, have been whittled down by rough agreement to a dozen or so volumes. The whole world knows *Robinson Crusoe*, if only partially; but it is a creation that exists very nearly in its own right—so that the 'literary critic' of a daily paper, who recently confessed that he had forgotten that Defoe wrote the book, joins hands with thousands to whom it scarcely occurs that the book had an author at all. The fame of *Moll Flanders*, persistent but for a period somewhat furtive, now stands deservedly and unashamedly high, followed at a little distance by *The Fortunate Mistress and Colonel Jack Captain Singleton* has not been republished since Aitken's excellent edition at the end of the last century; but the *Memoirs of a Cavalier*, the *Journal of the Plague Year* and (since Prof. G.D.H. Cole rescued the original text) the main part of the *Tour Through the Whole Island of Great Britain,* are easily obtained in standard editions. Of the works that require to be hunted out in second-hand bookshops, the most sought after are probably the *Apparition of Mrs. Veal, The Shortest Way with the Dissenters, the Essay upon Projects, The Compleat English Tradesman and A. Plan of the English Commerce,* possibly also the curious *History of the Devil.* With few exceptions the tracts and pamphlets are left to the specialist, or tasted in selections and anthologies such as those of Henry Morley, John Masefield, and Professor W.P. Trent of Columbia University, to whose influence is due much of the great interest now shown by American scholars in the inexhaustible subject of Defoe and his writings. Among American contributions the publication of a fascimile edition of the complete Review is of particular value, since the best of Defoe's journalism was previously unknown except by the occasional quotations of scholars. As for Defoe's verse, on which at one stage in his life he would have wished his fame to be based, we are content with the quantitative estimate that he wrote more lines than Milton. Only The True-Born Englishman stands out memorably with the rough vigour of its early attack on racial snobbery. The success of this defence of William of Orange gave great and natural satisfaction to its author, who put out his own collected (or selected) editions in 1703 and 1705 as the *Writings of the Author of the True-Born Englishman.* And it is with a reading of this satire that the B.B.C. has elevated Daniel Defoe among the Wits and Beaux of its Third Programme.

Defoe is indeed the one writer of his time who might prompt a passing reference to so modern a development as broadcasting. Of none of the great Augustans does one feel, as one feels instinctively with Defoe, that he might have adapted himself without too much effort to the age in which we live. He would no doubt have abandoned his versification by now, finding no fashion to which he cared to aspire; and pamphlet-literature no longer holds the field. But there are other fields which he would surely have had the energy to invade; and he would have found a Press, daily and weekly and monthly, avid for fact and for sensation or for a twilit association of the two. In economic, political, military, and scientific affairs Defoe's eager curiosity would not, perhaps, find the climate of today less congenial than his own. If theological controversy has lost its vogue we are not less beset than his generation by problems of belief and action, by encroachments upon liberty of thought, by conflicts of loyalty involving State and Church and individual. Above all he would have found, after the long picnic on Parnassus, that writing is a trade again. The ivory tower, like other stately homes of England, is too expensive and too troublesome to maintain. We are back with Defoe, forced to find a market beyond that of the literary cliques, or with his successor Fielding who declared that he had to choose between being a hackneywriter or a hackney-coachman. We can imagine that Defoe would not be altogether surprised that the domestic servants whom he found so unsatisfactory have now disappeared, so that 'kitchen-reading' gains a new significance and the practical lessons of Crusoe a new value.

In the corner of this freshly colonized kitchen stands the loudspeaker-extension, for we too live in a 'projecting age.' The commerce of words, with broadcasting, advertising, the cinema, and the daily newspapers, is not fertile in masterpieces; nor would Defoe's contemporaries have thought it at all likely that his works would be read two centuries after his death. The aristocracy of letters showed neither indignation nor sympathy when he stood unjustly in the pillory. Only Alexander Pope (and that in a private conversation very different from the tone of the *Dunciad*) came near a shrewd judgment:

> 'The First Part of *Robinson Crusoe* is very good. De Foe wrote a vast many things; and none bad, though none excellent, except this. There is something good in all he has written.'

The technical qualities of Defoe's writing have long been acknowledged. If we turn to him today with a new interest, it is to one who all his life lived on his precarious luck, who sought with admirable persistence an outlet for his words and a living for his family, and found an unexpected immortality. There is nobody quite like Defoe in the literatures of other lands. Even in the abundant variety of English he is unique; outside the main stream, perhaps, but a tributary of capital importance.

THE SHORTEST WAY TO THE PILLORY

With few great writers are life and work so intricately, so intriguingly bound up as with Defoe. Incomplete as is our knowledge of what happened to him at several stages of his long activity, most of what we do know, or can infer, is of value in the appreciation of his writings. The elements of his exclusion have been seen in his upbringing as a Dissenter, and to a smaller degree in his bent for business. But it is going too far to imagine an intellectual solitude comparable to the physical solitude of Crusoe. He was too constantly committed to his own and his nation's business to be thought of in brooding isolation. 'Time,' he observed pointedly in his old age, 'is no more to be unemployed than it is to be ill employed.' If the tinge of melancholy that we find in his greatest work (but seldom elsewhere) was a reflection of his own disposition, then it must seem that he appeased it as Crusoe did, by action. Buoyancy and vigour, courage at its best and bounce at its worst, are what we encounter repeatedly in Defoe's reaction to circumstance as well as in the flow of polemics and journalism that began in right earnest in his thirty-seventh year.

Of the crises that played their part in the direction of his energies, the first was the bankruptcy of 1692. Within two years of that considerable catastrophe he was on the fringe, at least, of the Court of William and Mary. Within six years he had published his first important pamphlets as well as the *Essay Upon Projects,* and held a Government appointment. By 1702 he had prospered afresh, this time as a manufacturer and employer of labour—when King William's horse stumbled upon the fatal molehill to provoke another climax in Defoe's affairs. In the second year of Queen Anne's reign he was in prison and the pillory, his business in pieces, his house and coach and library sold up. But it was after this experience that he stepped into the confidential service of Robert Harley and the new Government. This time, though he would still take commercial chances when they came to him, his fortunes were finally committed to his pen.

The period at which Defoe found himself in royal favour was of some general interest in literary history. Since he speaks of 'attending' Queen Mary when she was planning the garden of Kensington Palace (Wren having just built the south front and one wing), his emergence from disaster and disgrace had indeed been phoenix-like; for the Queen died in December 1694, two years after his crash. The Revolution led to significant changes in the situation of English writers, in their professional prestige and in their sources of income. The foreign king was not himself, by inclination or knowledge, a patron of letters. 'Charles II loved literature without paying for it,' says Professor Beljame; ' James II paid for it without loving it; William III neither loved nor paid.'[3] But William's first Ministers included men who did love literature; moreover the new political climate, in which public opinion was a factor of some significance and conciliation a constant need, gave writers a social and political value that was worth paying for. It is at this time that government appointments, not always sinecures nor always very lucrative, begin to figure in the literary biographies. Matthew Prior was an Ambassador and a Gentleman of the Bedchamber; the essayist Steele secured a succession of posts; the philosopher Locke was a Commissioner of the Board of Trade, Isaac

Newton Director of the Mint, William Congreve Commissioner of Hackney-Coach and Wine Licences; and Daniel Defoe was Commissioner of the Glass Duty during the four years of its operation from 1695 to 1699.

This does not mean that Defoe was one of the literary élite, although John Dunton mentions him in the same sentence with Swift and the Poet Laureate Tate. He was never a member of the Kit-Cat Club, where poets and playwrights, often of middle-class origin, met the new Whig aristocracy on familiar terms. But he had his contacts in political society (Sutherland suggests that his patron was Charles Montagu, Earl of Halifax, to whom there is a letter of Defoe's in the British Museum). And he must have made those contacts, at this stage, as a business man with financial and political ideas. He had friends who stood by him, no doubt, while he was striving to compound with his creditors, and he had prepared himself to take advantage of the first chance that should arise to gain the ear of the powerful. At Bristol or wherever he took refuge, he had begun work on a series of proposals on public affairs which was finally published in 1698 as *An Essay Upon Projects*.

It was, he says, the losses and depredations which the war with France at first brought with it (to himself among others) which caused such a proliferation of ideas good and bad, on every hand, directed to the raising of money. But he goes back to 1680, and to a few earlier instances including Noah's Ark, to trace 'the art and mystery of projecting' and 'the projecting hurnour.' He distinguishes between 'new inventions and projects . . . improvements of manufactures or lands, which tend to the immediate benefit of the public and employment of the poor,' and on the other hand the innumerable fantastic but exciting ideas that were current in his day. Yet he allows that the latter, when occasionally successful, enter the serious category, as for instance Sir William Phipps' salvage of

£200,000 in silver from a sunken Spanish ship. He also exposes dishonest projects, and makes the first of many protests against the excesses of stock-jobbing. This latter craze, he says, 'was at first only the simple occasional transferring of interest and shares from one to another, as persons alienated their estates; but by the industry of the Exchange brokers, who got the business into their hands, it became a trade, and one, perhaps, managed with the greatest intrigue, artifice, and trick that ever anything that appeared with a face of honesty could be handled with.' One may suspect that Defoe had himself been bitten.

There are other complaints in the book of malpractices and business disadvantages of various kinds under which the author had perhaps laboured. But there is a wind of enterprise blowing through it, an exhilarating sense of what it may have felt like to live in a society confident of having more to look forward to than to look back upon. It gave the *Essay Upon Projects* appreciative Victorian readers who saw the springs of their own civilisation glimmering through its pages. In our own day it has still the appeal of freshness and intelligence, and a considerable personal interest; for in any attempt to condense an 'essential Defoe' from the formidable mass of his writings, the *Essay Upon Projects* demands to be included.

The book has separate papers on banking, insurance, the bankruptcy laws, the highways, education, and other matters; and there are proposals or 'projects' for an income-tax, a pension-office, a charity lottery, and a system for registering, almost for nationalizing, all seamen. The extent to which Defoe was really an innovator in these 'particular thoughts' has been disputed; but the force of the writing, the mingling of shrewdness and daring, are certainly striking. Some of his ideas were obviously already in the air in this speculative period. Other projectors had caught up with him here and there during the four or five years between first composition and publication, and the Bank of England was established while his mind ran on such an institution—or rather on an improved version. Elsewhere he shows himself ahead of his time; for example in his demand for a system of good highways to replace the muddy lanes over which he had ridden on his business; in his recommendation for the more humane treatment of the insane (the new Bethlem Hospital had been opened at the south end of Moorfields in 1676); in the idea (scarcely likely to endear him with the new rich) of a close investigation of private estates to make taxation more fair and less evadable; and certainly in the plea for feminine education in the chapter *Of Academies*.

In this chapter Defoe has three proposals to make, and none of them without interest. The first is for a society or academy under royal patronage to vie with the celebrated Academy established in France, so that the English tongue should be polished and refined to appear no whit behind the French, but 'as it really is, the noblest and most comprehensive of all the vulgar languages in the world.' The Defoe who writes thus seems to stand somewhere between the youthful aspirant to polite literature and the creator of the 'homely plain English' of his later and greater period. He wants to introduce 'purity and propriety of style,' but he is wary of the pedantry and affectation that such a project might in its turn produce—'hard words, and long unusual coupling of sentences, which sound harsh and untunable to the ear, and shock the reader both in expression and understanding.' These are the faults of scholars, and he would exclude also from his society such specialists in speech as clergymen, physicians, and lawyers. He had, one would think, an idea of what he was after, but no very clear plan of getting it.

Defoe's second educational proposal lays down the organization, expenditure, and curriculum for a Royal Academy for Military Exercises. He notes the changes since the Civil Wars in the military art and practice, 'which now differ as much from what they were formerly as long perukes do from piqued beards, or as the habits of the people do now from what they were then.' Always in Defoe we meet this feeling for change. 'It is evident,' he says of his own times, 'what an improvement the English nation has made during this seven years' war.' But the costly length of warfare, with its encampments and sieges and waiting upon the foe, might be reduced by better training and a more efficient state of national readiness. He would like also to see musketry as much a natural exercise for youth as archery was formerly. He wants experimental grounds for ordnance and new inventions. He wants the English gentry to take a lead in training themselves and others. How often since Defoe's day have we heard words like these:

> 'It is a great hindrance to this nation, especially where standing armies are a grievance, that if ever a war commence, men must have at least a year, before they are thought fit to face an enemy, to instruct them how to handle their arms: and new-raised men are called raw soldiers.'

The third educational design, that for an Academy for Women, is notable not so much for Defoe's sketch of the form of a suitable establishment (one college 'at least in every county in England, and about ten for the City of London'), as for his advocacy of feminine education itself. His arguments are ingenious, amusing, and unanswerable. How much worse, he wants to know, is a wise woman than a fool? 'Does she plague us with her pride and impertinence? Why did we not let her learn, that she might have had more wit?' Every objection he smites, lightly but decisively. Eleven years before Dick Steele started his happy idea of The Tatler, touching graceful heights with his tribute to Aspasia (Lady Betty Hastings), Defoe had in his own mind the novel possibility of a woman whom to love might be a liberal education, provided that was what she had already been given. One need not dispute the sparkling achievement of the Tatler, nor the reformation in manners consolidated by Addison and the Spectator, to appreciate the significance of Defoe's short and early essay. The first forthright words state his case:

> 'I have often thought of it as one of the most barbarous customs in the world, considering us as a civilized and a Christian country, that we deny the advantages of learning to women. We reproach the sex every day with folly and impertinence, while I am confident, had they the advantages of education equal to us, they would be guilty of less than ourselves.'

The product of feminine education is presented in contrast with its horrid opposite:

> 'A woman of sense and manners is the finest and most delicate part of God's creation; the glory of her Maker, and the great instance of His singular regard to man, His darling creature, to whom He gave the best gift either God could bestow or man receive . . . Her society is the emblem of sublimer enjoyments; her person is angelic and her conversation heavenly; she is all softness and sweetness, peace, love, wit and delight . . . On the other hand, suppose her to be the very same woman, and rob her of the benefit of education, and it follows thus:

'If her temper be good, want of education makes her soft and easy. Her wit, for want of teaching, makes her impertinent and talkative. Her knowledge, for want of judgment and experience, makes her fanciful and whimsical. If her temper be bad, want of breeding makes her worse, and she grows haughty, insolent and loud. If she be passionate, want of manners makes her termagant and a scold, which is much at one with lunatic. If she be proud, want of discretion (which still is breeding) makes her conceited, fantastic and ridiculous. And from these she degenerates to be turbulent, clamorous, noisy, nasty and the devil.'

'It is but an essay at the thing,' says the projector, looking 'to those happy days, if ever they shall be, when men shall be wise enough.' And here is his final tribute to the sex:

> 'I cannot think that God Almighty ever made them so delicate, so glorious creatures, and furnished them with such charms, so agreeable and so delightful to mankind, with souls capable of the same accomplishments with men, and all to be only stewards of our houses, cooks and slaves. Not that I am for exalting the female government in the least; but, in short, I would have men take women for companions, and educate them to be fit for it.'

This sketch of perfected womanhood emerging from the license and cynicism of a male society comes from the pen which, twenty to thirty years later, was to give us those lively and unidealized portraits: Crusoe, independent of women; the gaol-bred Moll Flanders, 'debauched from her youth, nay, even being the offspring of debauchery and vice;' Colonel Jack, who 'was five times married to four whores;' and the Fortunate Mistress Roxana, who was in fact elegantly trained and (set out into the world having all the advantages that any young woman could desire to recommend me to others and form a prospect of happy living to myself.'

Defoe's concern with reform, as suggested by his plea for women's education, chimed well with the spirit of this time. That, no doubt, was one reason why it found expression. It responded also to the influence of the King and Queen. Kensington Palace itself might be thought of as a modest rural retreat after Whitehall with its urban freedom of manners; and the choice of the more grandiose Hampton Court as another royal residence was again in some sense a flight from London and the playhouse and the associations of a licentious society. After describing the progress of gallantry in previous reigns in his *Poor Man's Plea,* which appeared a few weeks after the *Essay Upon Projects,* Defoe proceeds:

> 'The present King and his late Queen, whose glorious memory will be daer to the nation as long as the world stands, have had all this wicked knot to unravel. This was the first thing the Queen set upon while the King was engaged in his wars abroad. She first gave all sorts of vice a general discouragement, and on the contrary, raised the value of virtue and sobriety by her royal example. The King having brought the war to a glorious conclusion and settled an honourable peace, in his very first speech to his Parliament proclaims a new war against profaneness and immorality.'

The peace was the Peace of Ryswick, concluded with France by England and her allies at the end of 1697, and it lasted—but only just—until the death of William and the accession of Anne in 1702. It was a period in Defoe's life when we should have said, did we not know what was to come, that he reached with remarkable speed the height of his achievement: a period upon which he himself looked back as one of unbounded hopes. In his devotion to William's memory, sometimes eloquent and touching, sometimes tedious, there is naturally an element of nostalgia for the good days when he walked with the highest in the land. Some writers have imagined a bond of deep sympathy between Defoe and the King, both slow to make friends, both men of the middle way, not altogether trusted by Whig or Tory, both Protestant in temper, disliking domestic strife most of all on religious issues but declared foes of 'the Devil, the Pope and Louis XIV.' In fact there is evidence of contact only, not of intimacy; and although Defoe. speaks of attending the Queen, it may not have been until the publication of the True-Born Englishman some six years after her death that he actually met the King. It is at least probable that some of his ideas were listened to by the King as well as by the politicians, and it is certain that all his writing during these years was devoted to causes which were William's causes also.

The reformation of society was one of them, but it was not the monopoly of Whigs and Dissenters. Jeremy Collier, whose famous *Short View of the Immorality and Profaneness of the English Stage* appeared in the same year as Defoe *Essay Upon Projects* and *A Poor Man's Plea*, was neither. He was not only a Tory churchman but a fierce opponent of the Revolution and King William, and this gave additional force to his vituperations against the stage and its supposed influence. Like Defoe, he had his experience of Newgate, but the same passionate words in the mouth of a Dissenter would have failed of their immediate effect, which Collier's did not. Defoe had been brought up to regard the Restoration theatre as an abomination, and later on he gave space in his Review to the usual sort of railing against the contemporary stage. But it is not literary criticism, and the drama obviously had singularly little interest for him, one way or the other. The brief reference in the Tour to the monument of 'old Shakespear' appears to be the conventional exception: 'the famous poet . . . whose dramatick performances so justly maintain his character among the British poets; and perhaps will do so to the end of time.' And though there is much to show that Defoe could write presentable dialogue, he was not (as was Fielding) trained in the theatre but in journalism. In the conflict precipitated by the *Short View* he was in no position to take sides, either with so rude a rebel as Collier or with the distinguished Wits who joined issue with him. The immorality and profaneness on which he preferred to turn his pen at this point were those of real life. The assault on intemperate language in particular is one of Defoe's recognisably Puritan activities; but the Puritan dress (at that time often seen as the uniform of a regicide or an anarchist) seldom fitted him very well. He was not wearing it when he wrote the *Essay Upon Projects*. He was garbed as a business-man, a man-abouttown, an official adviser, His Majesty's Commissioner of the Glass Duty. His views on women, as we have seen, are nearer to those of the Tatler and the *Spectator* than to any meeting-house moralizing; and the digression on bad language, in the same book, has a similar flavour. He prettily eschews the pulpit manner:

> 'I am not about to argue anything of their being sinful and unlawful, as forbid by divine rules; let the parson alone tell you that, who has, no question, said as much to as little purpose in this case as any other; but I am of the opinion that there is nothing so impertinent, so insignificant, so senseless and foolish as our vulgar way of discourse when mixed with oaths and curses; and I would only recommend a little consideration to our gentlemen, who have sense and wit enough, and would be ashamed to speak nonsense in other things, but value themselves upon their parts, I would but ask them to put into writing the commonplaces of their discourse, and read them over again, and examine the English, the cadence, the grammar of them, then let them turn them into Latin, or translate them into any other language, and but see what a jargon and confusion of speech they make together.'

This literary view of profanity, though it leads him into pedantry, is interesting in Defoe; no less so when he gives, as an example of what is to be avoided, a piece of conversational small change from the mint of the future storyteller:

> '"Jack, God damn me, Jack, how do'st do, thou little dear son of a whore? How hast thou done this long time, by God?" and then they kiss; and the other, as lewd as himself, goes on:
>
> '"Dear Tom, I am glad to see thee, with all my heart; let me die. Come, let us go take a bottle; we must not part so; prithee let's go and be drunk, by God."'

Swearing, drunkenness, and sundry other misdemeanours were scheduled for suppression through the magistrates and justices. The King proclaimed the policy, and in return a loyal Parliamentary address called for the example to be set in high places. Defoe supported this with considerable verve in his *Poor Man's Plea* of 1698. It is a good radical piece on the theme of one law for the rich and another for the poor: 'the small flies are catched, and the great ones break through.' Magistrates themselves, complains the 'Poor Man,' are often found wanting in virtue and manners, and 'punish a man for drunkenness, with a *God damn him, set him in the stocks!*' Though Defoe, as usual, did not sign this pamphlet there was probably no secret of its authorship, and he acknowledged it a few years later by including it in his first collected volume. He stands in this instance in the somewhat dangerous character of a man of the people:

> 'My Lord Mayor has whipt about the poor beggars, and a few scandalous whores have been sent to the House of Correction; some alehousekeepers and vintners have been fined for drawing drink on the Sabbath-day; but all this falls upon us of the mob, the poor plebeii, as if all the vice lay among us: for we do not find the rich drunkard carried before

my Lord Mayor, nor a swearing lewd merchant fined, or set in the stocks.'

The plebeian who thus talked was later to be rewarded by the mob with a kind reception in the pillory. On the other hand such treatment of the officers of justice may have opened up a short road for getting there. Six years later, in 1702, Defoe was still more outspoken with his verse satire *The Reformation of Manners*, in which individual justices, magistrates, and clergymen were indicted for viciousness in stinging terms and under the thinnest of disguises.

The effective reform of society was carried out, as it had to be, under the influence of men free from the suspicion of Dissent. But Defoe returned to this role from time to time, and more particularly (as we might expect) in his old age. To his late maturity as a writer belongs that pious and once popular domestic manual, *The Family Instructor*, which found a place not only in humble homes up and down the land but also in the nursery of the children of George I. This appeared four years before Robinson Crusoe, which gave a whole sequel to moralizing. Close upon *Moll Flanders*, in 1722, came the dialogue treatise on *Religious Courtship*; and in Defoe's sixty-seventh year, in 1727, when he was writing on trade, apparitions and approaching war, he produced not only the theological dialogues of *A New Family Instructor*, but also 'a treatise concerning the use and abuse of the marriage-bed' under the resounding title of *Conjugal Lewdness*, or *Matrimonial Whoredom*. Again in the following year his *Augusta Triumphans*, a new and elderly essay upon projects, numbered among its proposals the proper care of unwanted children, the prevention of street robberies in London, the reduction of the immoderate consumption of gin, 'clearing the streets of impudent strumpets, suppressing gamingtables and Sunday debauches.'

We shall come to these books later, and to the great human stories of which Charles Lamb, searching for the moral element, was satisfied to declare:

> 'In no other book of fiction, where the lives of such characters are described, is guilt and delinquency made less seductive, or the suffering made more closely to follow the commission, or the penitence more earnest or more bleeding, or the intervening flashes of religious visitation, upon the rude and uninstructed soul, more meltingly and fearfully painted. They, in this, come near to the tenderness of Bunyan.'

The question of Defoe's moral sincerity as revealed in his writings has been endlessly debated. It was raised often enough in his own lifetime, and before he had written his tales of thieves and molls. What, said his critics, about the lay-preacher's private life?

Defoe pointed out more than once that 'the man who has been sick is half a physician,' and he was prepared in serious moments to acknowledge himself not only in error but at fault. But against the imputation of some of the weaknesses that he castigated he did on one occasion openly defend himself. In 1703, in the preface to one of his reforming satires, he declared:

> 'But if I must act the Pharisee a little, I must begin thus: God, I thank thee, I am not a drunkard, or a swearer or a whoremaster, or a busie-body, or idle, or revengeful, etc., and I challenge all the world to prove the contrary.'

At the time of this challenge, one who later called himself Benjamin Norton Defoe was in his infancy. If we are to believe the story, he was the bastard of an oysterwench.

Nobody can be quite sure now whether that story is true. Pope helped to give it circulation, but it came from Richard Savage, the disreputable or perhaps tragic character to whom Samuel Johnson later gave fame in one of his first works. Defoe was nearing seventy before the matter was aired, and it may be more than a coincidence that his *Augusta Triumphans* (1728) had just then made what was taken for a reference to Savage in its proposal for a Foundling Hospital—Savage having given himself out as the needy love-child of an earl. Smarting, perhaps, under what was intended as a charitable solicitude, Savage may at this point have retorted with the story of the oyster-girl and baby Benjamin. Benjamin Norton Defoe, a hack-journalist, certainly existed, stuck to the name and passed it down to a grandson who was hanged at Tyburn for highwayrobbery towards the end of the century. If this malefactor really had in him the blood of Daniel Defoe, chronicler of his kind, then Daniel Defoe had two sons called Benjamin; for his good wife Mary bore him a boy who was thus named. He was her second son, the first having been called Daniel. There were also four daughters, Hannah, Henrietta, Maria, and Sophia. Two other little girls, Mary and Martha, seem to have died young.

It is only in his later years that his household relationships are known to have afflicted Defoe. It must, presumably, have cost him more than a few cares to bring up a family, but we know nothing of them in detail, nor whether he showed himself the wise and affectionate parent whose portrait he drew in family manuals. His constant activity, his restlessness, are well enough understood; and therefore there may be a note of personal regret in his later advice to the young tradesman: 'If he has a family, he will make his excursions upstairs, and no further.' That he made many excursions with oyster-women hardly seems likely—indeed the reiteration of this lowly but useful occupation throws a little suspicion on his detractors. One such excursion, it might be thought, would be refreshingly human in so human a writer. But to dismiss Defoe briefly as 'uxorious,' as a modern biographer of Steele has done, is the wildest guess-work.

The episode of the furtive liaison, if liaison there were, is assigned to Defoe's second period of comparative prosperity, when he had bought back his carriage and horses and paid off most of his debts beyond the agreed amount. This time he was an employer, the owner and manager of a brick and tile factory at Tilbury. It was on the north side of the Thames just in front of the Fort, then a large and strong construction 'which may justly be looked upon,' says Defoe in his *Tour,* 'as the key of the river of Thames, and consequently the key of the city of London.' In the same book he describes the marshy tracts where his brickfields were established as 'held by the farmers, cow-keepers, and grasing butchers who live in and near London,' so his property here may possibly have been a family inheritance. His bricks and tiles, at all events, were good bricks and tiles, if we accept the testimony of his enthusiastic Victorian biographer Lee, who picked up some specimens in the railway workings of 1860. They had to be good to make their way against the Dutch product in the rebuilding and extension of London; and we know of at least one public contract, for Greenwich Hospital, which Defoe's political position no doubt helped him to secure. There are references in the *Review* and elsewhere to this enterprise, trouble with the workmen, and so on, and from these we learn that Defoe was keeping a hundred artisan families and making at one time a profit of £600 a year.

Into his new business went his salary as Commissioner of the Glass Duty, and such presents as he received from King William. The King may not have ranked high as a literary patron, but Defoe had other services to offer. It may well be that his journeys through the country in this reign served the same purpose as they certainly did in the next one, that of collecting confidential information on the state of opinion. There are hints, tantalizing enough, of a high advisory standing, beginning with the 'eminent persons' with whom Defoe had been concerned so soon after his bankruptcy, 'in proposing ways and means to the Government for raising money to supply the occasions of the war.' Somewhat later, being of opinion that trade should be re-opened with France despite the war, he 'had the honour [he recalled much later in the *Review*] to defend this opinion, and give my reasons for it, before the House of Commons and before the Privy Council in the late reigns.' He insisted that the Glass Duty Commission was given him without any solicitation in 1695. In the same year, in October, The *Post-Boy* carried his name, previously Daniel Foe, for the first time as Daniel De Foe, in the capacity of managing trustee of a royal lottery—an assignment suggesting already some public standing.

But there were literary services to the King—some of the best that Defoe ever rendered to anyone. After the Peace of Ryswick in 1697, the cry was at once raised that William's experienced army must be disbanded. The old fear of a standing army as a danger to civil liberties was then relatively new and powerful. We can see its symbolic effects today in the fact that the Navy and the Air Force are in name 'Royal', but not the Army. In the sixteen-nineties there were people living who had seen the Stuart armies in the field, and many who had resented the military power of Cromwell. William had needed troops behind him before the new constitution was settled. Once settled, it was for Parliament to consider when an army should be raised for foreign service. The militia, it was urged, was sufficient for home security without a mercenary army quartered upon the land.

Defoe, calmly and reasonably, cut this and other contentions to pieces in his *Argument showing that a Standing Army, with consent of Parliament, is not inconsistent with a Free Government.* This, and a lesser pamphlet on the same subject, (*A Brief Reply to the History of Standing Armies in England*), appeared in 1698, the year of The *Poor Man's Plea* and the *Essay Upon Projects*—in the latter of which, as we have noticed, he had had things to say about military training. No less modern in their ring were the words in which he now showed that the fruits of victory on the Continent would be thrown away if England disarmed herself on a point of principle while France prepared for the next campaign.

'Some people talk so big of our own strength, that they think England able to defend herself against all the world. I presume such talk without book; I think the prudentest course is to prevent the trial.'

Defoe was not the only advocate of a small regular army with parliamentary authority. Nor, this time, was he the first in the field. A battle of pamphlets had preceded his own, and he was on the winning side. Nevertheless, this is a work not to be forgotten. Two years later he pleaded, in a poem called The Pacificator, by no means above his usual level of versifying, for a truce in the literary conflict between the Men of Sense and the Men of Wit. In the best of his hundreds of pamphlets—and the *Argument for a Standing Army* is among the best as well as among the first—Defoe exhibits himself as a Man of Sense, a compatriot of Locke, his senior by twenty-eight years. There is nothing passionate in it, and there is nothing involved. But the quiet skill in the contrivance of telling answers to exactly those objections which would be sincerely raised; the air of detachment, of talk for its own sake about an interesting and topical subject; the plain man's thought in the plain man's language: these and other qualities led William Minto to write in 1887:

> 'To persuade the mass of the freeholders was his object, and for such an object there are no political

tracts in the language at all comparable to Defoe's. He bears some resemblance to Cobbett, but he had none of Cobbett's brutality; his faculties were more adroit, and his range of vision infinitely wider. Cobbett was a demagogue, Defoe a popular statesman. The one was qualified to lead the people, the other to guide them. Cobbett is contained in Defoe as the less is contained in the greater.'

The plain man spoke again in November 1700, in a tract lucidly entitled: *The Two Great Questions Consider'd. I. What the French King will do, with respect to the Spanish Monarch.II. What Measures the English ought to take.* These two great questions, which had to be 'further consider'd' by Defoe just over a fortnight later, in reply to the objections which in those days got so rapidly into print, were occasioned thus: The King of Spain died childless, and in a death-bed will bequeathed his throne to the Duke of Anjou, second grandson of Louis XIV. Louis was pledged by treaty to make no claim upon the Spanish monarchy either for himself or his heirs, and had agreed to a different arrangement. The first question, therefore was whether he would break his pledge. If he did so, the coalition so patiently built up by William to preserve the balance of power in Europe would either collapse or have to fight again, and that was the second question. If the French King accepted this legacy for his grandson, must there be a War of the Spanish Succession?

The Tories, at this time steadily gaining influence, said no. There was the last war still to be paid for, and England should now be kept out of foreign entanglements and rely upon the protection of her fleet. Defoe, staunch for William's statecraft, saw France and Spain uniting under one ambitious monarch to dominate the world, 'when a French garrison is planted at Cadiz and the French fleet brings home the plate from Havana,' with England's American colonies cut off while the French 'have a free commerce from Quebec to Mexico behind ye;' and French 'pirates' in the Channel ports from Brittany to Flanders. His eyes were on the overseas trade, which was not, as a rule, the first interest with the Tories; and when he tried another approach in the following January it was again unimpressive to the extreme opponents of the war policy, a few of whom were Jacobites and saw in Louis XIV the protector and supporter of the exiled Stuarts. For this time, in *The Danger of the Protestant Religion Consider'd*, Defoe talked of a religious war and dropped mundane argument for challenging appeal. No man, he said, had the right to remain neutral in this great struggle.

If William and his supporters spent sleepless nights contriving checks on the aggrandisement of France, Louis XIV was no less concerned with his Ministers in escaping the death-grip of the alliance that threatened France's northern and eastern frontiers, and in saving his navy and his trade from the maritime menace symbolized by a Dutch King on an English throne. Divided counsels in England helped him. Though William had secured his standing army, it was much reduced from effective strength and the question of parliamentary supplies for a new war (a question which did not, of course, trouble Louis) was in grave doubt. Elections were due in February 1701, and Defoe prepared for them by addressing 'the good people of England' in his *Six Distinguishing Characters of a Parliament Man*. But the tide was still running the other way. Louis disposed of a whole series of undertakings and recognized his grandson in the Spanish succession. The new English Parliament, undismayed, pressed William to do the same. French troops took the offensive by occupying fortresses over the border of the Spanish Netherlands and holding their Dutch garrisons to political ransom. It was dismissed as the business of the Dutch. So confident was the newly elected Tory majority that when five gentlemen of Kent brought to Westminster a constitutional petition on behalf of the freeholders of their exposed county they were arrested.

This was the famous Kentish Petition, imploring Parliament 'to have regard to the voice of the people' and vote supplies for the defence of the realm 'before it is too late'. It may have been a party manœuvre, but it had secured popular backing, and it was certainly high-handed to take the spokesmen into custody. A fortnight later the protests took shape in another deputation to the House of Commons. Its leader, 'guarded with about sixteen gentlemen of quality' presented the Speaker with a paper and the party withdrew. The Speaker was Robert Harley, later Earl of Oxford. The leader of the deputation was Daniel Defoe. The paper was *Legion's Memorial to the House of Commons.*

Of several different accounts of this dramatic business, there is the one provided by Defoe's own *History of the Kentish Petition*, published in August of that year 1701 and hardly likely to distort an event that had so many witnesses. It was a brief encounter between Defoe and the man for whom he was later to employ his pen so busily. And the *Memorial* itself, in a style of indignant and extremely daring eloquence rare with Defoe, may well have stuck in Mr. Speaker Harley's memory. In the House at large, according to one witness, it struck terror. In this document that *required and demanded* a change of policy, we do not hear merely the voice of Whigs out of office and skirmishing to get back. The Kentish Petitioners had been seized for much less, and *Legion's Memorial* proposed that the thanks of the House should now be given to them for their gallant appearance 'in behalf of their country.' Looking at it historically, it is at this moment in behalf of his country that Defoe appears, and in a character different from the tolerant, pacifying, sensibly persuasive rôle that he so often played politically. Suddenly, dangerously, even nobly, he is a fanatic. 'You are not above the People's resentments,' he declares to a House elected in virtue of his respected Constitution yet tainted by the 'corruption' and 'stockjobbing' which he denounced in other pamphlets at this time. And finally:

> 'For Englishmen are no more to be slaves to Parliament than to a King. Our name is LEGION, and we are many.'

Not long afterwards, the House having risen and the Petitioners being free, Defoe was a guest at a banquet given to them by the citizens of London, before their triumphal journey back to Maidstone. The Tories had undoubtedly been shaken. By September King William was in a position to conclude his Grand Alliance with the United Provinces and Hapsburg Austria. It was signed for him by Marlborough, whose military genius was almost alone to save the combination from disaster. And the next thing that happened was the death on 16 September of the former King James II. This was a moment of critical importance in Jacobite politics, and Defoe was at once ready with a tract on *The Present State of Jacobitism Considered*. Louis XIV, alarmed by the coalition, took a step by which he must have hoped to widen the split in England, but in fact it was to unite the people in support of William's war policy. On the very day of James's death, Louis recognized James's son, the Stuart Pretender, as lawful sovereign of England. And in October came a pamphlet from Defoe, his last service in William's lifetime, of which the irony is sufficiently indicated in the title: *Reasons against a War with France; or an argument showing that the French King's Owning the Prince of Wales (the Pretender) as King of England, Scotland and Ireland, is no Sufficient Ground of a War*. It consists, of course (in that inverted manner of which Defoe was a master) of the demonstration of reasons for a war with a foreign despot who presumed to arrange the succession to the English throne. And one of these reasons, pleasantly insinuated, was that such a war would prove profitable, since it offered a chance of laying hands on the riches of Spanish America. The division of the Spanish colonies, as Louis had for some time expected, had been written into the treaty of the Grand Alliance. 'All the news from England and Holland,' Louis had written in February 1701, 'points to the fact that the chief design of the two nations is to undertake enterprises in the New World.' The Tories at that time, who designed nothing but to stay in their tight little island, would have been indignant to hear it. But the French King himself was helping to push matters to the point at which, in February 1702, Defoe could lay before William a detailed plan for attacking the Spanish possessions in America, embellished with his own widely-gathered geographical knowledge. How much in the change of mood in England had been contributed by Defoe's pamphleteering cannot be known. It may have been, as it seemed to him to be, very little. It was Louis XIV's insulting support of the Jacobites that had enabled William to dissolve Parliament and to find the next one belligerent at last. 'Of all the nations in the world,' observed Defoe, 'there is none that I know of so entirely governed by their humour as the English.'

The work that brought Defoe into familiar terms with William has not yet been described. This was the celebrated *True-Born Englishman*, a long poem which appeared in January 1701, ran into nine editions in the same year and was frequently reprinted—not only by Defoe but in pirated editions which he calculated lost him the proceeds of 80,000 copies. Over nearly all of Defoe's verse time has drawn a charitable veil. *The True-Born Englishman* scored its great success in a reign in which Dryden was old and Pope a child, a time of innumerable and barbarous pseudo-pindarics, with Nahum Tate the laureate and Prior the only poet who has survived. The verse is rough, but it has lines that startle by their point and vigour, and it is sustained by a shrewdly provocative central idea. Defoe in this poem springs to the defence of his hero the Stadtholder-King against the whispers and the publications of a rising xenophobia.

> He had what God could give or man desire
> Till pity roused him from his soft repose,
> His life to unseen hazards to expose;
> Till pity moved him in our cause t'appear;
> Pity! that word which now we hate to hear.
> But English gratitude is always such,
> To hate the hand which doth oblige too much.

The poem was occasioned by a satire by John Tutchin, a journalist who was to have more than this one brush with Defoe. Tutchin had roundly stated that it was 'intolerable for a true-born Englishman to be governed by a Dutch King.' Defoe flared up with the withering enquiry: what is a true-born Englishman?

> A Turkish horse can show more history
> To prove his well-descended family.

The proudest of the English nobility could trace their pedigree only to some French soldier who came over with the Norman bastard to conquer an already 'amphibious ill-born mob.'

> These are the heroes that despise the Dutch,
> And rail at new-come foreigners so much,
> Forgetting that themselves are all derived
> From the most scoundrel race that ever lived;
> A horrid crowd of rambling thieves and drones,
> Who ransacked kingdoms and dispeopled towns,
> The Pict and painted Briton, treacherous Scot,
> By hunger, theft and rapine hither brought;
> Norwegian pirates, buccaneering Danes,
> Whose red-haired offspring everywhere remains,

Who, joined with Norman-French, compound the breed
From whence your true-born Englishmen proceed.
And lest by length of time it be pretended
The climate may this modem breed ha' mended,

Wise Providence, to keep us where we are,
Mixes us daily with exceeding care.
We have been Europe's sink, the jakes where she
Voids all her offal outcast progeny.

Proceeding with his catalogue of miscegenation, in language which his opponents weakly replied he must have learned from some 'Billingsgate Amazon', Defoe had no difficulty when he reached the reign of Charles II.

The royal refugee our breed restores
With foreign courtiers and with foreign whores,
And carefully repeopled us again,
Throughout his lazy, long, lascivious reign . . .
This offspring, if one age they multiply,
May half the house with English peers supply;
There with true English pride they may contemn
Schomberg and Portland, new-made noblemen.

In the defence of William, he must also defend the favourite counsellors whom the King brought over with him, such men as Frederick de Schomberg, made Duke of Schomberg, and William Bentinck, made Earl of Portland.

It is all laid on with a will, and Defoe's own admiration for a fluid society is turned inside out to make his point.

Wealth, howsoever got, in England makes
Lords of mechanics, gentlemen of rakes:
Antiquity and birth are needless here;
'Tis impudence and money makes a peer.

Innumerable City knights, we know,
From Bluecoat Hospital and Bridewell flow;
Draymen and porters fill the city Chair,
And footboys magisterial purple wear.
Fate has but very small distinction set
Betwixt the counter and the coronet.
Tarpaulin lords, pages of high renown,

Rise up by poor men's valour, not their own. Great families of yesterday we show, And lords whose parents were the Lord knows who.

The English 'humour' that was to change confusion into resolve at a slight from the King of France, took a swift and enormous fancy to the derisive couplets of their very English countryman. There was a shower of ripostes, of course. Defoe, writing anonymously as usual, had taken care to make it clear that he was not a Dutchman. Fame made his authorship well known, and his resounding attack on English incivility was met by the assertion that he was 'the spawn of both nations, a loathsome thing, shap'd like a toad with spots and scabs' —the mole on Defoe's chin being a favourite item with the caricaturists of the pen. But this was part of the common exchange of literary and political London. What mattered was that everybody read *The True-Born Englishman,* thousands praised and quoted it, Dunton advertised Defoe's name with those of Swift, Tate, and Le Motteux, as 'the great writers of the age!' King William sent for him, recognizing the value of a wildly popular lampoon aimed at his detractors. When Defoe came to publish his first collected writings in 1703, they were put out as those of 'the Author of *The TrueBorn Englishman.'* For long it was his proudest title.

The King had need for such support. Whatever his qualities, the gift of popularity was not among them. Defoe was near the truth in suggesting that the sense of obligation in the nation that had summoned him made William disliked—chiefly, as was to be expected, by the Tories who were given leisure and security to regret the sacrifice of principle whereby they had acquiesced in the Glorious Revolution; but even the Whigs felt uncomfortable sometimes in the presence of their nominee, reserved but strong of will, dark and proud and brooding. Beyond the parties there was, of course, a general national acceptance, disturbed only when some sectional interest, the Dissenters or the City of London, seemed to be claiming William as their own. Defoe had no doubts about it. He was Defoe's King, the Protestant King, the honest, hard-working, god-fearing monarch of all Englishmen who were the same. The quality of Defoe's pamphleteering in these years owes something, at least, to the fact that his basic views and loyalties were broadly engaged. That February day in 1702 when William's horse stumbled at the gallop on a molehill in Hampton Court Park, fatally throwing its rider, became for Defoe sacred to an immortal memory. Throughout the publication of his *Review* the day was marked each year by an article of praise and gratitude. 'Can an Englishman go to bed or rise up without blessing the very name of King William?' One, at least, could not.

But when *William* died, with war just round the corner though not yet joined, there were sundry trueborn Englishmen who toasted, not the architect of the Grand Alliance but the horse which had thrown him and 'the little gentleman in black velvet' that had provided the opportune molehill. Defoe rounded on them, and the seven editions in twelve months of his satire *The Mock Mourners* suggest that he was not alone in his hero-worship.

One of the ornaments of William's reign, in Defoe's eyes, had been the Act of Toleration. By the Tories and the Anglican interest, however, the Dissenters were still, and for long to come, seen as a potential danger to Church and State, and most public offices were denied to them. By the letter of the law, the holding of office required occasional conformity—that is, the taking of Communion now and then—with the rites of the Established Church. Some Dissenters began to take advantage of this soon after the Revolution, quietening their consciences, for professional reasons, towards an occasional appearance in Church. Defoe's conscience, elastic in some ways, was notably rigid on this point, and when in 1698 a Dissenting Lord Mayor of London drew attention by attending an Anglican service one Sunday morning and a Dissenters' conventicle, in full regalia, the same afternoon, there shortly appeared on the bookstalls *An Enquiry into the Occasional Conformity of Dissenters in Cases of Preferment.* Apt as always with scriptural quotation, Defoe found his text in the challenge: 'If the Lord be God, follow Him, but if Baal, then follow him.' Reading the tract now, it seems a vindication of logic as much as of belief—the Man of Sense again. It was not the true Dissenters, for they would not for any reason take Communion, whom he sought to expose: it was the fellow-travellers of Dissent, those politically rather than religiously inclined, those indeed whose existence justified a measure of exclusion in the laws. Such appears to have been Defoe's attitude, but his tract opened a breach between himself and the community in which he had been reared.

That was in Janurary 1698, before the appearance of Defoe's first great political pamphlets. There was no immediate reply to the *Enquiry into Occasional Conformity.* Its offence to Dissenters, many of them upright and able men, who had thus 'played hide-and-seek with the Almighty,' was in the publicity it gave to the practices; and they were probably disinclined to invite any more of the limelight. In 1702, just after Queen Anne had come to the throne, Defoe reprinted his pamphlet.

But with the accession of Anne the wind was blowing the other way. She fulfilled William's foreign policy by maintaining the Grand Alliance and declaring war against

France within a fortnight of her accession. But in the new House of Commons Tories outnumbered Whigs by more than two to one. The Lords were still packed with the late King's friends, but Tories and High Churchmen knew that they had the Queen's favour, which indeed she had indicated in her speech from the throne—a mistake which Defoe respectfully but repeatedly pointed out. She had missed a great opportunity he held, of uniting the nation. Despite her formal undertaking to maintain the Act of Toleration, it was at once put about that 'now we had a Church of England Queen, and the Dissenters must all come down.' The celebrated 'High-Flier' Dr. Sacheverell said as much in a sermon at Oxford, and the House of Commons prepared severe legislation against all office-holders who had taken the Sacrament for the purpose and afterwards attended any non-Anglican service or meeting.

Occasional Conformity was the practice that Defoe had attacked. Now came a Bill against it, tension between the Commons and the Lords, fierce feeling whipped up throughout the country, intemperate speeches and sermons, the burning down' of conventicles, and the foreign war almost unregarded in the excitement. Defoe's contribution was to publish anonymously, in December 1702, his celebrated pamphlet *The Shortest Way With The Dissenters.* This time it was no poor man's plea but the righteous indignation of a High Tory seeking to be rid at last of an intolerable nuisance.

'No, gentlemen, the time of mercy is past, your day of grace is over; you should have practised peace, and moderation, and charity, if you expected any yourselves.' We have heard none of this lesson for fourteen years past. We have been huffed and bullied with your Act of Toleration; you have told us that you are the Church established by law, as well as others; have set up your canting synagogues at our church doors, and the Church and members have been loaded with reproaches, with oaths, associations, adjurations, and what not . . .'You have butchered one king, deposed another king, and, made a mock king of a third, and yet you could have the face to expect to be employed and trusted by the fourth . . . Your management of your Dutch monarch, whom you reduced to a mere King of Clouts, is enough to give any further princes such an idea of your principles as to warn them sufficiently from coming into your clutches; and God be thanked the Queen is out of your hands, knows you, and will have a care of you.' Of course it is ironical, but why should it appear so at the time, when the politico-religious feud was being prosecuted every day in similar, or even more violent, terms? Even today, did we not know the author and the circumstances, we might find ourselves temporarily impressed by the sustained argument. The Dissenters had claimed they were a numerous part of the nation. Here are the answers:

> They are not so numerous as the Protestants in France, and yet the French King effectually cleared the nation of them at once, and we don't find he misses them at home. . . .
>
> The more numerous the more dangerous, and therefore the more need to suppress them. . . .
>
> If we are to allow them only because we cannot suppress them, then it ought to be tried whether we can or not; and I am of opinion it is easy to be done, and could prescribe ways and means, if it were proper; but I doubt not the Government will find effectual methods for the rooting the contagion from the face of this land.'

The ways and means that Defoe would find, in the character of the author of this remarkable work, are presented in a series of bloodcurdling innuendoes. 'I do not prescribe fire and faggot,' he announces, but shortly afterwards observes:

> 'Moses was a merciful, meek man, and yet with what fury did he run through the camp, and cut the throats of three-and-thirty thousand of his dear Israelites that were fallen into idolatry. What was the reason? It was mercy to the rest to make these examples, to prevent the destruction of the whole army.'

The legislative proposals that had caused such a commotion were mere trifling, 'foolish handling of them by mulcts, fines etc.' If the Government armed itself with really severe powers, says the author contemptuously, most of the Dissenters would be frightened into obedience.

'If the gallows instead of the counter, and the galleys instead of the fines, were the reward of going to a conventicle, to preach or hear, there would not be so many sufferers. The spirit of martyrdom is over; they that will go to church to be chosen sheriffs and mayors would go to forty churches rather than be hanged.'

'If one severe law were made and punctually executed, that whoever was found at a conventicle should be banished the nation and the preacher be hanged, we should soon see an end of the tale.'

And with a highly disturbing allegory he approaches his peroration:

> 'Alas, the Church of England! What with Popery on one hand, and schismatics on the other, how has she been crucified between two thieves!
>
> 'Now let us crucify the thieves. . . .'

This is Sacheverellism run mad. But Sacheverellism was in fact running mad at the time. The irony was too thin to be perceived at first (the frequent references to Her Majesty's responsibilities have a most engaging subtlety). *The Shortest Way With The Dissenters* is superb in its species, and a mental refreshment in our own heresyhunting age. In Defoe's day it may in the end have done much to blunt the face of the intended intolerance: and that, naturally, was Defoe's object; for though he could tease his fellow-Dissenters on the score of Occasional Conformity, the smell of real persecution made him a different being. But from his own point of view, *The Shortest Way* was the rashest thing he had ever penned. It raised for him two sets of enemies like the two thieves of his Biblical simile. Once his authorship was known, the frightened Dissenters who had already been peppered by him with one charge of shot concluded that he had gone over to the enemy's camp: or if, on reflection, this could not be so, there yet must remain a suspicion of so brilliant, volatile, and unaccountable a pen. The High Tories, on the other hand, at first applauding the anonymous blasting of the Dissenters and then, discovering the audacious hoax upon their own excesses of intolerance, had the best of all reasons-humiliation—for hating its author.

In a sense Defoe had placed himself aptly between the extremists. The Defoe that we know, with his whole work before us, the sensible, moderate, civilized man who is there under so many disguises, here makes a gesture as convincing as it was imprudent. More than that, the personal crisis which this publication precipitated was in some degree the means of producing the riper author who is still loved and read. Professor Trent went so far as to say that without it the world would not have had *Robinson Crusoe*.

That being so, the rewards of research into these years 1702 and 1703 must be great. The facts that have so far been yielded can be briefly summarized. *The Shortest Way* appeared on 1 December 1702. On 3 January 1703 a warrant for the arrest of Defoe was issued by the Earl of Nottingham, one of the Secretaries of State, and on 10 January the London Gazette carried a notice offering £50 reward for information leading to the arrest of the 'middle-sized man, about forty years old' who has been itemized at the beginning of this book—a description which perhaps deliberately omitted any reference to Defoe as an author. Four days later an order was issued for seizing the manuscript and all stocks of the pamphlet from the printer, Croome. On 24 February *The Shortest Way* was declared seditious in the Assizes, and ordered to be publicly burned by the hangman. On 20 May Defoe was arrested in the house of a French weaver of Spitalfields and taken to Newgate Gaol (the informer's claim to his £50 reward has been preserved).

Defoe had been in hiding for four and a half months. The veil on one incident of that period was lifted by John Tutchin shortly afterwards when he described an encounter of Defoe in Hackney Fields with an unnamed man who recognized him. Instantly Defoe drew his sword, forced the man to his knees and made him swear 'that if he ever met him again he should shut his eyes till he was half a mile off him.' More is revealed in letters written by Defoe from his refuge, from April onwards, to his friend William Paterson—the correspondence is among the Portland MSS published in 1897 by the Historical Manuscripts Commission. Paterson, one of the founders of the Bank of England, became Defoe's secret intermediary with the moderate Tory Robert Harley, then rapidly coming to the fore in politics. But Defoe had already been appealing to Nottingham himself, pleading 'a body unfit to bear the hardships of prison and a mind impatient of confinement . . the cries of a numerous ruined family, the prospect of a long banishment from my native country.' He wished to throw himself upon the Queen's mercy, and offered his military services, without payment, in any troop of horse in the Netherlands; 'and without doubt, My Lord, I shall die there much more to her service than in a prison.' To such and more abject (though not unreasonable) pleas Defoe later said that his wife added her own, gaining admittance to the Earl of Nottingham only to be offered a bribe (which she refused) to betray her husband.

Reading these vain appeals, one remembers the man who two years before had marched into the House of Commons with a document infinitely more provocative, on the face of it, than *The Shortest Way With the Dissenters.* The triumph of *Legion's Memorial* and the favour of King William in the last thirty years may both have unbalanced Defoe. With William dead and his memory slighted, the author of *The True-Born Englishman* had drawn boldly on the most powerful resources of his irony in the preservation of fair comment and of the late king's Act of Toleration; and now he fully recognized the fury of the storm that he had raised. He knew what threatened him. The pillory, Sir W. Besant has recorded, 'was sometimes as fatal as the gallows, and far more terrible.' Ear-cropping had been abandoned (which makes Pope's later dig at 'earless' Defoe gratuitous), but the pilloried man was at the mercy of the mob. Defoe may have seen Titus Oates taken down nearly dead after his first day of the punishment, and in known cases after his time it proved fatal. In the Portland MSS we find these frank and moving words in one of Defoe's letters to Paterson:

> 'Gaol, pillories and such like, with which I have been so much threatened, have convinced me I want passive courage, and I shall never for the future think myself injured if I am called a coward.'

Dreadful as was the menace of the pillory, one is tempted to think that the 'numerous ruined family' may have been an equal anxiety to Defoe, who did not lack active courage. And perhaps the 'mind impatient of confinement' provided the most brooding anxiety of all through those months of hiding that were ended by the denunciation in the weaver's house.[4]

From his arrest until his trial in July, Defoe had seven weeks in which to consider his defence and enlist what support he could. His legal adviser William Colepeper (he had been one of the five Kentish Petitioners) counselled him to admit the authorship of *The Shortest Way,* plead guilty, and throw himself upon the Queen's mercy (as Defoe was to argue thereafter, if his pamphlet were seditious, then so were the sermons and speeches of Sacheverell and the High-Fliers whom he had parodied). But this played straight into the hands of his accusers, who wanted only this confession to proceed to an exemplary revenge. The precise complaint against the offender is a little obscure; Sir Simon Harcourt, the Advocate-General, described Defoe as 'paving his way with the skulls of Churchmen,' a quaint inversion of the literal sense of the tract; but the punishment was all that had been threatened. Defoe was sentenced to pay the crippling fine of 200 marks, to stand three times in the pillory, to be lodged in Newgate during the Queen's pleasure and thereafter to find sureties for his good conduct during another seven years.

Somebody was after Defoe's blood, and many attempts have been made to explain who, and why. In part, no doubt, it was a wild blow at the Dissenters themselves, little as they relished Defoe's complex intellectual exercise on behalf of Toleration. It was certainly also a High Tory attempt to destroy a dangerous man, a champion of Dutch William, a supposed tool of the Whigs, a man with too popular a pen who had offered affronts more direct than that of which he stood accused. But there was another and an important element in this vindictiveness which has been little noticed until recently,[5] though John Dunton's contemporary *Life and Errors* had offered a useful hint. In this book Dunton says of Defoe:

> 'The world is well satisfied that he is enterprising and bold; but alas! had his prudence only weighed a few grains more, he would certainly have wrote his *Shortest Way* a little more at length . . . Had he written no more than his *True-Born Englishman,* and spared some particular characters that are too vicious for the very originals, he had certainly deserved applause . . .'

There are no 'particular characters' in *The Shortest Way*. There are some in the *True-Born Englishman*. There are plenty, and vicious enough, in that versesatire *The Reformation of Manners. The Poor Man's Plea* had broadly appealed for the reform of those who administered justice. *The Reformation of Manners* had been peopled with judges and aldermen, named or nearly so, and charged in a picturesque vocabulary with intemperance, profanity, corruption, lechery or—worse still—the would-be lechery of the senile. It was an exercise, no doubt, in a fashionable manner. But even in a free-spoken age, the man who has dealt thus with the officers of justice would do well not to have to appear before them.

The savage sentence passed, a struggle began to mitigate or avoid it, and in these manoeuvres the prisoner's political importance developed significantly. For one thing Robert Harley was now considering the approach made to him by Paterson on Defoe's behalf, and Harley was a rival for the power of the Earl of Nottingham. Harley, Nottingham, the Lord Treasurer Godolphin, the Quaker William Penn, Colepeper, Queen Anne herself, all were involved in the case of the seditious pamphleteer. Nottingham visited him in prison, vainly trying, it seems, to uncover the confidences of the late King and the Whig Party. Defoe himself was taken to Windsor for examination.

Opinions on the Queen's part in the whole affair vary, but Defoe certainly never bore her a grudge and was afterwards perfectly loyal.

The pillory was not to be avoided, but it could be cheated. The famous episode of Defoe's popular reception in the instrument of shame and torture makes an even better story when we realize that he had prepared for it, though his success may have outrun his expectations. The agile mind and the indefatigable pen that had got him into the worst situation in his life were briskly engaged to get him out of it. While in hiding from Nottingham's men he had written and printed two pamphlets, one a 'brief explanation' of what had been intended in *The Shortest Way With The Dissenters,* the other *King William's Affection to the Church of England Examin'd.* Neither had saved him. In the middle of that month of July when his fate hung on the comings and goings of Ministers and their intermediaries, Defoe published from prison a 'satyr upon himself' in a thousand lines of verse called *More Reformation.* And by more than a coincidence the day finally fixed for his appearance in the pillory, 29 July, was the publication day of two other works, *The Shortest Way to Peace and Union* and *A Hymn to the Pillory.* Copies of these and other writings were on sale in the nearby streets and at the very foot of the pillory where their author was exposed. Both were revised later on when Defoe made up his collected volumes; and this gave him the chance of putting his accusers in the wrong by pointing out that they did not proceed against him for the defiant *Hymn to the Pillory* when they had him fast in their power. It is gallant doggerel, this *Hymn to the Pillory,* but it rises in passages to more than that, displaying both dignity and wit as Defoe first honours the 'hieroglyphic state machine' for the virtuous men that had stood in it before him, and then proposes a catalogue of those who might more fitly be punished. It ends with the celebrated lines:

> Tell them the Men that placed him here Are scandals to the times, Are at a loss to find his guilt, And can't commit his crimes.

Of this audacious broadsheet Professor Sutherland says warmly: 'It is the declaration of a man who expects fair play, and who believes that he will get it from his fellow-citizens if it is denied him in the courts of law.' From his fellow-citizens, as he stood there with head and arms locked, Defoe got flowers and friendliness instead of abuse and unsavoury missiles. According to a contemporary reference, they 'halloo'd him down from his wooden punishment, as if he had been a Cicero that had made an excellent oration in it, rather than a Cataline that was exposed and declaimed against there.' The demonstration was repeated at his second exhibition, and on the third day it reached extraordinary enthusiasm, with garlands and toasts and all the acclamation of a hero. This was at Temple Bar: and Fleet Street, which owes so much to Daniel Defoe, should remember it.

The mob that thus helped him to turn the tables upon his enemies was the same that had riotously attacked Dissenters' meeting-houses and was ready to cheer Dr. Sacheverell and the bigots of the High Church party. That Defoe captured them for three days may have been partly due to the work of Whig politicians, discreetly whipping up opinion in relief at Defoe's refusal to betray their secrets and in hopes of discomforting the Tory Government. Yet however brief, it was a personal and not an artificial triumph. The reckless appeal of the *Hymn to the Pillory* must have made its impression. At the bottom of the whole business, it was doubtless realized, lay the joke that had been played on those in high places. And if such papers as the *Poor Man's Plea* were among the works of Defoe being hawked through the crowd, then it is not difficult to imagine the mood in which a plain, outspoken and plucky citizen was saluted.

Certain contemporaries saw more than that in the business. In the following year Nottingham was out and Harley was in, and the rumour went about, *post hoc ergo propter hoc,* that the enigmatical Defoe, of whom almost anything came to be believed, had been for some time past in Harley's counsels, and his pay: indeed that the whole sequence of sedition, trial, and punishment had been precipitated, if not engineered, for the purpose of raising a hornet's nest about the Government. The correspondence in the Portland MSS, however, with Defoe seeking patiently to secure Harley's interest, makes this impossible to believe. It also disposes of the idea that *The Review* was started in Newgate—as maintained by his nineteenth-century biographers and, less excusably, by some recent writers. Defoe was free by November 1703, little more than three months after he had stood in the pillory, and *before* Nottingham was replaced by Harley as Secretary of State. How much he actually composed in prison is uncertain, though he did assemble some of his writings into the *True Collection of the Writings of the Author of the True-Born Englishman.* What matters more, surely, is first that Newgate gave him the scenes and the people, perhaps the ideas also, that later inspired *Moll' Flanders* and other human narratives of the unrespectable; and secondly that his experience throughout this whole year, the rank injustice of his usage and the shifts that were necessary to resist it, left a mark upon him. He had been in the jungle and had learned some of the cunning of the hunted.

The man who saved him from his prison sentence was, as we shall come to understand, a man whom Defoe could have served even had he not been under the necessity of rescue. After the vain attempt to placate the inveterate Nottingham, Defoe had shown good judgment in turning, or trying to turn, to Robert Harley. That Harley's good offices required considerable wooing was in part due to the complex animosities of the political situation, and in part to Harley's own intelligence. The man who was to assemble the Harleian Library of books and manuscripts was certainly among the first to recognize the political value of recruiting able pens; but the choice of Defoe, a Whig, a Dissenter, possibly eccentric, probably dangerous—was not an obvious one. Harley proceeded cautiously, and by means calculated to ensure an obligation to which Defoe might remain loyal. It was first necessary to convince the Lord Treasurer Godolphin (whom Defoe, incidentally, had lampooned in the *TrueBorn Englishman*) that the writer would on the whole be safer as friend than as enemy. When that had been accomplished, Harley sent to Defoe in Newgate, by word of mouth, the non-committal message: 'Pray ask that gentleman what I can do for him.' Defoe's reply was equally discreet: 'Lord, that I might receive my sight.' Perhaps, at this moment of exhilarating decision, he had opened his Bible and pricked a text, if we may use so sceptical an expression, at random.

Memorably it should have ended there. But there was still the Queen's pardon to secure; and since there was a danger now of Defoe's fine being paid for him by others, Harley stood to lose his gratitude if he did not finish the matter off. Once Godolphin had talked the Queen to the point of pardon, she was generous. She settled Defoe's fine and the costs of his discharge and she also sent a liberal present to his family. They needed it, for the brick and pantile business was in ruins with the collapse of Defoe's credit. He estimated that this meant a loss of £4,000 to him, which may have been an exaggeration. But it did mean that from now on he was to live mainly by his pen.

NOTES

1. See the bibliography in the *Cambridge Bibliography of English Literature.*

2. Cf. Defoe *Fortunate Mistress (Roxana)*: 'Thus his project of coming to bed with me was a bite upon himself, while he intended it for a bite upon me.'

3. Beljame, ed. Dobree: *Men of Letters and the English Public in the 18th Century*; 1948.

4. It is curious how the shade of William Cobbett dogs that of Defoe. Cobbett's 'most famous and seditious libel' of more than a century later, though furiously sarcastic where Defoe was subtle, was likewise an exaggerated distortion of an actual excess—the flogging of the Ely mutineers. Defoe had to hide: Cobbett merely retired to the country, but to await with equal misgiving a sentence which would not include the pillory. Cobbett had shown himself bold enough in Pennsylvania. At the prospect of Newgate and a heavy fine he was prepared for almost any concession if he could have avoided martyrdom. 'Indeed,' remarks his most recent biographer, W. Baring Pemberton, 'it is arguable whether any man upon whom a family depends, is justified in playing such a role.'

5. See, for example, J.R. Moore's Defoe in the Pillory (Indiana University Publications, Humanities Series, No. 1).

2

Defoe and the Art of War

—Maximillian E. Novak

Few lines in Defoe's writings are more startling to the modern sensibility than those that appear near the beginning of his "Introduction" to An Essay upon Projects where he attempted to define the nature of the "Projecting Age" in which he lived. After noting the advances in science that had distinguished the Restoration, he remarked:

> The art of war, which I take to be the highest perfection of human knowledge, is a sufficient proof of what I say, especially in conducting armies and in offensive engines. Witness the new ways of mines, fougades, entrenchments, attacks, lodgments, and a long et cetera of new inventions which want names, practised in sieges and encampments; witness the new sorts of bombs and unheard-of mortors of seven to ten ton weight, with which our fleets, standing two or three miles off at sea, can imitate God Almighty Himself, and rain fire and brimstone out of heaven, as it were, upon towns built on the firm land; witness also our new-invented Child of Hell, the machine, the machine which carries thunder, lightning, and earthquakes in its

> bowels, and tears up the most impregnable fortifications.[1]

There is an energy in this passage that appears to revel in the destructive powers of the new mortars that had created such devastation during the War of the Grand Alliance, and this raises questions about Defoe's seeming insensitivity to the terrible battlefield casualties suffered by England at Landen, Steenkirk, and Namur. We tend to think of Swift's terrifying picture of warfare in Gulliver's Travels or of Smollett's description of the bodies floating in the water at Cartagena as the normative, humane criticism of warfare that might be expected of the best writers of this period. As for the "Art" of warfare, Trajano Boccalini addressed that in his Adivices from Parnassus. A group of scholars object to the notion of applying such a term usually reserved for superior mental activities. Even the butchers protest. The judges decide: "That the Trade of War, tho often necessary, is yet is cruel and inhuman, that 'tis not possible to render it honorable by any fine Titles or specious Applelations whatsoever."[2] If Defoe held different attitudes, we would want to know how different they really were and whether his ideas changed after 1697, particularly when he was writing his major fictional works involved with warfare such as Memoirs of a Cavalier and Colonel Jack.

Even within An Essay upon Projects, Defoe hardly seems like a warmonger. He writes mainly as an apologist for William III. Returning to his praise of the advances made in the technology of warfare, in the proposal for a military academy ("the most noble and most useful proposal in this book" [133]) Defoe defends William for recruiting foreign officers for the English army. He did so, Defoe argues, only because most Englishmen lacked the skill needed to conduct the new warfare that emerged during the War of the Grand Alliance. As for the war itself, Defoe acknowledges that William had led England into "the bloodiest war this age has known" (134). How was the spilling of so much blood to be defended? Some recent critics have praised the Jacobite position on William as a lover of war and a tyrant, showering accolades upon Dryden for his supposed detestation of war and his opposition to the military ventures of William.[3] Were the twenty-four years of warfare between 1689 and 1713 as silly and futile as Southey's famous poem on Blenheim would suggest? I would like to suggest that it was not, but this is an essay on Defoe and not a general discussion of warfare during the period.[4] Here I want to examine the dominant attitude toward war during this period through an analysis of Defoe's interest in what he called the "art of war"; and secondly, I want to glance at a few of his more striking depictions of warfare to see what they reveal.

First of all we have to avoid glorifying Jacobite propaganda against the War of the Grand Alliance and the War of the Spanish Succession as if it were a forerunner of the movement for peace in America during the time of the Vietnam War. Dryden's favorite prince, James II, then Duke of York, was the subject of Dryden's adulation in Annus Mirabilis, a poem in which he glorified the destruction of the Dutch fleet and its sailors. His major aim as a poet was to write an epic which exalted the military exploits of his subjects. Dryden's depiction of William III as a bloodthirsty tyrant in his poems, plays, and prefaces composed after the Glorious Revolution was little more than name calling by a poet who had lost the prestige and power that he had under James.[5] And like most Jacobites, he seems to have been ready to endure the slaughter that surely would have ensued were James to attempt an invasion of England. Since there was some danger in overt attacks upon William III and his government, Dryden and his fellow Jacobites carried on a subtle political warfare, putting forward the cause of James II on every possible occasion through parallels, fictions, and fables. They were not opposed to war. They merely wanted a different government ruling England and used dissatisfaction with the war as a satiric weapon. Andre Corvisier says of European society in the time of Defoe that it still recognized the practice of the arts of warfare as the highest form of human activity aside from religious worship.[6] This was not entirely true of England, but many regarded William as a genuine military hero and admired his attempt to restore English pride in the military, which had never recovered entirely from the Civil War. As for a truly pacifist stance, it must have been limited to the Quakers and a few other sects. Both the belief in a right to self-preservation that formed the basis of the social contract among the proponents of natural law and the glorification of the nation and its monarch favored by adherents of absolute monarchy viewed war as a necessary part of contemporary political existence.

Defoe's advocacy for a military academy in his Essay upon Projects was certainly political. Although never acknowledged, it represented what may be the earliest document in the Standing Army Controversy that was to burgeon over the next two years. Its publication coincided with the rumors about a peace throughout 1696, rumors that took palpable form through the Treaty of Ryswyk in 1697. A military academy presupposes the existence of some kind of standing army, and Defoe was to repeat a number of his arguments from this section of An Essay upon Projects in his tracts supporting a standing army written during 1697 and 1698 As John Keegan has suggested, the kind of discipline provided by regular regiments represented a dramatic change in the warfare of the eighteenth century.[7] The arguments of the Classical Republicans may have won a political victory at the time, since William's army was almost completely disbanded by Parliament, but the regiments established under William were a major force in winning the spectacular victories of the War of the Spanish Succession. If Defoe's contact with William III at this time may have been exaggerated by some biographers, it is nevertheless true that he was writing as a Court Whig, recently in the employ of the government. And if he needed any other political motivation, he would naturally have supported any war against Louis XIV whose persecution of Protestants, particularly the Huguenots, was a shaping element in his view of the English government's treatment of the Dissenters.

Defoe suggests that experiments conducted by his military "colleges" ought to be published in the same manner as the experiments of the Royal Society, yet despite his emphasis on a curriculum that would stress mathematics and the particular arts of contemporary warfare and despite the interests of members of the Royal Society such as John Evelyn in Defoe's Child of Hell" (32), the new, powerful mortars that were used in the War of the Grand Alliance, it would probably be a mistake to overemphasize the scientific side of Defoe's interest in warfare. True enough, he was fascinated by explosions, whether those caused by gasses in wines or in the eruptions of volcanoes. He frequently offered what he considered to be scientific reasons for such events, but as Corvisier suggests, the populace of the times loved to hear the roar of cannons. Defoe's fascination seems to have been at least partly pure wonder.

This element of wonder emerges in Defoe's occasional tendency to romanticize the role of the soldier. He does so despite framing his depiction within boundaries that acknowledged the horrors and hardships of war. In An Essay at Removing National Prejudices against a Union with Scotland (1706), he conjured up one of his many scenes that attempt verbally what Jacques Callot had etched so brilliantly in Les miseres et les mal-heurs de la guerre (1633), describing "the Groans of the murther'd innocents, the Cries of the Widows and Mothers for their Husbands and Children, the Despair of flourishing

Families, ruin'd and undone; with their Fields over run, the Barns and houses plunder'd and burnt, their Cattle driven away, and their whole Substance destroy'd."[8] He often refers to soldiering as a "Trade" or "Profession," to courage as mere habituation to danger— something learned with time, and to modern war as a contest won by the longest purse. And he devoted three issues of the Review for October 1709 to illustrating the ways in which plague, famine, and blood were the inevitable consequences of combat.

But his admiration for the military hero—Gustavus Adolphus, William III, and Marlborough—was genuine enough. It is even apparent in Historical Collections, the selections from his childhood readings he presented to his future wife, Mary Tuffley. There, the military hero, whether Alexander the Great or Gustavus Adolphus and his followers, have a surprisingly large role. Defoe's offer to go as a volunteer to Flanders with a "troop of horse" and lead them against the French in the War of the Spanish Succession as an alternative to a prison sentence for having written The Shortest Way with the Dissenters, does not sound like the bargaining of a Cornhill tradesman, as Defoe's most recent biographer has suggested, so much as the decision of a man who saw himself as a potential soldier.[9] That he had ridden out of London to fight with the Duke of Monmouth in 1685, seems quixotic enough in a tradesman of twenty-five; that he should offer to do much the same at the age of forty-three suggests how deeply this self-conception was part of his character. Frank Bastian may have had difficulty providing the factual evidence for a Defoe who fought duels and dealt with pirates, but he did capture an important fantasy element in his personality.[10]

Whether this side of Defoe was restricted mainly to his fantasy life or not, he was certainly knowledgeable about various aspects of warfare. In his recent book on

King William's armies, John Childs quotes Defoe at length as providing the best description of the new kind of Warfare waged by Uncle Toby's "prodigious armies" in Flanders.[11] In his Essay upon Projects, Defoe contrasted contemporary methods to the violence inherent in warfare during England's civil war:

> We saw in England a bloody civil war, where, according to the old temper of the English fighting was the business. To have an army lying such a post as not to be able to come at them was a thing never heard of in that war; even the weakest party would always come out and fight—Dunbar fight, for instance; and they that were beaten today would fight again to-morrow, and seek one another out with such eagerness, as if they had been in haste to have their brains knocked out. Encampments, intrenchments, batteries, counter-marchings, fortifying of camps, and cannonadings were strange and almost unknown things, and whole campaigns were passed over and hardly any tents made use of.... now it is frequent to have armies of fifty thousand men of a side stand at bay within view of one another, and spend a whole campaign in dodging, or, as it is genteelly called, observing one another, and then march off into winter quarters. The difference is in the maxims of war, which now differ as much from what they were formerly as long perukes do from piqued beards, or as the habits of the people do now from what they then were. The present maxims of war are—Never fight without a manifest advantage And always encamp so as not to be forced to it. (134-35)

Although it was through such tactics that William Ill managed to hold his army together during the War of the Grand Alliance, Defoe's later praise for Marlborough as a general who did not hesitate to engage the enemy suggests that he had some misgivings about the new "maxims" of war.

Despite the cogency of his observations on warfare, it was as an effective writer about war, rather than as an early version of Von Clauswitz, that Defoe was to make his mark. Even before composing the military accounts in his memoirs and novels, Defoe gave special care to his accounts of battle. In his lively but shortlived journal, Master Mercury, he gave a brilliant account of Marlborough's victory at Blenheim, showing how he turned the tide at a time when the forces seemed to have fought to a standstill:

> . . . and thus the whole Armies were Engag'd with inexpressible Violence on every side: when the Duke of Marlborough finding all parts in a very good Condition, at the head of a great Body of Infantry, broke into the Centre, parted the two Armies; and falling with a Fury not to be resisted on the Horse of Marshal Tallards Left, put them into Confusion, and pushed them to the Rear of their infantry; who thus abandoned by their Horse were soon disorder'd, and then follow'd a terrible Slaughter, the Horse were pushed to that Extremity, that 30 Squadrons took [to] the Danube in the utmost Confusion, where very few of them escap'd.

All the Infantry that could make any Retreat rallyed in a Village which was in the Rear, where tho' they were surrounded by the English Army, and Charg'd on every side, they made a desperate Defence, till seeing the Cannon brought against them, they threw down their Arms and yielded at discretion; these amounted to 27 entire Battallions and 12 Squadrons of Dragoons.[12]

It is hardly necessary to point out how Defoe's style—his sentences that run on without stop until the end of the paragraph, his strong emphasis on verbs and verbals, his concreteness— lend to the description the feeling of men, horses, and cannon in violent motion. Words like "Fury," "desperate," and "Confusion" give the image of battle as a time of men functioning under the most extreme conditions, while, in Defoe's typical manner, he suggests that the events are beyond the power of words to describe. One element that is missing, interestingly enough, is the description of individual soldiers actually killing one another. The French cavalry forced into the Danube seem to disappear from the page as surely as they disappeared from life. Also notable is the relatively impartial point of view. While he celebrates England's victory in the separate "Reflector" section of this journal, his account also praises the bravery of the Duke of Bavaria and the French generals. Defoe had already mastered the trick of using a variety of angles of vision when describing an event. It was an ability he was to put to good use in his major fiction.

The narrators of Memoirs of a Cavalier and Colonel Jack strive for a certain objectivity, but both are partisans of what was, for Defoe, the wrong side. It was as if Defoe found his imagination most engaged when he assumed the role of a narrator very different from himself. The narrator of Memoirs of a Cavalier, of course, begins on the right side as an officer with the forces of Gustavus Adolphus in the Thirty Years War. It is the discipline of the forces under Gustavus (the famous "Swedish Discipline"[13]) that attracts him when he is still a neutral observer seeking a cause. He is horrified at the sacking of Magdenburg, describing it as

> . . . the dreadfullest Sight that ever I saw; the Rage of the Imperial Soldiers was most intolerable and not to be expressed; of 25,000, some said 30000 People, there was not a Soul to be seen alive, till the Flames drove those that were hid in Vaults and secret Places to seek Death in the Streets rather

> than perish in the Fire: . . . on a sudden I heard the dreadfullest Cry raised in the City than can be imagined, 'tis not possible to express the Manner of it, and I could see the Women and Children running about the Streets in the most lamentable Condition . . . In about an Hour's Time after this first Cry all was Confusion there was little shooting, the Execution was all cutting of Throats and meer House Murthers.[14] (44-45)

Magdenburg was a city under siege that had refused to surrender, and there were some writers on natural law and on the laws of war who accepted a degree of violence from the victors under these conditions, but the horrors that occurred after Tilly's troops entered shocked the sensibilities of the age.[15] Defoe's description is similar to those in his Journal of the Plague Year where the bodies of the victims are flung into the pits in a seemingly universal reign of death, and the phrase, "meer House Murthers," suggests something outside of war—the kind of murder committed by a group of ruffians who enter a house searching for booty and kill the inhabitants. It also hints at the disintegration of the army into individual criminals unrestrained by either law or discipline. Of similar import is his reference to this event as an "Execution." If the individual soldier behaved like a criminal; so the Emperor's officers, instead of being directed by some of the laws of warfare, behaved as if the inhabitants of Magdenburg were all malefactors to be subjected to the revenge of the offended Imperial state.

The sacking of Magdenburg, incidentally, plays a role in "The Farther adventures of Robinson Crusoe," for when Crusoe's crew decides to take revenge against a native village, they murder and burn in a manner that reminds Crusoe of this event.

> I never was at the sacking a City, or at the taking a Town by storm. I had heard of "Oliver Cromwell" taking "Drogheda" in "Ireland", and killing Man, Woman and Child. And I had read of Count "Tilly", sacking of the City of "Magdeburgh", and cutting the throats of 22000 of all Sexes: But I never had an Idea of the Thing itself before, nor is it possible to describe it, or the Horror which was upon our Minds at hearing it.[16] (3:95-96)

Defoe recognizes that such events occur during warfare, but they are part of the violence that humankind experiences in nature. From this standpoint, even the animals who attack Crusoe in the Pyrenees were capable of a kind of military order. Defoe did not disagree with Hobbes on the matter of the state of nature being a state of war. Crusoe's crew, like the soldier's in Tilly's army, revert to a state of brutality, killing everyone in sight, burning every structure. But this is not what Defoe thinks of as the "art" of warfare.[17]

In contrast to such uncontrolled violence, the Cavalier admires the "Discipline and Order" of the Swedish Troops. Although the Cavalier points to the mixing of infantry with cavalry as an innovation of the armies of Gustavus Adolphus, it is the balance and control that impresses him:

> I never saw an Army drawn up with so much Variety, Order, and exact Regularity since, tho' I have seen many Armies drawn up by some of the greatest Captains of the Age; the order by which his Men were directed to flank and relieve one another, the methods of receiving one Body of Men if disordered into another, and rally one Squadron without disordering another was so admirable; the Horse every where flank'd, lin'd and defended by the Foot, and the Foot by the horse, and both by

> the Cannon, was such that if those orders were but as punctually obey'd, 'twere impossible to put an Army so modell'd into any Confusion. (54)

During the civil war, the Cavalier fights alongside Prince Rupert whose forceful but undisciplined charges succeed in breaking the lines of the enemy. Unfortunately for the King's forces, these cavalry charges carried Rupert's men off the battlefield in a futile pursuit, while the battle was lost.

In his oblique manner, Defoe actually indulges in a praise of the Parliamentary army and of the "Swedish Discipline" which formed the model for the army of saints that governed England during the interegnum. Michael Walzer's book, The Revolution of the Saints stresses the relationship between the "military revolution" that took place during the seventeenth century and a new kind of soldier—one dedicated to a higher goal in religion or politics.[18] When Defoe joined Monmouth's rebellion in 1685, he might have noticed a few men wearing the uniform of Cromwell's New Model. As late as 1720, when Defoe published Memoirs of a Cavalier, praise of Cromwell or even the Parliamentary cause was still difficult. At almost every opportunity, High Church polemicists still presented the rebellion against Charles I as equivalent to Satan's revolt against God, and every January thirtieth brought out a rash of sermons reminding everyone of the certainty of this analogy. Defoe never made a frontal attack upon this religious position, however much he may have suggested that the idea was equivalent to blasphemy. But in his stated admiration for Fairfax at the end, the Cavalier (and Defoe) find a good substitute. Similarly, the praise of the Swedish army under Gustavus Adolphus is a good surrogate for any direct praise of that army of saints that had been the butt of so much humor during the past sixty years.

In much of this, Defoe's judgment was excellent. The Cavalier's two wars reveal a contrast between cavalry with infantry and cavalry used in an isolated haphazard fashion. Ultimately, it is the infantry that must hold the field, and Defoe seems to have understood this principle very well. His admiration for Swedish military techniques did not extend to Charles XII, whose refusal to support the Protestant cause in Europe was a cause of complaint from Defoe. Defoe also objected to Charles XII's attack on Russia, prophesying that all of Europe would come to regret that the Swedish monarch had taught the arts of modern warfare to the Russians. History certainly demonstrated that Defoe was correct in that opinion.

Defoe's presentation of warfare, aside from its political and economic dimensions, may be grouped into three categories: aesthetic, strategic, and pecuniary. All three play important roles in his two great war narratives, Memoirs of a Cavalier and Colonel Jack. The former showed Defoe's knowledge of warfare in the seventeenth century, but he had not yet succeeded in integrating the historical material and the experiences of his narrator with anything like a well defined character. The Cavalier has real feelings and emotions, yet he hardly steps beyond a certain character type— that of the good, fair minded soldier. But in some ways, Defoe is able to show the reader more about warfare in the period through a typical figure than in a work involving a more complex character and an angle of vision restricted by such a character.

What I call an "aesthetic" dimension to warfare appears in both narratives. At one point Jack avoids capture because he has decided to stroll out of Ghent to observe the "Beauty" of the fortifications around the city,[19] and we can detect in the Cavalier's admiration for the order of the Swedish forces something resembling an appreciation for a work of art— order, balance, control. And of the fortresses in Holland, Defoe's Cavalier remarks, "I spent some time in

Holland viewing the wonderful powers of art, which I observed in the fortifications of their town," (119). This aspect of the art of war is apparent enough in his Tour thro' the Whole Island of Great Britain. Defoe seldom describes any city without commenting on the fortifications, and this description is always involved in the possible scene of battle that might occur were some enemy to make an assault on London or Portsmouth. The contemplation of Tilbury Fort brings with it a narrative of the way in which the Dutch managed to sail up the Thames in 1667 to capture the Royal Charles and set fire to other ships in the English fleet. Similarly the discussion of the fortifications at Portsmouth contains within it an imagined scenes of an enemy attempting to make an assault and the consequent destruction of such a fleet. The power of the fortifications at places such as Sheerness or Harwich suggest an ability to resist all assaults, and there is a kind of appreciation for the ingenuity in building such structures, often in places that seem sandy and insecure. Such admiration for the beauty of fortifications does not extend to aged and crumbling castles. Dover's castle is depicted without nostalgia as ancient and useless.

The scenes of battle in both Memoirs of a Cavalier and Colonel Jack suggest Defoe's interest in military strategy. He has his Cavalier describe the battle of Leipzig, Gustavus Adolphus's greatest victory, in exact detail. If he allowed generalizations to hold for his description of the battle of Blenheim, here he is very much Defoe master of the circumstantial. The reader learns about the officers killed, the wiping out of entire regiments, and the King's heroic leading of the charge: In this Juncture came the King, and having seen what Havock the Enemy made of Cullembach's Troops, he comes riding along the Front of our three Brigades, and himself led us on to the Charge: the Collenel of his Guards, the Baron Dyvel, was shot dead just as the King had given him some Orders: When the Scots advanced, seconded by some Regiments of Horse which the King also sent to the Charge, the bloodiest Fight began that ever man beheld, for the Scotish Brigades giving Fire three Ranks at a Time over one anothers Heads, pour'd in their Shot so thick, that the Enemy were cut down like Grass before a Scyth; and following into the thickest of their Foot with the Clubs of their Muskets made a most dreadful Slaughter, and yet there was no flying. Tilly's Men might be killed and knocked down, but no Man turned his Back, nor would give an Inch of Ground; but as they were wheel'd, or marched, or retreated by their Officers.[20]

Defoe then proceeds to speak of the ferocious cuirassiers led by Baron Kronenburg, whom none of the Swedes wanted to fight and who left the battle intact,[21] in contrast with some troops who refuse quarter and die in the formation in which they had been placed.

Much may be learned from Defoe's account because he apparently knew a great deal. The major advance in warfare during the seventeenth century involved the greater efficiency and discipline of armies. The Scots who fire in three ranks represented this new discipline.[22] The faster that volleys could be fired, the more devastation could be created in the ranks of the enemy, and the idea of three ranks firing in order created the possibility that one line would always be firing while the others reloaded. The discipline of Tilly's is such that no one is moved enough by fear or the drive for self-preservation to turn and run. Courage, Defoe, suggests, might be rewarded by success or by death. The courage of the cuirassiers is rewarded by having everyone avoid them, and they "at last went off from the battle whole" (62). On the other hand, as we have seen, an equally courageous group of men perish.

Defoe's Cavalier never asks why these men behave as they do. These are the same men who behaved like savages at Magdenburg. Why were they capable of such bravery?

The Cavalier links the concept of courage to that of their "Dexterity" in managing their drills, their experience, and their "Discipline." (54). He is a true soldier in his taste for fighting, and when he goes to Holland to observe the manner of warfare carried on there, he makes a comment that throws light on Defoe's remarks upon what Defoe called the new,, way of fighting in his Essay upon Projects. The Cavalier notes that both the Swedes and the Imperialists were "free of their Flesh" (119), or willing to present their bodies to any kind of wounds. In contrast, he observes that the warfare waged by Prince Maurice was extraordinarily effective:

> Whereas Prince Maurice would lye in a Camp till he starved half his men, if by lying there he could but starve two Thirds of his Enemies, so that indeed the War in Holland had more of Fatigues and Hardships in it, and ours had more of Fighting and Blows: Hasty marches, long and unwholesome Encampments, Winter Parties, Counter-marching, Dodging, and Entrenching, were the Exercises of his men, and often times killed him more Men with Hunger, Cold and Diseases, than he could do with Fighting: Not that it required less Courage, but rather more; for a Soldier had at any time rather die in the Field a la Coup de Mousquet, than be starved Hunger, or frozen to Death in the Trenches.(119)

The Cavalier admits that Prince Maurice chose the best way to fight his adversary, since this method completely destroyed the power of the Spanish monarchy and impoverished the nation "till they are fallen from the most powerful, to be the most despicable Nation in the World" (120). As a soldier, the Cavalier judges this method lacking in "Gallantry," and he soon leaves Holland with feeling that he would find no "Relish" in such a war. The Defoe of An Essay upon Projects had to praise a method of fighting that was as effective for William III as it was for Prince Maurice, but there was enough of the soldier in Defoe to feel some sympathy for the lament of his Cavalier over such a pedestrian form of warfare.

The pecuniary interest of both Jack and the Cavalier puzzled me when I first came upon it. Both of Defoe's protagonists detail the loot they are able to obtain through finding money in the houses of civilians, among the possessions of those they have defeated, and through ransoming prisoners. In Memoirs of a Cavalier, the Cavalier's servant, George, finds enough money to purchase a commission and to raise himself to the status of a gentleman. After an action in which Colonel Jack distinguishes himself, he speaks of coming upon some money as something he liked much better than fighting. It seemed somewhat out of place in both works and I suggested that it was an import from the picaresque. I could understand the camp followers such as those portrayed in Simplicissmus, looting the corpses of the slain after battle, and it seemed appropriate enough for Defoe's pirates to be mainly concerned with the treasure and goods they could obtain from the ships they captured. But the Cavalier came from a good and wealthy family and Colonel Jack's chief aim in joining the French army was to become a gentleman. Was not such concentration upon the loot to be obtained through war beneath a gentleman? John Keegan's The Face of Battle showed me how little I knew. Keegan notes that the desire for loot has always been a strong force in war. And while he dismisses the idea that the desire for loot was the major force in keeping the common soldiers in place at Waterloo, he thinks that the suggestion is at least worth considering.[23]

Memoirs of a Cavalier is unquestionably Defoe's best fictional war memoir. But some two years later, in Colonel Jack, Defoe succeeded in Integrating these elements of fiction more fully and in some ways gave a better feeling of the kind of confusion that the individual soldier experiences in battle. Defoe also had a sense that he was writing in a different genre. At one point, Jack refuses to give a full account of a battle on the grounds that he was "not writing a Journal of the Wars" (214). Unlike the Cavalier, Jack becomes a professional soldier more to establish his vision of gentility than from any professional interest in warfare. In his first, brief fling at an army career, he decides to desert, wondering why anyone would get "knock'd on the Head at the Tune of Three and Sixpence a Week" (105). The older Colonel Jack, feels considerable pleasure in his career as a soldier not merely because his rank conveys the status that he was seeking but also because he is relieved to find himself possessed of a considerable amount of courage after having behaved with such trepidation toward some friends of his wife while in Britain.

We learn of Jack's newly acquired bravery at the battle of Cremona, but in Jack's relation of the encounter between the French forces and Prince Eugene, all that is offered the reader is some occasionally effective narrative history. Like the Cavalier, Jack can tell in detail only those parts of the war that he experienced personally. But whereas the Cavalier attempts something like a chronologically coherent narrative, Jack is almost entirely interested in what happens to him. Hence the accounts of battle and any clear history of the war tend to be swallowed up in Jack's participation in small skirmishes. We get a vivid picture of the giant Imperialist trooper who is killed and whose body falls on Jack but no very good idea of what is happening elsewhere. The modern reader has to greet with some relief the sequence of events that follow—Jack's being taken off as a prisoner of war and his subsequent encounter with the daughter of a burgher of Trent who seduces him and traps him into a marriage.

But Defoe seems to have enjoyed filtering this narrative of the Italian campaign through Jack's consciousness, and he may have been right in thinking that his readers would feel the same way. Contemporary readers may indeed have sensed that they were experiencing an exciting new way of reading, for Defoe does break up the temporal sequence of events leading to the battle of Luzzara. Although the outlines of the battle may be recovered from Jack's narrative, events are seen almost entirely from the standpoint of the French with whom Jack is fighting and through Jack's personal experiences.[24] After he has his arm broken and is half buried under the corpses of both armies, he misses the rest of the battle. Jack provides a brief summary of events, but he notes, "My Campaign was now at an End" (221); and indeed the angle of vision shifts to the fate of the prisoners. Defoe's method here, then, is very different from that in Memoirs of a Cavalier. The accounts of the battles are more personal, more a part of Jack's entire experience in which Jack's quest for happiness is the more dominant theme. Unlike the wars of the Cavalier, the war fought in the Po valley was a campaign that went nowhere, one in which the armies on both sides seemed to slip away in the deaths and various illnesses caused by campaigning in the marshy ground surrounding the river. Seen through Jack's eyes, it is a campaign dominated by small skirmishes and doubtful victories. Although the battle of Luzzara was counted among Prince Eugene's great triumphs, Jack questions such a judgment.[25] The Cavalier numbers his victories and defeats clearly. Jack's Italian campaign seems to prefigure his abortive military experiences with the Jacobites.

Defoe never abandoned his belief that a war with Spain might bring Britain countless wealth, but he did undergo a change in his attitude toward inventions in the art of war as the peak of human Ingenuity. Whereas the flintlock musket appeared ready to revolutionize the firepower of infantry at the end of the seventeenth century, no like technical advance was to appear during the succeeding decades. Defoe returned to a praise of the advances in the art of warfare in his History of the Principal Discoveries and Improvements in Useful Arts (1726), but he devotes more space to the scientific discoveries of Boyle and Newton.

He considered war as an aspect of politics and trade in a mercantile state, and so, for the most part, did everyone else. If he avoided descriptions of heads being blown off and tended to use euphemisms to describe the way whole regiments might be destroyed by canon fire, he succeeds in conveying the horrors of the battlefield well enough. Certainly he was far from ignorant about the conditions of war. Madman, his truth speaking character in the Review, argues that "War is a Madness of itself."[26] For its victims, it brings "FAMINE and BLOOD" (6:343), and Defoe estimates that 3,724,000 people had died directly or indirectly by the effects of warfare in Europe. Defoe also argued that for the soldier, war often brings incredible poverty and hardship. In his Short Narrative of the Life and Actions of His Grace John, Duke of Marlborough (1711), Defoe posed as an "Old Officer in the Army" to depict the life of the soldier and to attack those who complained about soldiers as mere pleasure seekers:

> But if they did but see them in a Rainy Season, when the whole Country about them is trod into Chaos, and in such intolerable Marches, Men and Horses dying and dead together, and the best of them glad of a bundle of Straw to lay down their wet and weary Limbs: If they did but see a Siege, besides the daily danger and expectation of Death, which is common to all, from the General to the Centinel; the Watches, the labours, the Cares which attend the greatest; the ugly Sights, the Stinks of Mortality, the Grass all wither'd and black with the Smoke of Power, the horrid Noises all Night

> and all Day, and Spoil and Destruction on every side; I am sure they would be perswaded, that a State of War, to those who are engag'd in it, must needs be a state of Labour and Misery.[27]

What siege had he seen? Had he been an eye-witness to a siege in Holland or in Germany? However much we would like to know the answer to such questions, the more important point is that he had the ability to recreate such a scene imaginatively and to wonder at the soldier's ability to endure such suffering. Defoe never ceased to admire the courage of the soldier, and along with the rest of contemporary Europe, he considered the state of war the natural condition of relations between nations.

NOTES

1. Daniel Defoe, *An Essay upon Projects*, in *The Earlier Life and Chief Earlier Works of Daniel Defoe*, ed. Henry Morley (London: Routledge, 1889), 31-32.
2. Trans. John Hughes, et al. (London, 1706), 128 (Advice LXXV).
3. James Winn, *John Dryden and His World* (Yale U. Press, 1987), 438-513.
4. For a more general discussion of warfare and the concept of the hero at this time, see my essay, "Warfare and Its Discontents," Eighteenth-Century Fiction 4 (1992): 185-205. It might be pointed out that Defoe's statement about the "art" of war appears to have attracted the attention of contemporaries. It is one of the few references from An Essay upon Projects in a commonplace book of the early eighteenth century. See the commonplace book of William Seller, Folger M.a.60, 336.
5. For an assessment of Dryden's motives, see Ronald Clayton, "Dryden's Advice to Danby," *N&Q*, n. s. 36 [vol. 206 cont. ser.] (1989: 447-50.
6. Armees et societes en Europe de 1494 a 1789 (Paris: Presses Universitaires de France, 1976), 13-31.

7. Argued forcefully by the eminent military historian, John Keegan, in an address to the Western Society for Eighteenth-Century Studies on 17 February 1990. A similar argument may be found in Geoffrey Parker's *The Military Revolution* (Cambridge U. Press, 1990), 72.

8. Part I (London, 1706), 19.

9. See Paula Backscheider, *Defoe* (Johns Hopkins, 1989), 101. Backscheider considers the suggestion absurd because she believed he had no legal grounds. The important thing is that this offer did not seem absurd to Defoe.

10. See Bastian, *Defoe's Early Life* (Totowa, New Jersey: Barnes and Noble, 1981), passim.

11. *The British Army of William III, 1689-1702* (Manchester U. Press, 1987), 255.

12. Issue number 4 for Thursday, 17 August 1704, reprinted in Augustan Reprint Society No. 183, ed. Frank Ellis and Henry Snyder (Los Angeles: William Andrews Clark Memorial Library, 1977), 14.

13. For an account of the influence of the "Swedish Discipline," see Michael Walzer, *The Revolution of the Saints* (New York: Athenaeum, 1969), 275-99.

14. *Memoirs of a Cavalier*, ed. James T. Boulton (Oxford U. Press, 1972), 44-45. All subsequent references to this work will be included, within parentheses, in my text.

15. In treating the horrendous massacres of the Aztecs and other Indians by the Spaniards, writers on natural law tried to define something like acceptable rules for nations at war. In his study, On the Indians and on the Law of War, Franciscus de Victoria argued (179) that under certain conditions it was considered "lawful" to hurt the innocent.

16. In The Shakespeare Head Edition of the *Novels and Selected Writings of Daniel Defoe* (Oxford: Blackwell, 1927), 3:95-96.

17. Somewhat closer to organized warfare in the state of nature than anything in Robinson Crusoe is the siege of

Captain Singleton's encampment in Africa by an assortment of wild beasts. Singleton also speaks of the elephants he observes marching "in a fair Line of Battle." Shakespeare Head Edition, 109.

18. Walzer is especially good in showing how the military metaphor taken from the ideal of the "Swedish Discipline" became pervasive in sermons and religious literature in the period before the conflict between Charles I and Parliament and how it prepared the way for the idea of Cromwell's army as the true representatives of the revolution. See Walzer (275-90).

19. *Colonel Jack*, ed. Samuel Monk (Oxford U. Press, 1965), 183.

20. *A Tour thro' the Whole Island of Great Britain*, ed. G. D. H. Cole (London: Peter Davies, 1927), 1:9-10, 122.

21. John Keegan has argued that during the eighteenth century, armies almost always had a body if troops, usually dressed in ferocious costumes of the savage eastern European soldiers. Their purpose was to terrify the opposing forces. By spreading fear, they served more as a form of psychological warfare than as a force effective in their own right. The cuirassiers, described by the Cavalier as being dressed from head to toe in black armor, appear to serve just this purpose. "Spreading Panic: The idea of Eighteenth-Century Battle," Plenary lecture before the members of the Western Society for Eighteenth-Century Studies at the Broadmoor Hotel, Colorado Springs, 17 February 1990. For pictures of cuirassiers, see Z. Grbasic and V. Vuksic, *The History of Cavalry* (New York: Facts on File, 1989), 13, 76, and 87.

22. See Geoffry Parker, *Military Revolution*, 19-24, 49-52.

23. *The Face of Battle* (New York: Viking, 1976), 115, 180-81.

24. Although the battle of Luzzara was sometimes counted among Prince Eugene's victories, Jean Du Mont admitted that the encounter resulted in few gains for either side. Since the French army withdrew from the field between 4 and 5 September, leaving Prince Eugene in possession,

it could and was claimed as one of his many victories. See Du Mont, Batailles gagnees par le serenissime Prince Fr. Eugen de Savoye (The Hague, 1725).

25. Prince Eugene's reputation as a general was challenged only by Marlborough's, but Prince Eugene's victories were spread over a greater period of time; and his reputation on the Continent was far greater. Du Mont admitted that the battle of Luzzara did not result in any great gains for either side, but he does point ot the withdrawal of the French army on 4 or 5 September as a sign that it could be claimed as a victory for Prince Eugene.

26. Review, ed. Arthur W. Secord, Facsimile Text Society No. 44 (Columbia U. Press, 1938), 5:151. Subsequent references to this work will appear within parentheses in my text.

27. (London, 1711), 41.

3

A Sermon by the "Queen of Whores"

—Marilyn Westfall

Daniel Defoe's Roxana seems to resist interpretation, though it has been scrutinized for its likeness to a trade manual, a spiritual autobiography, and a "'woman's novel.'"[1] Leopold Damrosch, for instance, remarks with some exasperation on his attempt to define Roxana's "inner logic": "We cannot know exactly what Defoe thought he was doing in this enigmatic novel, but we do know that it was his last. As one critic puts it, 'Defoe stopped when he reached the end.'"[2] One prominent debate concerns the novel's religious allusions, as when Roxana reflects: "So possible is it for us to roll ourselves up in Wickedness, until we grow invulnerable by Conscience."[3] At issue is the influence that Defoe's Puritanism exerted on the text. Polarized opinions on this subject emerge in two seminal studies of Defoe. In the monograph Economics and the Fiction of Daniel Defoe (1962), Maximillian Novak presents Defoe as guided by the religious precepts of Puritanism; Novak, thus, is not loath to pronounce Roxana "guilty of two economic sins: avarice and luxury."[4] Contrary to Novak, Ian Watt claims in The Rise of the Novel (1957) that

Defoe substitutes the literary schema of "formal realism" for Puritanism's providential order, making his writings "ethically neutral."[5] Roxana's unsatisfactory plot "denouement," Watt says, shows that Defoe "prefers and certainly achieves the inconsequential and the incomplete."[6] Recent studies tend to view Roxana as informed by Defoe's Puritanism, particularly in its sober tone, even while they suggest that the novel is a departure from strict religious discourse toward aesthetic expression. As Malinda Snow comments in "Arguments to the Self in Defoe's Roxana' (1994), "Defoe's narrative method encourages us to seek a 'right way' to talk . . . about our choices rather than seeking a right choice.'"[7] In The English Novel in History (1999), John Richetti concludes that, despite debate, Roxana's meaning remains ambiguous: "Some critics consider her agonized reflections as Defoe's warning about the moral decadence of early Georgian England, but others just as plausibly discount the chorus of guilty reflections as conventional moralizing."[8]

Diverging from current thinking on Roxana, this study affirms Novak's proposition that Defoe's Puritanism provides a template for a coherent analysis of the text. I contend that the novel's "inner logic" (to borrow Damrosch's phrase) is based on the sermon, specifically the Puritan jeremiad sermon. I place Roxana within the context of Defoe's other late works to subdue the notion that Roxana represents a dead end for Defoe, particularly concerning the moral content of his writing. I show, instead, that Roxana incorporates Calvinistic tropes decrying against luxury and promoting charity, rhetoric that also appears, for example, in Defoe's The Complete English Tradesman. Lastly, I argue that, as "the Queen of Whores," Roxana becomes an allegorical representation of England, which, according to the novel, is a nation prostituted by its nobles and king, whose behaviors are mirrored in the actions of commoners. As Novak observes, Roxands plot "revolves about the decline of Roxana's moral character, a decline that is contrasted with her worldly success. But although the focus of the novel is mainly on Roxana's hardening conscience, the course of her career implies the moral decline of the entire society."[9]

As a narrator, Roxana frequently digresses from her story to moralize about her lack of integrity. Her most poignant remark no doubt is the novel's closing line: "my Repentance seem'd to be only the Consequence of my Misery, as my Misery was of my Crime" (p. 330). From early on, however, she depicts herself as a reprobate. She says of taking her landlord's supposed charity in exchange for sex: "I did what my own Conscience convinc'd me at the very Time I did it, was horrible unlawful, scandalous, and abominable" (p. 39). Shortly afterwards, she reiterates: "so with my Eyes open, and with my Conscience, as I may say, awake, I sinn'd, knowing it to be a Sin, but having no Power to resist" (p. 44). She muses somberly a few pages later that "there can be no substantial Satisfaction in a Life of known Wickedness; Conscience will, and does, often break in" (p. 49). In retrospect, she sees herself as stricken by a "Disorder" (p. 277) for trying but failing to live outside the providential order. Also, her emphasis on conscience and the role it plays in memory seems predicated on the rhetoric, for example, of Richard Baxter in A Sermon of Judgement "Conscience will be an Accuser . . . It will be a Glass wherein every man may see the face of his heart and former Life."[10] In the same sermon Baxter forecasts that sinners' words will serve to condemn them: "out of their own mouth shall they be Judged. That very tongue that now excuseth their sin, will in their torments be their great Accuser."[11]

Roxana does condemn her past behavior. The face of her heart—the manner in which she speaks about and sees herself— is unforgiving and grimly ironic. She appreciates, for instance, that her "good Skin" masks her corruption, and she implores readers against using beauty as a "Bait": "God forbid any shou'd make so vile a Use of so good a Design" (p. 75). No longer concerned with preserving appearances, she calls herself "Queen of Whores" (p. 821). a "Carcass" (p. 741). and even a swine: "I went on smooth and pleasant: I wallow'd in Wealth" (p. 188). Looking at the glass that conscience holds out, she can now reflect "upon the Brutallity and blindness of Mankind" (pp. 74-5) by first confessing her own inhumanity. Roxana is a frank narrative about a brutish life, informed by a revived moral vision. In essence, therefore. the novel meets a claim made in the preface about Roxana's narration: "In the Manner she has told the Story... she makes frequent Excursions, in a just censuring and condemning her own Practice: How often does she reproach herself in the most passionate Manner: and guide us to just Reflections in the like Cases?" (p. 2). Like a sermon, Roxana is ethically charged and meant to stir the conscience of "the Virtuous Reader" (p. 3).

Like Roxana, the jeremiad sermon censures and condemns acts against conscience. Sacvan Bercovitch notes in The American Jeremiad that the jeremiad served as "a lament over the ways of the world"; it also "decried the sins of 'the people.'"[12] The sermon's basic purpose was to instill through appeals to conscience the fear of divine punishment. Baxter begins his Sermon of Judgement with an epigraph from 2 Corinthians: "For we must all appear before the Judgement Seat of Christ, that every one may receive the things done in his body; according to that he hath done, whether it be good or bad. Knowing therefore the terrours of the Lord we perswade men."[13] Another cleric, Edmund Calamy, in The Great Danger of Covenant-Breaking warns that God may chastise a people immediately: "Sin makes all Times dangerous; yet the Times be never so prosperous, yet if they be sinful Times, they are Times truly dangerous . . . It is sin that makes Afflictions to be the Fruit of GOD's revenging Wrath . . . and a beginning of Hell."[14] Roxana's increasing sense of doom dominates the end of her narrative. Feeling afflicted, she diagnoses herself as a "Malade Imaginaire," someone who "may as easily die with Grief, or run-mad with Joy" (p. 238). When Roxana and the Dutch Merchant examine their riches just prior to marriage, she suffers a paroxysm of conscience. She recollects her fright: "I trembled every Joint of me . . . Unhappy Wretch, said I to myself, shall my ill-got Wealth, the Product of prosperous Lust . . . be intermingled with the honest well-gotten Estate of this innocent Gentleman, to be a Moth and Caterpiller among it, and bring the Judgments of Heaven upon him" (p. 259). Suppressing her fears, she weds the Merchant, only to experience "a secret Hell within" and "a constant Terror . . . In a word, it never Lightn'd or Thunder'd, but I expected the next Flash wou'd penetrate my Vitals, and melt the Sword (Soul) in this Scabbord of Flesh" (p. 260). Examined within the context of the jeremiad, Roxana's torment is appropriate to her state of spiritual deterioration. Baxter admonishes habitual sinners in words attributed to God in Proverbs: "I will mock when your fear cometh: when your fear cometh as Desolation, and your destruction cometh as a whirlewind: when distresse and anguish cometh upon you: then shall they call upon me, but I will not Answer."[15] Roxana attempts to repent; she does not, however, receive the grace to believe in forgiveness. "I was not come to that Repentance," she recalls, "that is rais'd from a Sence of Heaven's Goodness . . . it was of another and lower kind of Repentance, and rather mov'd by my Fears of Vengeance" (p. 261).

In addition to disquieting people about spiritual waywardness, Puritan jeremiads extend the hope of salvation by prescribing specific reforms that secure a covenant with God. Bercovitch finds that American Puritans used the jeremiad "to direct an imperiled people of God toward the fulfillment of their destiny [and] to guide them individually toward salvation, and collectively toward the American City of God."[16] The English Puritans, as well, sought to sanctify their nation, as is evident in Edmund Calamy's England's Looking-Glasse: "The Lord in mercy ruinate our sinnes, and not the Nation! the same Lord worke a Nationall Reformation, and make you his Instruments in this great work! Much hath been done by you this way already . . . The Lord enable you to perfect what you have begun."[17] The Puritan "rhetoric of mission," according to Bercovitch, carried with it "a climate of anxiety that helped release the restless 'progressivist' energies required for the success of the venture"; the rhetoric also established "direction and purpose." These two elements, Bercovitch says, "define the ritual import of the jeremiad: to sustain process by imposing control and to justify control by presenting a certain form of process as the only road to the future kingdom."[18]

By inclining readers toward 'Just Reflections," Roxana promotes a constructive anxiety, an effect G.A. Stan describes as a "tension between sympathy and judgment."[19] The text, like the jeremiad, also presents a "certain form of process as the only road to the future kingdom"; the process, however, completely opposes the narrator's path of "prosperous Wickedness" (p. 106). Roxana, in fact, discourages readers from imitating her life's design. "I am," she says, "a Memorial to all who shall read my Story; a standing Monument of the Madness and Distraction which Pride and Infatuations from Hell runs us into; how ill our Passions guide us; and how dangerously we act, when we follow the Dictates of an ambitious Mind" (p.161). For English Puritans, the process toward salvation depended not on individual financial gain, which Roxana achieves, but on charity. The "future kingdom" was a commonwealth, in which-ideally-wealth benefited the poorest in the nation, by means of proper economic stewardship. As Margo Todd observes in Christian Humanism and the Puritan Social Order, the English Puritans advocated "the mediocritas in getting and spending, the doctrine of stewardship, and the demand for discriminate, rationalized secular poor relief."[20] Under this system, profit was legitimate if "it did not harm the interests of others." Todd notes that "profit is implicitly harmful if retained by the individual rather than invested in the common weal . . . When the businessman's yen for personal profit overcomes his responsibility to the commonwealth, his activity is interpreted as greed, and the wealth obtained by it is regarded as illegitimate."[21] The ideology expressed in Calamy's The Monster of Sinful Self-Seeking, Anatomized supports Todd's analysis. Calamy reminds his audience that riches "cannot be said to be our own properly, neither may we use them as we please, but according as God hath prescribed, therefore they are called another mans and not our owne." All things, including wealth, Calamy says, should be directed toward the "preservation and propagation of the Kingdome of Jesus Christ."[22] In The Great Danger of Covenant-Breaking. Calamy remarks that if men "drive their own Designs," they show "contempt of GOD and the common Wealth."[23]

Allusions to the commonwealth pervade Roxana, noticeably in the section where the brewer, Roxana's first husband, abandons her. Over several months she is reduced to poverty. She appeals to her husband's relations for help. She reports, however, that the family "sent me short and surly Answers; nor did any one of them offer to come to see me, or to see the Children . . . well perceiving that I was in a Condition that was likely to be soon troublesome to them" (p. 15). Just as family members resist giving aid, nurses employed by parishes fail to help poor children. Roxana tells of "Parish-Children being Starv'd at Nurse; of their being ruin'd, let grow crooked, lam'd and the like, for want of being taken care of" (p. 19). Roxana's narrative laments the demise of charity as promoted by the Puritans. In response to poverty, Baxter presents in his preface to The Crucifying of the World by the Cross of Christ a "Catalogue of Seasonable Good Works." The first assigned task is to "[e]inquire what persons, burdened wit h children, or sickness, or on any such occasion labour under necessities, and relieve them, as you are able, and find them fit."[24] John Calvin observes in The Institutes of the Christian Religion that one should regard charity, ultimately, as a gift to God: "If we believe heaven to be our country, it is better for us to transmit our wealth thither . . . But how shall we transmit it? Why if we communicate to the necessities of the poor; whatever is bestowed on them, the Lord considers as given to himself. Whence that celebrated promise, 'He that hath pity upon the poor lendeth to the Lord.'"[25] Calvin does not praise charity for its intrinsic merit, for to do so would contradict his doctrine that faith, not works, is the means to salvation. Rather, Calvin says, if Christians are charitable, God, in return, will extend to them salvation: "For all things that are bestowed on our brethren in a way of charity, are so many deposits in the hand of the Lord, which he, as a faithful depositary, will one day restore with ample interest."[26] Charity is an act of faith, securing the contract between God and the people.

Impoverished, Roxana decides to abandon her children on the doorstep of her husband's sister. Luckily, the sister's husband, who is not a blood uncle, takes the children in. The man says to his wife, who refuses to accept the children: "Come, Come my Dear . . . Charity is a Duty to the Poor, and he that gives to the Poor lends to the Lord; let us lend our Heavenly Father a little of our Children's Bread... it will be a Store well laid up for them" (p. 22). His dialogue is nearly identical to Calvin's tropes about charity. The wife had raved at him: "Would you have these Bratts come and eat up my Children's bread? . . . Charity begins at home" (p. 22). The man advises his wife: "don't shut up your Bowels of Compassion against your own Flesh and Blood" (p. 23). He warns her that hard-hearted indifference would be a "Reproach" against her, as her family had "once flourish'd" in the place where she now would permit her brother's children to starve (p. 24). He also relates a passage from Proverbs: "Whoso stoppeth his Ears at the Cry of the Poor, he also shall cry himself but shall not be heard" (p. 23). His sentiments and rhetoric both befit a jeremiad. Indeed, they are echoed in Calamy's sermon on self-seeking, where Calamy reminds his audience that "Our safety is more wrapt up in the publique welfare, than in our private."[27] They also resonate with Baxter, who instructs: "I should always prefer the Publick Good of Church or Common wealth, before the personal wealth of my posterity."[28]

Both Baxter's and Calamy's sermons complement Roxands narrative in other respects. Calamy dwells on the secret nature of self-seeking, calling it "an inward, invisible and spirituall sinne, that consumes England as a moth"; it is also a "Caterpillar that devours all the green things of the land."[29] In A Sermon of Judgement, Baxter remarks on the impossibility of concealing sins from God and conscience: "It is not possible that any should keep out of sight, or hide their sin and the evil of their actions, and so delude the Judge."[30] Roxands text incorporates the insect imagery found in Calamy's sermon: the character Roxana fears that her "ill-got Wealth" will act as a moth and caterpillar, devouring the Dutch Merchant's honest riches (p. 259). She also testifies that Providence intervenes so that "the most secret Crimes are, by the most unforeseen Accidents, brought to light and discover'd" (p. 297). Her story, of course, exposes the full extent of her narcissism, including her greed and vanity, as well as her need to preserve her "outwardly happy Circumstances" (p. 329). Accumulating a fortune through vice, she uses her money, not toward any common good, but instead to manipulate others for her own benefit, as when she purchases the loyalty of an impoverished Quaker woman, abandoned by her husband. She neglects her child by the merchant, and financially cuts off her son by the jeweler until he marries a woman of her choosing. She refuses to recognize her daughter Susan, and allows Amy to murder her. Roxana reflects that people may become "quite Lunatik with their Pride" (p. 235). Calamy observes that self-seekers often envision themselves as kings or deities, and "act from self as a principle, by self as a rule, for self as an end."[31] Like a feminine King Lear or a parody of the Calvinist God, Roxana is convinced that she can determine which of her children to sustain, which to cast off.

The subject matter and style of Roxana indicate a conservative trend in Defoe's late works. The commonwealth, the staple topic of the Puritan jeremiad, proves a significant issue for Defoe from the time of Roxana's publication in 1724 until his death in 1731. The Protestant Monastery (1727), for example, begins with a metaphor depicting the interdependence of English citizens: "A Commonwealth is a Machine actuated by many Wheels, one dependant on the other, yet the Obstruction of a small Wheel may stop the Motion of the whole: Every Man ought therefore as much as in him lies, to contribute in his Station, to the publick Welfare."[32] In The Complete English Tradesman (1725), Defoe accuses those who trade in luxuries of committing "rapes . . . upon nature" so that the rich might enjoy "eating fine." He then asks: "will anybody say that most of these people might not be better and more usefully employed for the good of the commonwealth?"[33] He also proposes restrictions in trade to improve England's moral climate: "I think something might be done, and suffered too . . . to that part of trade which is carried on to bad purposes . . . To be sure, the bad consequences of not stopping the evil, greatly outweigh the other consideration."[34] The Great Law of Subordination Consider'd (1726?) criticizes the gentry for ruining the morals of the common people through displays of "Riot and Luxury. "[35] In one of his final tracts, The Generous Projector (1731), Defoe condemns extravagance: "In short, the Luxury of the Age will be the Ruin of the Nation, if not prevented."[36] Defoe's apocalyptic forecasts are reminiscent of the jeremiad's rhetoric.

The subject of conscience, essential to Roxana's retrospective narrative, becomes the climactic focus of The Life of Jonathan Wilde (1725). In the brief biography, Defoe first indicates that the famous thief created a "Commonwealth like that of the Bees" from a band of "lawless People," demonstrating that a society prospers when people "make no Difference betwixt Meum and Tuum."[37] While Defoe praises Wilde's savvy and understanding of "the weak sides of Men," he by no means justifies crime, for he comments that Wilde suffers "a deplorable State of Mind" after he is condemned to death. Defoe then concludes: "Virtue only can give true Tranquility, and nothing can Support a Man against the Terrors of Death, but a good Conscience."[38] The same moral could also apply to Roxana the fortunate mistress, turned "such a sorrowful Penitent" (p. 75), yet unable to believe in her own contrition after a lifetime of vice. Like the jeremiad, both texts agitate for social change through the agency of a reader's conscience.

Defoe's religious upbringing and study for the ministry likely affected the homiletic tone of Roxana and his other late writings. In the biography Daniel Defoe: His Life, Paula Backscheider observes that the most significant event in Defoe's youth was his parents' refusing membership in the Anglican Church, and instead choosing to join the religious '"Dissenters."'[39] The name "Dissenters" designated the change in status for those once known as Puritans, for with the restored Stuart king and the re-established Anglican Church, Puritans became "dissidents."[40] Charles II proved anxious to retaliate against the Puritans who had executed his father and instituted in the place of the monarchy a commonwealth. During the first years of his reign, a series of decrees and acts expelled Dissenters from government, university, and parish positions, and also allowed for their persecution. In Defoe's biography, Backscheider notes that "Defoe was ten years old when Quaker children were put in the pillory, boys publicly scourged, children as young as twelve sent to Bridewell Prison at hard labor, and doors broken down in order to search houses."[41] The campaign against Dissent was conducted, in part, over the issue of conscience: the "sense of Divine justice,"[42] as Calvin defined conscience, had already permitted a revolution against the monarchy; it fostered the potential for further rebellion. Baxter, for instance, argues in his sermon The English Non-conformity that if the king demands his subjects to "live in Murder, Adultery, Perjury &c," then "the King must be forsaken."[43].

Defoe knew of these ideas, for he attended Newington Green Academy, a university for the children of Dissenters, where, as Backscheider says, he at least began the theological curriculum. [44] As regards a divinity student's education, Baxter in A Christian Directory requires for the "poorest library" nearly seventy-five religious texts; his list of books eventually extends to several hundred volumes.[45] According to Backscheider, Baxter's writings on "practical divinity" were required reading at Newington Green Academy, as were the "'best books both of the Episcopal, Presbyterian, and Independent Divines.'"[46] Defoe, therefore, had the opportunity to study religious discourse, including the rhetoric of the jeremiad. The headmaster and founder of the academy, Charles Morton, was one of two ministers whom Backscheider believes inspired Defoe throughout his life; the other was Samuel Annesley, a family pastor to the Foes. Though Dissenters faced imprisonment and even death, Annesley preached openly. He promoted both public service and "'Practical Godliness.'" This idealistic agenda, Backscheider says, evinces itself in Defoe's "last works" where he expresses his "desire to publish his beneficial ideas 'and leave, at least, a Testimony of my good Will to my Fellow Creatures.'"[47]

Despite his "good Will," Defoe attacks the lax morals of Anglicans and Dissenters alike near the time of Roxana's publication. The religious fervor that had characterized "the heroic age of Dissent" during the reign of Charles II had elapsed. Under the rule of George I, religious tolerance generally prevailed, but with the tolerance came a license in behavior that, in Defoe's opinion, allowed people "to indulge their Wickedness."[48] In The Great Law of Subordination, Defoe characterizes the nation during this era as drunken, commenting that "the Drunken Vice [is] the worst of all Brutality" contributing to "all Vice," including "Whoreing, Gameing, Thieving, Murther."[49] In The Dissenters, Michael Watts comments that, under George I, Nonconformists were "losing their reputation for 'superior virtue, and merit'" by "wasting time at plays, gaming tables, and dances."[50] Watts also points out that a young minister, Strickland Gough, criticized Dissent for its lack of "fashion." In his pamphlet, An Enquiry into the Causes of the Decay of the Dissenting Interest (1730), Gough recommends that "ministers pay less heed to the needs of the humble members of their congregations and more to the tastes of 'people of wit and politeness.'" He advises that "at the academies dancing masters should be employed 'to prune off all the clumsiness and awkwardness that is disagreeable to people of fashion.'"[51] Gough's plans to gentrify Dissent's membership compare very well with Roxana's description of herself at age 14: "I was . . . tall, and very well made; sharp as a Hawk in Matters of common Knowledge; quick and smart in Discourse . . . full of Repartee . . . Being French Born, I danc'd as some say, naturally . . . I wanted neither Wit, Beauty, or Money" (pp. 6—7). Roxana epitomizes Gough's improved Dissenter. The crassness of the times, the emphasis on fashion and vanity, even by a minister, occasioned the need for a jeremiad.

The fact that Roxana graduates from being a fashionable Protestant to a "Protestant Whore" (p. 69) is a mark against a society intoxicated with the notion that "Liberty is a Freedom to Crime."[52] In The Institutes, Calvin says regarding mistaken notions of liberty: "There is scarcely any one, whom his wealth permits to be sumptuous, who is not delighted with luxurious splendour in his entertainments, in his dress, and in his buildings . . . And all these things are defended under the pretext of Christian liberty."[53] Empowered by her wealth, Roxana takes the liberty to realize her deepest narcissistic desires, such as becoming "Mistress to the King himself (p. 161), a goal she easily achieves. She attends a masquerade, costumes herself in "the Habit of a Turkish Princess" (p. 173), and dances while the nobles shout, "Roxana" (p. 176)—which becomes her pen name. Afterward, she reports that "for three Years and about a Month, Roxana liv'd retir'd . . . with a Person, which Duty, and private Vows, obliges her not to reveal, at least, not yet" (p. 181). In her "'Sink of Wickedness,'"[54] she resembles an apocalyptic figure like the Whore of Babylon from Revelation, who was associated in English Protestant writings with the Catholic Church and forthcoming disasters.[55] Indeed, as Novak indicates, the luxury on which Roxana thrives was considered the "sign of a decaying state."[56] Her story shows a systemic weakening of Protestantism and the English nation because of vice. David Blewett notes that masquerades at the court of George I allowed "an indiscriminate mixing of classes and a considerable degree of sexual licence." For Defoe and many of his contemporaries, Blewett says, masquerades were "both symbol and cause of an alarming decline in morals."[57]

The figure of the harlot appears in Baxter's The Crucifying of the World by the Cross of Christ. She symbolizes both prosperity and the temptation to fulfill lusts. Just as a harlot entices through adornments, so the world is adorned "with the best cloathes" and "the most enticing garb." The lips of the harlot "drop as an honeycomb," Baxter says, but taste "as bitter as wormwood";

likewise, the "poyson of the world is covered by its sweetness."[58] Baxter's tropes are typical of sin's depiction in the jeremiad: not only is sin a poison, but it is also a disease from which one needs "spiritual recovery."[59] The secret nature of sin, particularly that of self-seeking, which Calamy calls "a great and hidden iniquity," makes it all the more insidious, as it "devours" from within.[60] For these Puritan ministers and for Defoe, sin slowly murders the individual, like syphilis. Roxana remarks several times that she is ill. She says for example of her "old lewd Favourite" (p. 207), her lover after her three-yea r affair with the king: "I began not to be sick of his Lordship only, but really I began to be sick of the Vice" (p. 200). After marrying the Dutch Merchant, she realizes that her mind is "distemper'd" by fantasies. "I had," she remarks, "two Assistants to deliver me . . . first, Amy, who knew my Disease, but was able to do nothing as to the Remedy; the second, the Merchant, who really brought the Remedy, but knew nothing of the Distemper" (p. 239). While the merchant is a positive and healing character, most of the men depicted in Roxana are spiritually diseased. They infect not only Roxana, but also England. Roxana comments on the morals of the king and his nobles, that "If the Sovereign gave himself a Loose, it cou'd not be expected the rest of the Court shou'd be all Saints" (p. 172). Calamy says of the example set by "the representative Body of the Nation": "Great men are the Looking-glasse of the Country where they live . . . If they be wicked, the whole Countrey is much the worser by them. The vices of Rulers are the rules of Vices . . . If the liver be tainted, the body is dropsie."[61]

Like pentimenti, the themes of the jeremiad affect the tones of Roxana's self-portrait. We might wonder, however, why Defoe's use of the jeremiad is so subdued, if he truly is concerned about England's spiritual health. Why would he even discourage our reading Roxana as a sermon by having the character state: "I am not to preach but to relate" (p. 49)? The preface indicates that authors are forced to modify both rhetorical style and subject matter. In the preface, three authorial figures, the relator, the writer, and an "I" assure readers that the story to follow is "true" based on the oral testimony of a "Beautiful Lady"; however, names cannot be revealed, nor the "Facts trac'd back too plainly" (p. 1). The "I" remarks that Roxana distinguishes itself from romances and other "Modern Performances of this Kind" in "this Great and Essential Article, Namely, That the Foundation of This is laid in Truth o Fact; and so the Work is not a Story, but a History" (p. 1). As the "I" claims, the main narrative begins with historical details: the year is 1683; the Huguenots are escaping religious persecution in France by fleeing to England. Although these facts imply that England is the haven of liberty, what the authors do not divulge is that, even as the Huguenots arrive, Charles II is persecuting Dissenters in England. By the time Charles's reign ended in 1685, an estimated 15,000 Dissenters had died; Defoe estimated that 8,000 had been imprisoned.[62] The authors' omission implies that Roxana could not be published if it contained this information. A comment in the preface, then, assumes great significance: "if we shou'd be always oblig'd to name the Persons, or not to relate the Story, the Consequence might be only this, That many a pleasant and delightful History wou'd be Buried in the Dark, and the World be depriv'd both of the Pleasure and the Profit of it" (p. 1). The authors must tell a story rather than name names, or their history will be buried. Defoe knew well the price to be paid for liberty of expression, as he was twice imprisoned for sedition. Roxana's narrative testifies to history, especially to religious history, in the guise of a story.

The jeremiad sermon fuses secular and sacred history in order to determine a nation's progress in realizing the kingdom of God on earth. This fusion is apparent in The Great Danger of Covenant-Breaking, where Calamy compares London with Jerusalem: "The King made a Covenant before the Lord . . . and he caused all that were present in Jerusalem . . . to stand to it . . . O that this might be the honour of this City! That we may say of it, London is a City keeping Covenant with God."[63] Roxana, instead, laments over a diseased nation and a populace that has lost its spiritual moorings through narcissistic indulgence. In the end, the narrator decries the hollowness of her "fortunate" life. Defoe tries to disturb readers, to guide them to "just Reflections" about a woman who would sacrifice all, including the life of her child, for money and glamour. The slow transformation of an Everywoman into a brute shows us the outcome we can expect when we accept wealth and social standing as commensurate with success.

NOTES

1. Bram Dykstra, *Defoe and Economics* (New York: St. Martin's Press, 1987); G.A. Starr, *Defoe and Spiritual Autobiography* (Princeton: Princeton Univ. Press, 1965); Paula R. Backscheider, "Roxana," in *Daniel Defoe: Ambition and Innovation* (Lexington: Univ. Press of Kentucky, 1986), pp. 182—214. Backscheider writes: "Defoe intended The Fortunate Mistress to be a 'woman's novel'" (p. 182).
2. Leopold Damrosch Jr., *God's Plot and Man's Stories: Studies in the Fictional Imagination from Milton to Fielding* (Chicago: Univ. of Chicago Press. 1985), pp. 211-2. Damrosch's reference is to Everett Zimmerman's Defoe and the Novel (Berkeley: Univ. of California Press, 1975), in which Zimmerman ascertains that the character of Roxana reveals "the limitations of [Defoe's] own and his previous characters' moral assumptions" (p. 186).
3. Daniel Defoe, *Roxana The Fortunate Mistress*, ed. Jane Jack (Oxford and New York: Oxford Univ. Press, 1988), p. 69. All subsequent citations will be from this edition and will appear parenthetically within the text according to page number.

4. Maximillian E. Novak, *Economics and the Fiction of Daniel Defoe* (Berkeley: Univ. of California Press, 1962). p. 134.
5. Ian Watt, *The Rise of the Novel: Studies in Defoe, Richardson and Fielding* (Berkeley: Univ. of California Press, 1957), p. 117.
6. Watt, pp. 104-5.
7. Malinda Snow, "Arguments to the Self in Defoe's Roxana," *SEL* 34, 3 (Summer 1994): 523-36, 534.
8. John Richetti, *The English Novel in History, 1700-1780* (London and New York: Routledge, 1999). p. 79.
9. Novak, *Realism, Myth, and History in Defoe's Fiction* (Lincoln: Univ. of Nebraska Press, 1983), pp. 112-3.
10. Richard Baxter, *A Sermon of Judgement* (London. 1672), *Early English Books, 1641-1700* (Ann Arbor MI: Univ. Microfilms International, 1990, Reel 1116), P. 16. All subsequent microfilm references share this publisher.
11. Baxter, *Judgement*, p. 30.
12. Sacvan Bercovitch, *The American Jeremiad* (Madison: Univ. of Wisconsin Press, 1978), p. 7.
13. Baxter, *Judgement*, p. 1.
14. Edmund Calamy, *The Great Danger of Covenant-Breaking* (London, 1706), *The Eighteenth Century* (Woodbridge CT: Research Publications, 1989, Reel 2977, No. 9), sig. A2.
15. Baxter, *Judgement*, p. 137.
16. Bercovitch, p. 9.
17. Calamy, *England's Looking-Glasse* (London, 1642), Early English Books (Reel 840), sig. A2. The sermon is noted in the index as C236; it was printed by I. Raworth in 1642; the page number is not noted, though the page that follows is noted (by hand) as 362.
18. Bercovitch, pp. 8, 23, 24.
19. G.A. Starr, *Defoe and Casuistry* (Princeton: Princeton Univ. Press, 1971), p. 165.

20. Margo Todd, *Christian Humanism and the Puritan Social Order* (Cambridge: Cambridge Univ. Press, 1987), p. 147.

21. Todd, p. 129.

22. Calamy, *The Monster of Sinful Self-Seeking, Anatomized* (London, 1655), Early English Books (Reel 308), p. 3.

23. Calamy, *Covenant-Breaking*, p.4.

24. Baxter, *The Crucifying of the World by the Cross of Christ* (London, 1658), Early English Books (Reel 524), sig. 13.

25. John Calvin, *The Institutes of the Christian Religion*, trans. John Allen, 2 vols. (Philadelphia: Presbyterian Board of Christian Education, 1936), 2:68-9.

26. Calvin, 2:69.

27. Calamy, *Self-Seeking*, p. 12.

28. Baxter, *Crucifying*, sig. d2.

29. Calamy, *Self-Seeking*, pp. 22, 31.

30. Baxter, *Judgement*, p. 10.

31. Calamy, *Self-Seeking*, p. 13.

32. Defoe, *The Protestant Monastery* (London, 1727), The Eighteenth Century (Reel 386), sig. A2.

33. Defoe, *The Complete English Tradesman*, in *The Novels and Miscellaneous Works of Daniel Defoe*, 2 vols. (London: Oxford, 1841; rprt. New York: Guinn Co., n.d.), 2:viii-246, 2:228-9.

34. Defoe, *Tradesman*, 2:229.

35. Defoe, *The Great Law of Subordination Consider'd* (London, 1726?), The Eighteenth Century (Reel 1561), p. 55.

36. Defoe, *The Generous Projector*, or a Friendly Proposal to Prevent Murder and other Enormous Abuses (Augusta Triumphans) (London, 1731), The Eighteenth Century (Reel 1380), p. 43. I let the joint title stand as it appears in the microfilm edition, though P.N. Furbank and W.R. Owens comment in the *Canonisation of Daniel Defoe*

(New Haven: Yale Univ. Press, 1988), that The Generous Projector is a rewrite of Augusta Triumphans (p. 80).

37. Defoe, *The Life of Jonathan Wilde* (London, 1725), The Eighteenth Century (Reel 908), pp. 16-7.

38. Defoe, *Jonathan Wilde*, p. 40.

39. Backscheider, *Daniel Defoe: His Life* (Baltimore: Johns Hopkins Univ. Press, 1989), p. 7.

40. John Spurr, "From Puritanism to Dissent, 1660-1700," in *The Culture of English Puritanism, 1560-1700.* ed. Christopher Durston and Jacqueline Eales (New York: St. Martins Press, 1996), p. 234.

41. Backscheider, *Daniel Defoe*, p. 10.

42. Calvin. 2:91.

43. Baxter, *The English Nonconformity, Truly Stated and Argued as under King Charles II and King James II* (London. 1690). Early English Books (Reel 524), p. 7.

44. Backscheider, *Daniel Defoe*, p. 15.

45. Baxter, *A Christian Directory*, 4 books (London, 1673), Early English Books (Reel 343), 3:922.

46. Backschelder, *Daniel Defoe*, p. 15.

47. Backschelder, *Daniel Defoe*, p. 17.

48. Defoe, Subordination. p. 18. In "Roxana's Georgian Setting," Rodney M. Baine concludes that Defoe "took advantage of the opportunity to make telling satiric thrusts by having his readers contrast the court of Charles II with that of George I—to the disadvantage of the latter" (*SEL* 15, 3 [Summer 19751: 459-71, 468).

49. Defoe, *Subordination*, p. 64.

50. Michael R. Watts, *The Dissenters*, 2 vols. (Oxford: Clarendon Press, (1978), 1:384.

51. Watts, 1:383.

52. Defoe, *Subordination*, p. 18.

53. Calvin, 2:83.

54. Novak, *Realism*, p. 110.

55. Marianne Gateson Riely, *The Whore of Babylon by Thomas Dekker: A Critical Edition* (New York: Garland Publishing, 1980), pp. 44-S.

56. Novak. *Economies*, p. 137.

57. David Blewett, *Defoe's Art of Fiction* (Toronto: Univ. of Toronto Press, 1979), pp. 124, 125.

58. Baxter, *Crucifying*, p. 164.

59. Baxter. *Crucifying*. p. 224.

60. Calamy, *Self-Seeking*, p. 22.

61. Calamy, *Looking-Glasse*, p. 44.

62. Cited in Harry Grant Plum, *Restoration Puritanism: A Study of the Growth of English Liberty* (Chapel Hill: Univ. of North Carolina Press, 1943), p. 51.

63. Calamy, *Covenant-Breaking*, p. 26.

4

Modern Panegyrick and Defoe's Dunciad

—D.N. DeLuna

When John Dryden in Mac Flecknoe ridiculed Thomas Shadwell with the lines "Thy Tragick Muse gives smiles, thy Comick sleep . . . Thy inoffensive satyrs never bite,"[1] he did not include a literary disaster which would, decades later, become the basis of a much-bandied satiric assertion directed at Sir Richard Blackmore: thy panegyrics wound. In one contemporary poem, entitled "To that Incomparable Panegyrist," Blackmore is advised, "Henceforth no more in thy Poetick Rage, / Burlesque the God-like Heroes of the Age." In another such squib, it is largely on account of Blackmore's injurious praise that the speaker would have him succeed Dryden's anointed dunces: "Let Bl re . . . To Fleckno's Empire his just Right maintain . . . / Let him . . . With Praise and Slander maul both Friends and Foes." Yet another lampoon of the day spoke of Blackmore's "Praise defaming."[2] Blackmore retaliated in kind when in 1700 he said of his detractors: "If I can escape the Defamation of their Panegyricks, I think my self very safe."[3] I cite moments from the literary battle begun in the mid-1690s between Blackmore and the Covent Garden

Wits, that group of literati which convened at Will's Coffeehouse and included Dryden, Samuel Garth, John Dennis, Joseph Addison, and a number of less reputable types, such as William Pittis and Tom Brown.[4] In 1700 the Wits brought out (mock) Commendatory Verses on the Author of the Two Arthurs and the Satyr against Wit, a volume of verse satires aimed at Blackmore, in which he is repeatedly accused of satirizing King William in his allegorical, pro-Nassovian Arthur epics, Prince Arthur (1695) and King Arthur (1697). The volume contains the above-mentioned satiric jibes, and it opens with a poem in which Blackmore is said to have "turn'd Bard, and . . . Burlesqu'd the Bravest, Wisest SON of Mars."[5]

The years of the Blackmore v. Wits paper war were years in which Jonathan Swift was preoccupied with writing his Tale of a Tub. Here Swift, who was a satiric onlooker rather than a participant in the fray, singles out both Blackmore and Dryden for attack. Much of this assault is focused on these authors' assiduous efforts in panegyric (particularly their prefatorial curtsies to large audiences of putative admirers and what Swift sees as their opportunistic handiness at writing dedications and at exalting patrons and important contemporary figures in heroic verse),[6] and much of the attack is carried out through ironic mimicry in the text proper and through Swift's conception and practice of panegyric in the Tale's dedications, in which an overly gracious Blackmore and Dryden are parodied.[7] Later in the Tale we have a moment intended to continue this early parody when we hear the speaker's claim that his entire book is "a little Panegyrick" "without one grain of Satyr intermixt"—"[I have] neither a Talent nor an Inclination for Satyr."[8] Swift produced with his Tale what we might refer to as a work of dramatic mock-panegyric satire.

In 1713 the third earl of Shaftesbury repeated in abstract and prosaic terms Swift's strike at panegyric that backfires: "in reality the Nerve and Sinew of modern Panegyrick lies in a dull kind of Satire; which the Author, it's true, intends shou'd turn to the advantage of his Subject; but which, if I mistake not, will appear to have a very contrary Effect."[9] In the 1730s Alexander Pope followed Swift in using satiric methods to expose such "modern Panegyrick."

We are likely to be most familiar with the achievement of Pope in this regard because a number of important twentieth-century critics have given it studied attention. Maynard Mack was the first to make much of the fact that a good deal of Pope's later satire ironically mimics the conventions of contemporary panegyric, the Epistle to Augustus being a prime example.[10] More recently, James Garrison has cited Swift's Tale and Pope's Augustus as evidence of an ignoble conception of panegyric which he finds to have become widespread in the early eighteenth century: "[panegyric] comes generically to imply its opposite, satire. It is this paradoxical conception of the genre that motivates Swift to propose . . . A Panegyrick upon the World . . . [and] Pope to do the same for George II in the 'Panegyric strains' of the epistle 'To Augustus.'"[11]

One effect of this attention to the Augustans' upending perspective on panegyric has been that of helping us better appreciate the satiric art of Pope and Swift. Modern critics, however, have wholly ignored Daniel Defoe's pioneering performance in mock-panegyric satire, on display in his Pacificator of 1700. This poem takes as its central subject the Blackmore v. Wits paper war, and in it Blackmore is made mock hero and satiric butt. It is Defoe, rather than Swift or Pope, who deserves credit for first showing early-eighteenth-century readers how a dramatic method could be used to accuse a panegyrist of producing satire.

In commentary that introduces the work in the Yale Poems on Affairs of State, Frank Ellis suggests that Defoe's poem may be worth reading only because it is possible that Pope may have been inspired by this work about literary personalities of the day: "Although there is no evidence," Ellis writes, "it is not difficult to imagine Pope's mind working over this material and conceiving The Dunciad."[12] In what follows, I treat Defoe's "Dunciad" with no such patronizing condescension. Rather, I show it to be an arresting, verbally intricate performance in mock-panegyric satire—a feat only later matched by A Tale of a Tub and the Epistle to Augustus and The Dunciad.[13] A brief review of Blackmore's epic art—which is parodied throughout The Pacificator—and its contemporary reception furnishes an important context for understanding Defoe's mock-panegyric achievment.

Blackmore took a maverick approach to the vocation of poet when he published Prince Arthur in 1695. It was the admittedly part-time recreational work of a prestigious City physician, who even boasted of having had no prior training in the lesser literary genres.[14] The work itself was maverick because it was nakedly propagandistic, an epic remarkable for its transparent allegory paralleling Prince William's Glorious "delivery" of England and his martial victories in the charge at Killiecrankie and in the Battle of the Boyne with Arthur's struggle with the Saxons, his assumption of power in England, and his later martial triumphs in Ireland and Scotland. For the first time, epic form now appeared purely an instrument used to elevate and compliment a contemporary monarch. In short, Blackmore had flagrantly adapted the epic to political ends. And he repeated this feat two years later in his sequel King Arthur (1697), where, again using allegory, he applauds English victories in the Nine Years' War, celebrates King William's survival and punitive handling of the 1695 Barclay Assassination Plot, and commends his recent efforts to negotiate a peace treaty with France.[15]

The Arthur poems were popular successes on which the Jacobite Dryden could only reflect with bitter irony. He would have recalled that he had conceptually pioneered Blackmore's marriage of epic and panegyric in his preface to Annus Mirabilis, in which he stated that the "same images serve equally for the epic poesy, and for the historic and panegyric, which are branches of it."[16] He would have recalled, too, that King Arthur's struggles against the Saxons were a subject he himself had contemplated for an epic he would now never write. Finally, Dryden would have remembered that his own King Arthur had been produced in 1691—an anti-Williamite play (on which Blackmore drew for his Christian machinery and for his character of the evil Norse wind god Thor).[17]

Dryden's public quarrel with Blackmore was, nonetheless, focused primarily on artistic rather than political matters. In the dedication to his Aeneis of 1697, he aimed oblique defaming remarks at Blackmore's histrionic heroics ("fustian"), his alleged "bladdered greatness," and his newly acquired admirers in "warm young men" who are "partial and ignorant."[18] In 1700 he attacked his Cheapside rival more openly, first in his Preface to Fables, where he ironically comments that he will refrain from denigrating the Arthur poems since "nothing ill is to be spoken of the dead,"[19] and next in his prologue to Vanbrugh's revised Pilgrim, where he keeps to the same note, stating "all the former Fustian stuff he [Blackmore] wrote,/Was Dead-born Doggrel, or is quite forgot."[20] But Dryden's attack on Blackmore was more extensive yet, for it can rightly be said to take in the sum of anti-Blackmore works produced by his impressionable satellites at Will's, productions that include John Dennis's hostile Remarks on Prince Arthur (1696), Samuel Garth's Dispensary (1697), and the Commendatory Verses (1700).[21]

Blackmore did not lie passive while the Wits so repeatedly attacked him. Indeed, he used the prefaces of his Arthur works to provoke them, and in his preface to King Arthur he seems especially bent on impugning their literary credentials. While the Wits voiced their disapproval of the Arthur poems as art, Blackmore (who played a particularly active role in the day's moral reform movement)[22] warred against their poetry and artists' lifestyles on moral grounds: Dryden's lewd plays, poets who shirk the role of moral reform activist, and men who assume no other vocational responsibility than that of coffeehouse wit and author.[23] In November of 1699 these charges were marshaled in A Satyr Against Wit, Blackmore's most aggressive lambasting of Dryden and his acolytes, especially Garth—a Dublin version of the poem added the subtitle "Design'd an Answer to a Poem Stil'd the Dispensary."[24]

Defoe's Pacificator appeared in mid-February of 1700, only a few months after the publication of Blackmore's incendiary Satyr Against Wit.[25] Defoe's poem is about the paper war itself, which is imagined in terms of martial combat between (Blackmorean) "Sense" and (Covent Garden) "Wit." Defoe chronicles the literary feud in mock-heroic style, touching on such highlights as Blackmore's aggressive preface to Prince Arthur ("Heroic Nokor [Blackmore] made the first Attack, / And threw Drammatick Wit upon its Back" [lines 63-4]),[26] Dennis's harsh Remarks on Prince Arthur ("A Storm of Words the Hero overtook" [line 71]), Jeremy Collier's reformist Short View of the Immorality and Prophaneness of the English Stage ("C_____r came next" [line 89]), and Garth's Dispensary ("Florid G_____h was General of Horse" [line 207]). A turning point in the poem comes when we receive a late report ("News, hasty news" [line 193]) of Nokor/Blackmore's devastating strike with his Satyr Against Wit, an offensive said to have left the Wits in utter defeat and Nokor/Blackmore "Encamp'd in the Field of Victory" [line 307]). Framing this metaphorical battle narrative is a call for peace. The poem opens with witty alarmist rhetoric about

England on the brink of civil war (of which "The Pen's a certain Herald" [line 41]). At the work's conclusion, negotiation of a Parnassan peace treaty is urged, one feature of which is the proposed assignment of generic provinces—for example, "D[ryde]n to Tragedy," "Hymns for [Nahum] T[at]e," "Let C[ongrev]e write the Comick" (lines 419-23). Defoe himself was neither a Blackmore epigone nor a Dryden satellite. Like Swift, he was a satirist writing about the feud from an outsider's vantage. At various moments in The Pacificator he quite openly attacks Dryden and his followers, as when he speaks of the Wits' "Licentious Arms" of "Burlesque, Bombast, and Bawdy-Song" (lines 172, 175). At other points he singles out particular Wits for derisive hits, as when he characterizes Dennis as a critic who "find[s] out all Mens Errors but his own" (line 158), delivers a slurring comment about Garth's borrowing from Boileau ("'Twas a dull fancy in him to think fit, / To polish English Sense with Foreign Wit" [lines 231-2]), and takes an anti-Catholic swipe at Dryden, whom he shows performing ludicrous, superstitious precombat rites ("General D[ryde]n, with a Pious Rage . . . First Sacrific'd to the Emperor o' th' Moon" [lines 284-6]).

It is, though, Blackmore who is the poem's principal satiric butt, and the methods by which Defoe pursues this target are subtle and elaborate, especially when compared to the simple ways by which he attacks the Wits. One method frequently relied on involves the use of puns and ambiguous constructions to invite subversive, satiric readings of lines. When read casually, certain lines exalt Blackmore, but when read closely they pointedly ridicule him, wholly contravening the more accessible meaning. This technique of verbal sabotage derives much of its intended comic effect from the reader's repeated detections of Defoe's false elevation of his victim- merely pretending to tender praise with one hand while using the other to ridicule.

These lines from the poem's climactic battle scene refer to Blackmore's attack on Dryden and his epigoni with his Satyr against Wit:

> [Nokor/Blackmore's] Squadrons in Poetick Terror shone
>
> The strong Brigades of his Heroic Horse, Dreadful for Sense, for Pointed Satyr worse, in fiery Raptures flew.
>
> (lines 295-300)

Read at their most accessible level, these lines compare the Satyr against Wit to a martial hero's impressive troops and so suggest the power and effectiveness of Blackmore's Satyr. However, an attentive reader comes to pause at such locutions as "Poetick Terror," "Dreadful for Sense," and "for Pointed Satyr worse," and eventually sees meanings that exactly reverse the commendations which Blackmore at first seemed to be receiving: "Poetick Terror" can of course mean that the verse of A Satyr against Wit is so bad as to shock the artistic sensibilities of its readers; and "Dreadful for Sense, for Pointed Satyr worse" can refer to Blackmore's lack of lucid statement and feeble satire—all qualities that seem to follow naturally from the work of a verse satirist whose art turns on nothing more controlled than "fiery Raptures." Also, in the line "The strong Brigades of his Heroic Horse," a careful reader might find the suggestion that Blackmore the satirist (no less than the epic poet) relies on "hoarse" heroics. Dryden in his Aeneis has Neptune characterize Aeolus as a king of "boast and bluster" "With hoarse Commands."[27] And Pope in The Dunciad, in depicting the dunces' braying contest in book 2 (which, incidentally, Blackmore wins) has Dullness announce the prize of a drum for the man "'whose hoarse heroic base / Drowns the loud clarion of the braying Ass.'"[28]

Here and elsewhere Defoe's verbal sabotage is bound up with another of his poem's satiric maneuvers: tendering a satiric fiction of Blackmore victimized when made the heroic subject of his own epic panegyric. The martial language of The Pacificator everywhere recalls that of Blackmore's epics. The lines we have just been examining, for instance, echo innumerable similar lines in the Arthur poems—e.g., "In resplendent Arms Prince Arthur shines, / Darting bright Terrour thro' the Saxon Lines"; "Valiant Troops awful Pomp display"; "Showers of Death flew pointed"; "the generous Courser . . . Flew wild about."[29] It is within this chamber of echoes that Defoe ironically elevates Blackmore, and the result is the fiction of Blackmore being gored by his own epic poetry. Defoe's implied satiric assertion is that the Arthur poems are indeed panegyrics which wound the hero they would praise-no gain from a bad poet's praise (Nec prave factis decorari versibus opto).[30]

Defoe's subtly rendered satire on Blackmore has gone unnoticed by modern commentators on the poem, a number of whom have even claimed that the work shows partisanship toward Blackmore: that Defoe "openly sympathizes with" (Albert Rosenberg), is "friendly to" (Robert Krapp), places himself "solidly on the side of" (Harry Solomon), and "champions" (Theodore Newton) him.[31] It is as if these commentators only observed The Pacificator's surface inflations of its "hero." They might have been more cautious had they recalled that Defoe attacks Blackmore in other works, in his True-Born Englishman (1701), for instance, and in his Reformation of Manners (1702).[32] One would think, moreover, that their reading of The Pacificator would have been guided by what we know to be Defoe's habit as a controversialist of discomfiting readers of opposing views—a habit most notoriously indulged in his Shortest Way with the Dissenters of 1702, which provoked angry replies from Church Tories and Dissenters alike.[33]

Perhaps one cause contributing to their misreading of The Pacificator is that they all fail to note Defoe's parodic play with Blackmore's Arthur poems, which can be observed not only in Defoe's martial language, but also in his poem's plot and overall structure. Defoe's paper-war narrative is modeled after Blackmore's martial narratives, a resemblance contemporaries would have been alerted to at the start of Defoe's account by such details as Nokor/ Blackmore's leading troops of "Old Brittons" newly arrived from a conquest in "the Neustrian Strand"—Neustria being, in the Arthur poems, both a reference to the Merovingian kingdom and an allegorical code word for Holland. Defoe's opening battle episode, moreover, which describes Nokor/ Blackmore and his troops overtaken by "A Storm of Words" recalls the (Aeneid-like) opening of Prince Arthur, where Arthur/William of Orange and his men encounter a devastating storm as they sail from "the Neustrian Coast"[34] to Albion.

A subsequent section of The Pacificator, which describes the Wits' cruel ravaging of the English countryside, recalls the Arthur poems' colorful sketches of reigns of tyranny and lawlessness, which feature despots and their ministers plundering, raping, murdering, and often eating innocent country folk.[35] And what follows this section is Defoe's madly excessive mid-poem cataloguing of conquered Wits ("C[ongrev]e . . . Soldiers Bred in Flanders, / With D[enni]s, D[urfe]y, T[uchi]n, Dull M[otteau]x . . . / G[ildo]n, Tom B[row]n, and many a Subaltern . . . / Mock-Wits, Beau-Wits, and Wits in Masquerade . . . / The Witty D[avenan]t appeared there too" [lines 268-77]; and so on for seventy-five lines), behind which contemporary readers would have recognized Blackmore's spectacularly long warrior lists, which sometimes take up almost a full book in his epics. Finally, in The Pacificator's preclimactic scene, featuring Dryden sacrificing to the Emperor of the Moon, contemporaries would have been reminded of the Arthur poems' superstitious (anti-Catholic) prebattle rituals performed by the archvillains Octa/James II (who, in Prince Arthur, invokes the aid of the pagan Merlin) and Clotar/Louis XIV (who utilizes the arts of the wicked sorceress Maneton in King Arthur).[36]

Defoe, then, parodies Blackmore's Arthur poems in a thoroughgoing fashion, his particular aim being to satirize Blackmore the panegyrist. He signposts this emphasis by structuring his poem according to the conventions of classical panegyric.[37] These conventions are also evident in Blackmore's epics, which commemorate important public events, use a lofty style, and stress the ideal of national harmony. As readers of The Pacificator eventually learn, the poem presents itself as having been written on the occasion of Nokor/Blackmore's overwhelming victory over the Wits with his Satyr against Wit—i.e., the poem's climactic episode, (in which "The Troops of Wit . . . Are Slain, Disper-c'd, Disgrac'd, and Overthrown" [lines 304-5]). This event, we also glean, has inspired the timely pacificating overtures in the framing sections of the work, overtures that sound the traditional panegyric theme of national reconciliation ("if we this Destructive War permit, / Britain will find the Consequence of it" [lines 314-5]). Thus, as in classical verse panegyric, The Pacificator commemorates a public occasion and delivers a political lecture. Also conforming to conventions of classical verse panegyric is the content of The Pacificator's political lecture, which consists of both an address to the general public and an offering of oblique counsel to Nokor/Blackmore. This advice takes the form of the speaker's suggestion that it is in Nokor/Blackmore's best interest to negotiate a peace now, from the position of strength afforded by his recent victory. For, it is cautioned, if he should continue to prosecute the war, he risks defeat, since the Wits are now "arm[ing] at an unusual rate . . . / Recruits from every side come in amain . . . [and] / Their strong Detachments o'r Parnassus range, / And meditate on nothing but Revenge" (lines 318, 321, 327-8). Furthermore, we hear that if the war continues,

> Britain will find the Consequence of it, A Dearth of Sense, or else a Plague of Wit. (lines 315-6)

(A "double-take" is required on 316, so as to note the false antithesis.)

But such counsel should not be registered by us at face value only, because what follows the poem's last general call for an end to the hostilities is a series of proposed peace terms, one of which is this recommended method of forestalling Parnassan boundary disputes:

> To their own Province . . . all confine, Doctors to Heal, to Preaching the Divine;
>
> D[urfe]y make Ballads, Psalms and Hymns for T[at]e: Let P[rio]r Flatter Kings in Panegyrick, R[atcli]ff Burlesque, and W[icherl]y be Lyrick: Let C[ongrev]e write the Comick, F[o]e Lampoon, W[ess]ly the Banter, M[ilbur]n the Buffoon.
>
> (lines 417-24)

In this passage generic territories are parceled out in a fairly exhaustive way. But there is no property for Blackmore. Indeed, once we ask what Blackmore would gain, Defoe's satiric wile obtrudes itself: confining "Doctors to Heal, to Preaching the Divine" might deprive a number of Wits of their literary practices (for instance, Garth, Dr. James Drake, and the preacher-turned-Wit James Smallwood), but it would also take away Dr. Blackmore's poetic practice, and perhaps on two counts, he being a physician and moral reformer (as Dryden put it, "no one Category can contain him; / A Pedant, Canting Preacher, and a Quack, / Are Load enough to break one Asses Back").[38] What is more, Defoe's proposal systematically confers on others every genre in which Blackmore had practiced: "Psalms and Hymns" with his contributions to Nahum Tate's Miscellanea Sacra (1696),[39] "Flatter[ing] Kings in Panegyrick"—or "Burlesque"—with his Arthur poems, and "Lampoon" with his Satyr Against Wit (1699).[40]

Commentators have found it interesting that Defoe would consign the province "Lampoon" to himself, and no critic has yet explored the possibility that his skills as a satirist justify this literary (territorial) claim.[41] One might point out that his later satiric performances in such works as The True-Born Englishman (1701) and Jure Divino (1706) won him the reputation of being one of the most engaging political poets of the period. I suggest that the claim to superiority in satire is justified by the show of intricate verbal wit and sophisticated mock-panegyric design on display in The Pacificator- the very locus of the claim. This suggestion may seem perverse, especially in view of what has become almost a tradition of twentieth-century disparagement of Defoe's prenovelistic literary skills.[42] While the satiric Pope has been viewed as the age's consummate poetic craftsman, Defoe's satiric verse has been denounced as hurriedly written and dully plain. This assessment of Defoe is even manifest in Defovians' pronouncements on The Pacificator,[43] and, in at least a few cases, their negative judgment seems to rest primarily on a reading that is blind to the poem's mock-panegyric contents, and is focused instead on its mock-heroic aspect. James Sutherland, for example, considers this aspect its "most interesting feature"; and both he and Paula Backscheider compare The Pacificator unfavorably to Swift's Battle of the Books. Defoe's notion of a military contest between rival literary coteries, Sutherland writes, "reminds us of Swift's more fully developed satirical fun in The Battle of the Books." Backscheider remarks, similarly, that Defoe's mock-heroic conception is exploited by Swift "with more range and humor."[44]

Close scrutiny of The Pacificator's opening battle episode, where the mock-heroic element is at its most pronounced, should afford an excellent opportunity of putting these statements of Sutherland and Backscheider to the test. Consider these lines:

> Great Nokor does the Men of Sense Command,
> Prince Arthur Trailes a Pike at his Right Hand
>
> And . . . the Bloody Combat undertakes, His [Nokor's] Sence was good, but see what Fate Decrees! His hasty Talent threw him on his Knees, A Storm of Words the Hero overtook, Disorder'd all his Lines, and all his Squadrons broke.
>
> (lines 61-72)

As we know, Defoe here represents the Blackmore v. Wits paper war in mock-heroic fashion; and, as commentators have noted, his mock-epic has an allegorical component in that it allusively renders a sketchy narrative of specific events in the paper war.[45] Two such events are being referred to above: the "Combat" refers to the publication of Prince Arthur in 1695, and the "Storm of Words" refers to the publication of John Dennis's scathing Remarks on Prince Arthur (1696).[46] For the reader acquainted with these works, Defoe's allusions gain in comic force. For the "Bloody Combat" at line 67 remarks on the sensationalistic "blood-and-guts" quality of Blackmore's epics. And the "Disorder'd . . . Lines" and "Squadrons broke" at line 71 describes the dislocations performed on the lines and stanzas of Prince Arthur by Dennis, who employs in his Remarks a method of close textual criticism. But to read the poem only in this mock-heroic light would be to overlook the considerable skills Defoe shows in ridiculing Blackmore. Let us register briefly how the lines quoted above take on a new complexion when patiently sifted and enjoyed as mock-panegyric satire.

Defoe, of course, elevates Blackmore to a martial hero of (mock-) epic proportions. His "hasty Talent" and "Hero[ic]" stature are pointed up; and in line 67 the legendary Arthur is described as a subordinate of this "great" Nokor/Blackmore. And we should notice that Defoe is at the same time ridiculing Blackmore the poet, whose "hasty Talent" (said to have thrown him on his knees [line 69]) must hobble him in the literary field. At line 70 we see Nokor/Blackmore besieged by "A Storm of Words," an action that suggests that Blackmore's planned epic suffered severely from Blackmore's own "Storm of Words," hasty fustian that disordered lines and even whole stanzas. Dryden, in translating Persius's first satire, speaks of bad authors whose work "is Fustian, and the Numbers lame. / All Noise, and empty Pomp, a storm of words."[47] This scenario of Blackmore the poet being defeated, like a vanquished soldier, by his own hastily produced bombast is developed further through details that exploit the scene's satiric and farcical potential. In line 68 ("[Nokor/Blackmore] the Bloody Combat undertakes") Defoe puts two senses of "undertakes" into play to stress just how poorly Blackmore the poet controls language. The most obvious meaning of the word, in context, is "begins" (Blackmore initiates the combat); but another meaning is its obsolete sense of "seizes upon by craft" (the combat entraps Blackmore unawares). The OED documents this latter meaning with an illustration from Malory's Morte Darthur, the chief literary source of Blackmore's Prince Arthur ("Tristram endured . . . grete payne, for sekeness had vndertake hym" [9.37.400]). In lines 68 and 70 Defoe uses structural and verbal symmetry ("[Nokor/Blackmore] the Bloody Combat undertakes . . . A Storm of Words the Hero overtook") to activate this latter meaning, since it pushes alert readers to laminate (in their minds) "overtook" with "took unawares."

Defoe further suggests Blackmore's disaster at the hands of his own wayward words through ambivalent use of the verb "broke"- in "A Storm of Words the Hero overtook / Disorder'd all his Lines, and all his Squadrons broke" [lines 70-1]). The subject of this verb can be "Storm of Words," so that Defoe's sense is, at one level, that Blackmorean bombast threw the verse of Prince Arthur into total disarray. But since "Squadrons" may also be the subject of "broke," this sense is underwritten in a vivid way, so that we are presented with an image of the very stanzas of Prince Arthur responding to Blackmorean poetic incompetence by flying into disorder, breaking their ranks, as it were.

We have not been led to expect such intricate verbal play from Defoe's poetry. But it is everywhere discoverable in The Pacificator once we view it as mock-panegyric satire. It is unfortunate that Ellis, in the volume of the Yale Poems on Affairs of State that includes The Pacificator, depreciates Defoe the satiric poet for his "directness" ("not a virtue in art") and careless haste ("'too much haste to correct'"); and, rather than properly assessing Defoe's accomplishment in the context of state affairs verse, he concludes: "Defoe evolved a kind of stripped-down poetry of statement that is heard again in Cowper, for example."[48]

In the 1940s Maynard Mack did much to counter Matthew Arnold's opinion that Pope had, along with Dryden, developed versified prose. Some twenty years later, Ellis, I think, has rather obviously displaced Arnold's famous assertion about Pope onto Defoe. Mack, in 1944, initiated what would become a major reappraisal of Pope's satiric verse when he prescribed, "We must read Pope's poetry with the most scrupulous attention, weighing every word."[49] For "Pope," read also "Defoe."

NOTES

1. Mac Flecknoe, in *The Works of John Dryden*, ed. H. T. Swedenberg et al. (Los Angeles and Berkeley: Univ. of California Press, 1955-), 2:59, lines 198-200. Unless

otherwise indicated, all quotations from Dryden are taken from this edition, and will be referenced parenthetically in the text.

2. Commendatory Verses, on the Author of the Two Arthurs and the Satyr against Wit; By Some of His Particular Friends, in Richard C. Boys, Sir Richard Blackmore and the Wits, no. 13 (Ann Arbor: Univ. of Michigan Press, 1949), pp. 71, 73, 104. This volume of verse is reproduced in full in Boys's book. All quotations from it follow Boys's edition—cited hereafter as Commendatory Verses.
3. Richard Blackmore, *A Paraphrase on the Book of Job* (London, 1700), "Preface," sig. a[1.sup.r].
4. Detailed accounts of the Blackmore v. Wits paper war can be found in Boys's Sir Richard Blackmore and the Wits, pp. 2-31; Harry M. Solomon, Sir Richard Blackmore (Boston: Twayne, 1980), pp. 34-5, 59-74, 76-83; notes by Edward Niles Hooker in *The Critical Works of John Dennis*, 2 vols. (Baltimore: Johns Hopkins Univ. Press, 1939-43), 1:447-8; and Albert Rosenberg, *Sir Richard Blackmore: A Poet and Physician of the Augustan Age* (Lincoln: Univ. of Nebraska Press, 1953), pp. 39-70.
5. Commendatory Verses, pp. 67-8.
6. See esp. *A Tale of a Tub*, in *The Prose Works of Jonathan Swift*, ed. Herbert Davis, 14 vols. (Oxford: Basil Blackwell, 1939), 1:18, 43, 115-6. For commentary on Swift's satire on Blackmore and Dryden in these (cited) pages and in other moments in the Tale, see Herbert Davis, *The Satire of Jonathan Swift* (New York: Macmillan, 1947), pp. 30-2; notes by A.C. Guthkelch and D. Nichol Smith in their second edition of the Tale (Oxford: Oxford Univ. Press, 1958), pp. 30, 182-3; Edward W. Rosenheim, "Swift's Satire in A Tale of a Tub" (Ph.D. diss., Univ. of Chicago, 1953), pp. 136-8; and Rosenheim, *Swift and the Satirist's Art* (Chicago: Univ. of Chicago Press, 1963), pp. 85-8.
7. On this parody, see my references to Davis, Guthkelch and Smith, and Rosenheim.
8. *A Tale of a Tub*, pp. 29-30, 32. These page numbers refer to Davis's edition.

9. Anthony Ashley Cooper, *Characteristicks of Men, Manners, Opinions, Times*, 2d edn., 3 vols. (London, 1714), 1:226. This passage is quoted and commented on by Aubrey Williams in Pope's "Dunciad" (London: Methuen, 1955; rprt. Hamden CT: Archon Books, 1968), pp. 12-3, and by James Garrison in *Dryden and the Tradition of Panegyric* (Los Angeles and Berkeley: Univ. of California Press, 1975), pp. 34-5.

10. Maynard Mack, "'Wit and Poetry and Pope,'" in *Pope and His Contemporaries*, ed. James L. Clifford and Louis A. Landa (Oxford: Clarendon Press, 1949), pp. 33-4. Aubrey Williams built on Mack's point by insisting that Pope closely imitates his models. For example, Williams states that Pope in the Epistle to Augustus is doing "nothing more, in one respect, than what Eusden and Cibber did innocently and uncritically in their birthday odes" (p. 12). Hugh Kenner flamboyantly concurred with this contention in his Counterfeiters: An Historical Comedy (Bloomington: Indiana Univ. Press, 1968; rprt. Baltimore: Johns Hopkins Univ. Press, 1985): "It was in the course of transmuting the second George into Augustus that Pope made his principal contribution to the theory of counterfeiting, so stunning an insight that he was to spend much of the seven years that remained to him recasting the Dunciad by its light. He discovered Pop Art." According to Kenner, the Epistle to Augustus sustains two possible readings, one that detects satiric irony and one that does not: "If it is signed, say 'Ambrose Philips,' or not signed . . . trifling flaws become bubbles in a torrent of adulation. Pope's signature does not merely accept responsibility for the libel, it creates the libel" (pp. 92-3).

11. Garrison, p. 36.

12. Frank Ellis, commentary in *Poems on Affairs of State: Augustan Satirical Verse, 1660-1714*, ed. George deF. Lord, 7 vols. (New Haven: Yale Univ. Press, 1963-75), 6:158; hereafter cited as "the Yale POAS."

13. Twentieth-century critical discussion of The Pacificator has been spare. The poem has largely been ignored by

scholars, and what attention it has received has, on the whole, been cursory and dismissive. Paul Dottin and James Sutherland never discuss the work in their biographies of Defoe (Dottin, *The Life and Strange and Surprising Adventures of Daniel De Foe*, trans. Louise Ragan [New York: Macaulay, 1929]; Sutherland, Defoe [London: Methuen, 1950]). Brief glosses on the work include those in John Robert Moore, *Daniel Defoe: Citizen of the Modern World* (Chicago: Univ. of Chicago Press, 1958), p. 233; Sutherland, *Daniel Defoe: A Critical Study* (Cambridge MA: Harvard Univ. Press, 1941), pp. 93-6; Frank Bastian, *Defoe's Early Life* (London: Macmillan, 1981), p. 221; and Paula Backscheider, *Daniel Defoe: His Life* (Baltimore: Johns Hopkins Univ. Press, 1989), pp. 73-4. There has been only one scholarly article fully devoted to the poem: Albert Rosenberg, "Defoe's Pacificator Reconsidered," *PQ* 37, 4 (October 1958): 433-9.

14. On the Arthur poems as recreative endeavors, see Blackmore's preface to *Prince Arthur* (London, 1695), sig. c2r, and his preface to King Arthur (London, 1697), p. v.

15. For a detailed account of the topical allegory in *Prince Arthur* and *King Arthur*, see Solomon, pp. 42-3, 52, 55; and Roberta Florence Brinkley, *Arthurian Legend in the Seventeenth Century* (Baltimore: Johns Hopkins Univ. Press, 1932), pp. 176-83.

16. Dryden, "An Account of the Ensuing Poem," 1:53.

17. Dryden mentions having contemplated using Arthur's warring with the Saxons for an epic in his "Discourse concerning the Original and Progress of Satire" (1692), 4:22-3. A superb political reading of King Arthur is that by David Bywaters in *Dryden in Revolutionary England* (Los Angeles and Berkeley: Univ. of California Press, 1991), pp. 75-93.

18. Dryden, "Dedication of the Aeneis," 5:327. I am indebted to Solomon's discussion on p. 61 of his Twayne Blackmore of Dryden's oblique hits at Blackmore in this dedication.

19. Dryden, "Preface," Fables, in *The Poems of John Dryden*, ed. James Kinsley, 4 vols. (Oxford: Clarendon Press, 1958), 4:1462.

20. Dryden, "Prologue," *The Pilgrim* (London, 1700), sig. A[2.sup.v]. For a fuller account of Dryden's attacks on Blackmore, see Solomon, pp. 57-61 and Rosenberg, Blackmore, pp. 54-5.

21. On this point, see Solomon, p. 62. Concerning the possibility that Dryden influenced Dennis's writing of the Remarks on Prince Arthur, see H.G. Paul, *John Dennis: His Life and Criticism* (New York: Columbia Univ. Press, 1911), p. 29. I would suggest that the strategy of focusing on the alleged artistic shortcomings of Blackmore may have had much to do with the fact that Dryden and his Will's epigoni did not all agree in political outlook. Dryden, for example, would have shared common political ground with the colorfully outspoken Jacobites Tom Brown and William Pittis. John Dennis and Samuel Garth, however, were staunch Williamites.

22. Blackmore, it seems, was an eminence in the S.P.C.K. See *A Chapter in English Church History: Being the Minutes of the Society for Promoting Christian Knowledge for the Years 1698-1704*, ed. Edmund McClure (London: Society for Promoting Christian Knowledge), pp. 3, 6, 7, 12, 111.

23. For commentary on Blackmore's moralistic assaults on the Wits—on Dryden in particular—in his prefaces to his epics, see Solomon, pp. 59-61.

24. This Dublin edition was published in 1700.

25. Luttrell's copy of The Pacificator specifies 15 February as the publication date. This copy is now in the Clark Library. On Luttrell's dating notations, see James Osborn, "Reflections on Narcissus Luttrell," *The Book Collector* 6, 1 (Spring 1957): 21-3.

26. My text for The Pacificator follows Ellis's edition in vol. 6 of the Yale POAS. However, I retain Defoe's use of "blank-names," which Ellis does not, although he reproduces them in his textual notes to the poem (6:754).

27. Dryden, *Aeneis*, 5:349, lines 201-2.

28. Pope, *The Dunciad*, in the Twickenham Edition, ed. John Butt et al., 11 vols. [in 12] (New Haven and London: Yale Univ. Press and Methuen, 1939-69), 5:307, lines 233-4.

29. *Prince Arthur*, 3d edn. (London, 1696), book 8, p. 217; *King Arthur*, 4.100; *Prince Arthur*, 4.111; *King Arthur*, 4.103. I have chosen the third edition of *Prince Arthur* as my text because Defoe, writing his poem in 1700, may have had easiest access to it.

30. Horace Ep. 2.1.266.

31. Rosenberg, Blackmore, p. 48; Robert Krapp, "Class Analysis of a Literary Controversy: Wit and Sense in Seventeenth-Century English Literature," *Science and Society* 10 (Winter 1946): 80-92, 87; Solomon, p. 75; Theodore F.M. Newton, "Blackmore's Eliza," *Harvard Studies and Notes in Philology and Literature* 18, 1 (Winter 1935): 113-23, 114.

32. See, in the Yale POAS, Defoe's *The True-Born Englishman*, 6:297, line 954; and his *Reformation of Manners*, 6:444, lines 1146-51, and 6:415-6, lines 389-415, which satirize Blackmore while they attack a merely apparent "parallel" target, one Richard Blackburne. For corroboration of this, see, in the Yale POAS, Defoe's *More Reformation* [1703], 6:579, lines 769-70.

33. On this habit of Defoe's, see Maximillian E. Novak, "Defoe's Use of Irony," in Irony in Defoe and Swift, intro. H. T. Swedenberg, William Andrews Clark Memorial Library (Los Angeles and Berkeley: Univ. of California Press, 1966), pp. 10-7; and Novak, "Defoe's Shortest Way with the Dissenters: Hoax, Parody, Paradox, Fiction, Irony, and Satire," *MLQ* 27 (December 1966): 40217, 412-3. See also my essay, "Ironic Monologue and 'Scandalous Ambodexter Conformity' in Defoe's Shortest Way with the Dissenters".

34. Prince Arthur, 1.3.

35. See, for example, *Prince Arthur*, 4.101-5, and *King Arthur*, 1.4-9.

36. See *Prince Arthur*, 7.202-7, and *King Arthur*, 12.316-9.

37. For a fine discussion of the conventions of classical panegyric, see Garrison, pp. 63-82.

38. Dryden, "Prologue," *The Pilgrim*, sig. A[2.sup.v].

39. Blackmore's particular contributions to Tate's Miscellanea Sacra bear no signature, but convincing identification of them can be found in Rosenberg, Blackmore, p. 41 n. 4.

40. In The Pacificator Defoe even proposes granting to another poet a genre he anticipated Blackmore would be working in: "Banters on the Sacred Text" (line 449). Blackmore, as many Londoners knew, was soon to publish a Williamite allegory using the biblical Job story, and in fact his Paraphrase on the Book of Job was published only weeks later than The Pacificator, in late February or early March, 1700 (on this dating, see remarks by Ellis, 6:188 [n. 17]). In Defoe's poem, such "Banter" would, under the terms of the recommended treaty, be monopolized by Samuel Wesley, a Blackmore satellite and author of the pro-Williamite epic, *The Life of Christ* (1694). For some contemporaries, Blackmore's Job must have seemed a significant departure from the earlier Arthur poems, since Blackmore in this work rejects the imitation of classical (hence pagan) models (see his preface to Job, sigs. [Bb.sup.r-v]); but for others, it was more of the panegyrical same. The Wits penned such epigrams as "On Job [King William] Travesty'd by the City Bard" and "On Job newly Travestied by Sir R_____Bl_____," and such lines as, "What Spouse and Satan did attempt in vain, / The Quack will compass with his murdring Pen, / And on a Dunghil leave poor Job again," and "Job . . . does in your Poems Languish / And suffer almost hellish Anguish" (*Commendatory Verses*, pp. 85, 90, 105, 129). One contemporary, Elizabeth Thomas, committed this faux pas when asking for Job at her bookseller's: "instead of asking for his Paraphrase, I enquired for his Satire on JOB, which mightily offended some Friends of Sir Richard's that were in the Shop" (Richard Gwinnet, *Pylades and Corinna* [London, 1731], 2:178-9; quoted in Solomon, p. 91). In The Pacificator, if all the proposed treaty's stipulations were to be agreed upon and obeyed,

including the one relating to banters ("No Banters on the Sacred Text admit" [line 449]), Wesley, a Blackmore epigone, would be exiled to a sacred banter land, but Blackmore would not even gain so much ground.

41. See, for.example, Sutherland, p. 96, and Mary Campbell, Defoe's *First Poem* (Bloomington: Principia Press, 1938), p. 1.

42. Maximillian Novak has done much to counter the opinion that Defoe's prose fiction lacks detailed verbal sophistication and care. In the preface to his *Realism, Myth, and History in Defoe's Fiction* (Lincoln: Univ. of Nebraska Press, 1983), he finds one component of Defoe's literary genius in "the often-underestimated complexities of his style and language" (p. xiii)- a claim especially well supported in his chapter "'Unweary'd Traveller' and 'Indifferent Monitor': Openness and Complexity in Moll Flanders."

43. According to Sutherland, the poem would have been more effective as satire if Defoe "had taken a little more care with it" (p. 96). Frank Bastian would concur, since for him the poem looks like "the kind of thing that Defoe could have thrown off in a few winter evenings" (Defoe's Early Life [London: Methuen and Co., 1981], p. 221). Other appraisals by Defoe scholars are, typically, just as lukewarm, if less specific: "not without longueurs" (Ellis, 6:158); "a mediocre poem" (Newton, p. 114); "calculated to divert the family circle at Christmas-time" (William Freeman, *The Incredible De Foe* [London: Herbert Jenkins, 1950], p. 125); "by no means above his [Defoe's] usual level of versifying" (Francis Watson, *Daniel Defoe* [London: Longmans, 1952], p. 90).

44. Sutherland, p. 95; Paula Backscheider, *Daniel Defoe: Ambition and Innovation* (Lexington: Univ. of Kentucky Press, 1986), p. 22.

45. On this, see Rosenberg, "Defoe's Pacificator," pp. 433-44.

46. For corroboration, see Solomon, p. 75, and Ellis, 6:163 n. 71.

47. Dryden, *The Satires of Persius*, 6:261.

48. Ellis, 6:260, 261. I realize that the formalist criteria of the New Criticism brought by Ellis to his appraisal of Defoe's poetry here fails to reckon with the values of effective political verse- as shown in the works of such Dryden scholars as Michael McKeon, Steven Zwicker, and Phillip Harth. In my forthcoming book, "Defoe and the Business of Satire," I discuss how Defoe uses hermeneutically challenging satiric art to gain readers for his political propaganda.

49. Maynard Mack, "On Reading Pope," *College English* 7, 5 (February 1946): 263-73, 263.

5

Robinson Crusoe as Narrative Theologian

—Daniel E. Ritchie

Daniel Defoe's three volumes of Robinson Crusoe (1719-20) appeared at a time of great change in biblical hermeneutics. As described by one of the founders of "narrative theology," Hans Frei, western reading of the Bible up to the eighteenth century was "strongly realistic, i.e., at once literal and historical, not only doctrinal or edifying" (Eclipse 1). Under the pressure of the historical-critical method, however, historical readings of Scripture began to split apart from the "edifying" ones. I hope to show that Defoe's volumes reflect both the earlier, unified reading of Scripture, and the contemporary split. In the first and most well-known volume, Robinson Crusoe reflects an earlier reading of Scripture. There, the biblical narratives are considered "true" in that Crusoe comes to recognize the authority of biblical narratives for the purpose of reinterpreting his past life and for shaping his future life. He comes to understand his own life story as he learns to interpret it with respect to sacred stories. That is, Crusoe learns to "read" his life by orienting his own patterns of experience with respect tc the stories of Scripture, rather in the manner of recent narrative theologians. By contrast, the second and third volumes (and especially their prefaces) give evidence of the hermeneutical shift taking place. There, Defoe becomes extremely concerned about the "truth"—by which he means the historical verifiability—of the narrative and his fictional character. Rather in the manner of the emerging historical-critical readers of Scripture of the early eighteenth century, Defoe's reading of his own novels begins to separate their "edifying" meaning from their historically unverifiable fictions.

The split between "the edifying" and "the historical" has had large consequences for the reading of Scripture since the eighteenth century. Those consequences may be seen in church history in the split between "the historical Jesus" and the "Christ of Faith." They may also be seen in the Enlightenment assumption, still held by many religious liberals and conservatives of today, that the fictive elements of a narrative cannot have any claim to truth (see Green 81). Having recognized the fictive elements of Scripture, liberals have sought to locate biblical meaning in various kinds of nonhistorical areas (myth, existential affirmation, etc.), while conservatives have labored all the harder to verify the historical accuracy of Scripture. Both sides, however, share the assumption that the "plain sense" of sacred history would, in principle, emerge from a scientific reconstruction of the biblical world and its events, particularly the events of the life of Jesus. Recent narrative theologians have contested these assumptions. While acknowledging fictive elements, they have asserted the "history-like" character of biblical narrative, as distinct from the mythical character of Greek legends (see Frei, Eclipse 11-12). "[The] `plain sense' of biblical stories is not their historical reference," writes narrative theologian Garrett Green, "but their narrative meaning. Quite simply, the meaning of the texts is the story they tell—`fictive' elements and all!" (91).

In this essay I hope to demonstrate that the terms of recent narrative theology may give us a way of understanding why Robinson Crusoe has pleased more readers than its sequels.[1] In the first volume of Robinson Crusoe, the pre-critical hermeneutics of Scripture—the assumed unity of the Bible's narrative meaning and fictive elements—translates into the way Crusoe interprets his own life. I hope to show, however, after the first volume, that Defoe becomes immersed in disputes that parallel those of the emerging, critical reading of Scripture, especially when he shows concern about the split between the edifying and the historical significance of his story. Along the way, I hope to show that it is more fruitful to "historicize" the novel by restoring Crusoe's pre-critical reading of his life through the perspective of biblical narrative than by recent attempts (suggestive though they are) to view it in terms of imprisonment, cannibalism, or Crusoe's own acquisitive desires.[2]

Along with H. Richard Niebuhr, Stephen Crites, and Erich Auerbach, Hans Frei is viewed as one of the founders of narrative theology. Frei saw that in pre-critical readings of Scripture, neither Christian doctrines nor the historical events recounted in the Bible had any significance apart from the larger narrative context in which they occurred. The world described by the narratives of the Bible was considered to be the "primary world," from which everything else derived its significance. In his well-known contrast between the effect of Homeric fiction and that of biblical literature, Erich Auerbach wrote,

> The Bible's claim to truth is not only far more urgent than Homer's, it is tyrannical—it excludes all other claims. The world of the Scripture stories is not satisfied with claiming to be a historically true reality—it insists that it is the only real world, is destined for autocracy. All other scenes, issues, and ordinances have no right to appear

> independently of it, and it is promised that all of them, the history of all mankind, will be given their due place within its frame, will be subordinated to it. (12)

Before the rise of the historical-critical method, there was ultimately only the one, single world of the biblical narratives, wrote Frei, and it was the reader's duty to find his or her story in it (Eclipse 2-3). In Stephen Crites's explanation, the "sacred stories" of a culture "are not like monuments that men behold, but like dwelling places. People live in them" (295). And when people begin to tell their own stories—"mundane stories," in Crites's terms—those stories attain their resonance as they clarify the contemporary world with respect to the culture's sacred stories (296-97). In the Enlightenment, however, the rational inquiry of the historical scholar, independent of the traditional interpretations of the Church, came to be viewed as the authoritative means of arriving at the literal meaning (or "plain sense") of the biblical text. To be sure, doctrinal statements about the Trinity or Creation, for instance, could still be made. Personal significance could still be derived from Scripture. But both doctrine and personal significance were, in principle, divorced from historical inquiry by Enlightenment scholars. Many of those scholars often believed in Christian doctrine and took its personal significance quite seriously; but they made the "true" meaning of the Bible entirely dependent upon their inquiries into the historical factuality of the scriptural narratives. The miracles, legends, and saga-like elements of the Bible were consequently relegated to positions of little importance. As Frei writes, when the value of a text came to be partly or wholly dependent upon its historical veracity, the narrative threatened to split. In his controversial writings of 1724 and 1727, for instance, the deist Anthony Collins maintained that because the literal sense of Isaiah 7:14 refers to a young woman in the days of King Ahaz, Matthew's claim to find the verse fulfilled in Christ's birth (Matt 1:22-23) is meaningless (Eclipse 66-69).

As the eighteenth century progressed, there was no longer "one story" in the Bible, no longer a single narrative in which one was challenged to find one's own story. Rather, there were numerous fragments, some of which were probably historically accurate, others not. The religious meaning of these fragments changed more with reference to prevailing intellectual trends rather than in continuity with the interpretations given by the community of Christians down through the ages.

Recently, narrative theologians have sought to bring together both historical-critical and pre-critical ways of reading Scripture. This kind of reading attempts to restore some of the ways of Bible reading that most of Defoe's audience took for granted. For instance, the meaning of a text is not detachable from the stories it tells (see Placher 8). In the face of modern critical readings and postmodern suspicious readings, the narrative theologians seek a "hermeneutics of restoration" (Frei, Theology and Narrative 130). They seek a "second naivete" that locates the "plain sense" of Scripture not in its historical reference but in its full narrative meaning. Remarkably, for a movement so closely related to literary hermeneutics, narrative theology has been largely ignored by scholars who deal with earlier fiction.[3]

Defoe was part of a Protestant culture that was vigorously intellectual and energetically literary. During his time, the split between historical-critical and doctrinal-personal readings began to show itself. One can see it in Defoe's growing unease about writing a story that is "not true"—that is, fictional. He tried to keep up the pretense that Robinson Crusoe (like his later fictional characters) was a real man. When Defoe was derided by Charles Gildon for having written an allegory, he responded by accepting the criticism: "The story, though allegorical, is also historical," he wrote in the preface to Serious Reflections (ix). By the time he wrote the preface to the third volume, however, we see Defoe straddling the emerging gap between the historical realism of a story and its meaning.

We know from J. Paul Hunter and G.A. Starr that the narrative shape of Robinson Crusoe derives from Puritan literature. The basic pattern involves the Lord's providential doings before conversion, conversion itself, recovery, decay, and the subject's present position (see Starr 40). These autobiographies saw the Christian life as a narrative whole, often as a journey, in which the climactic moment was conversion.

Every Christian's life was therefore both typical and unique: the unique events of one's own life answered to the types provided by biblical narratives. The biblical narratives were accepted as true, "literally" true, without an independent inquiry into their historical factuality. Moreover, the one story of the believer's life answered to the "one story" of the Bible. Thus, the truth of Pilgrim's Progress rested, for contemporary readers, on the believable correspondences between the stories of the Bible, of Christian and his family, and of the readers themselves.

Recent narrative theology sees life in similar terms: "Christian narrative emerges from the collision between an individual's identity narrative and the narratives of the Christian community" (Stroup 95). "Collision" emphasizes the "disorientation and reinterpretation" that spiritual transformation causes. In the first volume of Robinson Crusoe, Crusoe's life frequently collides with biblical types or narratives. These collisions produce the most striking illuminations of his sinfulness, his setbacks on the road to conversion, and later, his spiritual maturity. In this novel and in contemporary spiritual autobiographies, the reader could ultimately come to see that even the disasters of the believer's life were necessary for some providential purpose.

Robinson Crusoe appeals to its audience in a way that is analogous to the way biblical narratives have appealed to their audiences: most readers do not puzzle over the empirical truth of Crusoe's adventures any more than Bible readers puzzle over miracles. The audience finds the events "history-like," to use Auerbach's phrase. These events are "indispensable to the rendering of a particular character . . . or a particular story" (Frei, Eclipse 14). In short, there is a unity between narrative and meaning in this earlier reading of Scripture and in Robinson Crusoe, without any prior investigation of the narrative's historical verifiability.

An example from Psalm 78, which later has great significance for Crusoe, may help to clarify this unity. The Psalm recapitulates the history of the exodus and God's providential care for the people of Israel. In the opening twelve verses, however, the psalmist gives the reason for telling the story: by rightly hearing the story, our children may trust in God. Unlike the Israelites of the exodus, they may remember his works and keep his commandments (vs. 8). It does not occur to the psalmist, any more than it occurs to Crusoe, to inquire into the historicity of his narrative and to base its meaning only on the verifiable details. The whole psalm is a unity whose meaning is inseparable from the story it tells.

This kind of unity has evaporated by the time Defoe writes his preface to volume three. There is a gap between narrative and meaning that the Psalmist—and the Crusoe of volume one—would not have recognized. In the later preface, Defoe defends the first two volumes of Robinson Crusoe because of the "moral and religious Improvement" they bring. But this preface (and volume three as a whole) makes a peculiarly modern distinction between the historically dubious tale of Robinson Crusoe and its allegedly true meaning, even as Defoe desperately affirms its historicity:

> In a word, there's not a circumstance in the imaginary story, but has its just allusion to a real story, and chimes part for part, and step for step with the inimitable Life of Robinson Crusoe . . . (Serious Reflections xi)

What is this "real story"? Many readers have seen in Defoe's own confinement in Newgate the "real history [that] is represented by a confined retreat in an island" (Serious Reflections xii). Paula Backscheider and John Bender, in particular, have shown the novel's relationship to both Defoe's imprisonment and contemporary views of the penitentiary. But more significant for my purpose is a prior question: why isn't the fictional Robinson Crusoe a "real story"? Why must there be an allusive relationship between the imaginary and the real, whether in Defoe's mind or in the minds of modern interpreters? The answer, with respect to Defoe, is that he has already begun to assume that "fiction" (including legend, saga, allegory, allusion) is the opposite of "real" and "true." If it cannot be empirically verified, the "fiction" is false, even if the moral of Robinson Crusoe is still true, as Defoe loudly asserts.

> Here is invincible patience recommended under the worst of misery; indefatigable application and undaunted resolution under the greatest and most discouraging circumstances; I say, these are recommended, as the only way to work through those miseries, and their success appears sufficient to support the most dead-hearted creature in the world. (Serious Reflections xii)

Defoe has come to believe that the moral truth of the novel can stand alone, apart from the "false" surrounding fictions. Earlier in the preface, however, he implies that true religious reflection depends upon historical verification in every particular.

> . . . [A]ll those parts of the story are real facts in my history, whatever borrowed lights they may be represented by. Thus the fright and fancies which succeeded the story of the print of a man's foot, and surprise of the old goat, and the thing rolling on my bed . . . the description of starving, the story of my man Friday, and many more most material passages observed here, and on which any religious reflections are made, are all historical and true in fact. (x-xi, emphasis added)

These words look back, in part, to the Puritan unease with fiction, familiar to English readers since Stephen Gosson's debate with Sir Philip Sidney. But the assumption that true religious meaning depends upon historical verification also looks forward. It looks forward to the assumed conflict between the origins (or reliability) of a text and its value. This conflict, which was just beginning to be felt in biblical criticism during Defoe's day, is already reflected by the preface: how can a narrative be true if its veracity is not susceptible to empirical investigations by a detached, rational observer? Defoe fears that if Robinson Crusoe is known to be fictional, it will also be considered meaningless.

I think it very likely that the audience for Robinson Crusoe has remained large, while that of the Farther Adventures and Serious Reflections is virtually non-existent, precisely because the conflicts in Crusoe's life are literally inseparable from the narrative's moral and religious meaning. In other words, Robinson Crusoe is "history-like" in that its representation of reality cannot be separated from its particular narrative. An early, influential biography by Walter Wilson (1830) corroborates this. Wilson, a dissenter, very much unites the realism of the novel with its religious significance:

> The fine sentiments that abound in Crusoe, its delicate touches, and pure morality, are not the least parts of its beauties, and give it a decided superiority over every other work of the same description. Whilst it instructs us in the development of the human powers, under the guidance of natural reason, it points to the Almighty as the source from whence man derives his capacities, and to whom his homage should be directed. The reader of Crusoe is taught to be a religious, whilst he is an animal being. But his lessons of this [religious] kind are no where out of place; they are closely interwoven with the story, and are so just and pertinent in themselves, that they cannot be passed over, but the attention is irresistibly rivetted to them as an essential part of the narrative. (Rogers 91)

Some of the most influential readings of Robinson Crusoe, beginning with that of Ian Watt, see the challenges before him as those of overcoming the environment and subjugating the persons with whom he comes in contact. But the deeper challenge is for Crusoe to learn to acknowledge God, and for his worldly actions to reflect a mature trust in Providence in each new scene of his life. The book is structured around Crusoe's growing trust in God. At each point where the narrative comes to either a lull or a point of high tension, Defoe invents a new series of incidents that push Crusoe to a higher level of trust in God.

In the early episodes of the novel, Crusoe passes up his many opportunities to learn from experience. Then, in the days following his shipwreck, Crusoe is beset by fear—the response considered by Defoe's contemporary Dissenters as the direct opposite to trusting in Providence. Crusoe still learns little. In the eight months after the shipwreck it becomes increasingly clear that Crusoe is going to escape starvation. But achieving a state of relative prosperity is not the climax of the narrative. The climax comes in the ninth month, when Crusoe falls deathly ill of a fever and dreams of an angel holding a spear: "Seeing all these things have not brought thee to Repentance, now thou shalt die," says the angel (87). At this point Crusoe's conscience begins to awaken. As a first step, he is led to acknowledge God's existence and providential control over nature. He even acknowledges his own misspent life. But these acknowledgments are the products of Crusoe's "natural" theology, the spiritual insight he can achieve without God's direct help. A saving knowledge of God must come from divine revelation. At this point we can start to see how Crusoe's pre-critical reading of Scripture works, especially the unity of story and meaning that it assumes.

As Crusoe begins to recover, he finds a Bible. Between doses of his medicine, Crusoe "opened the Book casually," reading the first words he finds: "Call on me in the Day of Trouble, and I will deliver, and thou shalt glorify me" (94; Ps. 50: 15). Crusoe now begins to consider the possibility that his identity is captured and explained within the narratives of Scripture:

> The Words were very apt to my Case, and made some Impression upon my Thoughts at the Time of reading them, tho' not so much as they did afterwards; for as for being deliver'd the Word had no Sound, as I may say, to me; the Thing was so remote, so impossible in my Apprehension of Things, that I began to say as the Children of Israel did, when they were promis'd Flesh to eat, Can God spread a Table in the Wilderness [Ps.78: 19]? (94)

There are three parts to the "plot" of Psalm 50:15: calling on God, being delivered, and glorifying God. As he returns to health, Crusoe can now see how God has continually delivered him. "But I had not glorify'd him," he realizes (95-96). During his very next Bible reading, Crusoe places himself among the audience that listens to the testimony of Peter and the apostles: "[Christ] is exalted a Prince and a Saviour, to give Repentance, and to give Remission" (Acts 5:31). This verse calls forth Crusoe's own prayer for repentance, and enables him to understand the "deliverance" of Psalm 50 "in a different Sense from what I had ever done before" (96). That is, he seeks (and finds) deliverance from the guilt of his past life, compared to which deliverance from the island would be a figure or analogy. The two passages in Psalms and Acts are quite brief, but their brevity does not diminish the effectiveness of the narrative sequence, as both Crusoe and recent theologians recognize (see Frei, Theology and Narrative 208). The continued popularity of Robinson Crusoe, especially among Christian readers, probably rests on moments like these, where the realism of the spiritual narrative is united with the realism of the island adventure. This unity makes Crusoe a biblical Everyman, recapitulating in his island existence the drama common to everyone who learns to trust God.

Beginning with his climactic conversion, Crusoe begins to find his world in the stories of Scripture. During the next decade he recognizes that his life is indeed described by Psalm 78:19—God's Table is spread in the Wilderness—as he learns to make clothes and pottery and becomes a baker and goatherd. He also comes back to Psalm 50: 15 during the next turning point of his life, a crisis that I shall discuss at length below, when he discovers a human footprint on the island and fear again threatens to overmaster him (153).

Equally important, Crusoe now begins to reinterpret his past life (before conversion) in terms of biblical narrative. As in other contemporary autobiographies, conversion is the most significant plot element of the story: the subplots make sense when viewed from its perspective. In parallel fashion, recent narrative theology helps one see how conversion becomes the central "plot" element in establishing the Christian identity of the individual believer. As George Stroup explains, the believer's past self-understanding comes into question at the moment of conversion and must be reworked. The previous elements of his life are reinterpreted, now as indispensable elements of a new self-understanding that is re-oriented around Christ (Stroup 116-17). As his identity is reformed by Christian narrative, Crusoe is able to look back at his original opposition to his father as his "original sin" (194). It is important to note that this mode of self-understanding provides Crusoe with a hermeneutic for his life story: now that his past and present life make sense in the terms of biblical narratives, he can see the truth of a fictional story like the Prodigal Son for his own life. In other words, Defoe's narrative does not make the Enlightenment distinction between empirically verifiable/true versus fictional/false. Instead, his character grants the claims that the "history-like" stories of Scripture make over the believer's life.

The biblical narratives provide a structure for Robinson Crusoe, but they are unobtrusive enough that many modern scholars may underestimate their importance. Instead, they treat Robinson Crusoe as a novel about economics and survival, in which theology provides Crusoe with a way to internalize his own desires (McKeon 323) or to rationalize his underlying capitalist manner of life (Watt 105-06). Michael McKeon, for instance, dismissively describes Crusoe's climactic reading of Psalms and Acts as listless experiments with "bibliomancy" (317)—a term that hardly does justice to Crusoe's later study of Scripture.

Even in the passages where Crusoe's economic concerns are prominent, his growing understanding of Providence is usually more fundamental. During his third year on the island, for instance, Crusoe's barley and rice crops are increasing so fast that "I really wanted to build my Barns bigger," he says (123). This would enable him to plant only once a year rather than twice. This plan—which he does not carry out—is almost certainly an allusion to the foolish man who longs for greater barns (Luke 12:18-21) The man in the parable—who never carries out his plan either—is not "rich toward God." Immediately thereafter, another plan begins to obsess Crusoe: to build an immense canoe to leave the island. The project costs him six months of fruitless labor, for Crusoe finds it impossible to move the huge craft from the construction site to the water (127). In reflecting on this, he alludes to Luke 14:28 in remarking "the Folly of beginning a Work before we count the Cost." The point of these allusions is that Crusoe is learning to interpret his own narrative by means of biblical narratives.

> As the fourth anniversary of his shipwreck approaches, he says that his "constant Study, and serious Application of the Word of God" had produced a different Notion of Things. I look'd upon the World as a Thing remote, which I had nothing to do with . . . and well might I say, as Father Abraham to Dives, Between me and thee is a great Gulph fix'd. (128; cf. Luke 16:19-31)

The word "as" is significant. It implies the possibility of a plurality of perspectives on just what "the real world" is. Crusoe invites us to accept his perspective—but his own perspective may be radically flawed, as recent historicizing work by McKeon and others tends to assume. Or (as I would maintain) Crusoe may not be capable of sustaining this perspective throughout his entire fictional, three-volume life. The large amount of religious material in volumes two and three may not have the power of Robinson Crusoe because Defoe's narrator and characters no longer face fruitful collisions between one's ordinary perspective and the perspective offered by Scripture.

The narrative theologian Garrett Green describes the significance of "as" in these terms:

> Kant called "is" the copula of judgment; we can call "as" the copula of imagination. In this quite technical sense, imagination is common to the natural scientist, the poet, and the religious believer. . . With the help of this concept of imagination as the "as" faculty, we can give conceptual precision to Paul Ricoeur's suggestive distinction between a "first" and a "second naivete." (Green 89)

For Crusoe, this "second naivete" means that he views the pre-shipwreck "world" as the distant, tormenting fires of Christ's parable. On the island, by contrast, there is an immediate connection between Crusoe's plans—whether to build barns or canoes—and their true value in God's eyes. The connection is that of Providence. In this setting, coveting more grain or wine or timber than he can use is obviously and immediately foolish, as Crusoe comes to realize. By contrast, prudential plans and temperate consumption are rewarded.

By this time, four years into his island existence, Crusoe is taking major steps on his pilgrimage. Although his steps are often backward as well as forward, he knows which direction is the correct one. His life frequently answers to Psalm 78, which prompts him to "admir[e] the Hand of God's providence, which had thus spread my Table in the Wilderness" (130). He is learning, through successes and follies, that his life can indeed run in the providential patterns of the Psalmists and gospel writers.

The significance of Crusoe's life is not reducible to the abstract values that he later identifies (prudence, temperance, etc.), nor to the ideologies of sociopolitical control identified by recent readers. Rather, prudence, temperance, and the other qualities Crusoe needs for a good life on the island have been developed through recognizing the intersection between the events of his life and the narratives of Scripture.

Crusoe's chief conflict has been to understand the narrative of his life in terms of the stories of the Bible. He treats the Bible as "true" in the sense that he gradually comes to recognize the authority of its stories for the purpose of reinterpreting his past life and shaping his future life. The earlier and more famous volume of Robinson Crusoe, in contrast with its sequels, gives us a picture of how a fiction becomes history-like when it appropriates the narratives of Scripture to establish the identity of its protagonist.

By his fifteenth year on the island, Crusoe appears to be leading a balanced Christian life. At this point, Defoe interrupts Crusoe's calm in a way that will force him back to Scripture so that he can attain a higher level of trust in God:

> It happen'd one Day about Noon going toward my Boat, I was exceedingly surpriz'd with the Print of a Man's naked Foot on the Shore . . . I stood like one Thunderstruck, or as if I had seen an Apparition. (153)
>
> Crusoe is immediately overwhelmed with a fear of cannibals. This "Fear banish'd all my religious Hope; all that former Confidence in God which was founded upon such wonderful experience as I had of his Goodness, now vanished . . ." (156).

As in his conversion, Crusoe looks back to Psalm 50:15 in the current crisis: "Call upon me in the Day of Trouble, and I will deliver, and thou shalt glorify me." But Crusoe finds himself unable to do this successfully. Instead, he thinks of releasing his goats and plowing under his grain. He begins to look upon his dwelling as a "castle," which he fortifies and conceals again, as he had done in the fearful days before his conversion. In short, the incident subjects him to "the constant Snare of the Fear of Man," and prevents him from "resting upon [God's] Providence" (159). After several wasted years, he begins to ask whether he should consider himself the executioner of the cannibals. "How do I know what God himself judges in this particular Case?" he asks (171). Since God alone is the "governor of nations," he concludes, he decides to avoid intervening altogether "unless I had a more clear Call from Heaven to do it, in Defence of my own Life" (173).

After this point, Crusoe makes no further advances in his outward manner of life (176). But as with his earlier crises the narrative is really leading in another, inner direction. It is leading Crusoe to renew and deepen his trust in God, through identifying the truth of his life with a fuller knowledge of Scripture. Since Crusoe already sees his own "mundane story" (to return to Stephen Crites' phrase) in terms of biblical stories, his next step will be different from the earlier ones. Crusoe is ready to understand how he is an active participant in providential history.

Although Crusoe achieves some peace of mind by deciding he will probably not attack the cannibals, his despair over the lack of society increases to near insanity. As the happiness of Crusoe needed interrupting after his first fifteen years, so his despair in the twenty-fifth year needs interrupting now. Crusoe goes so far as to consider breaking up a cannibal feast to get one or more slaves. At the very next visit of the cannibals, one of their victims escapes, running directly toward Crusoe as two of the cannibals pursue him. Crusoe kills one and the fugitive kills the other, leaving the fugitive free. Thus commences the relationship between Crusoe and his "man Friday," which continues for their final three years on the island. This is the first of several incidents in which Crusoe is able to understand himself as an agent of Providence, saving the lives of Friday and several others, one of whom is the captain of the ship that will return Crusoe to Europe.

Some modern readers have suggested that Crusoe treats Friday as little more than a slave. Defoe makes it clear, however, that Friday's "conversation"—their relationship as a whole, and not the services he provides—makes their years "perfectly and compleatly happy" (220). The first fifteen years charted Crusoe's growing ability to see how God had "spread a table for him in the wilderness." The next nine had forced him to come to terms with his fear of cannibals. The final three years show Crusoe capable of bringing the blessings of Providence to others, especially in the physical and later the spiritual salvation of Friday.

Defoe does not explore Friday's conversion in any detail. The narrative purpose of Friday's conversion is rather to lead to deeper growth in Crusoe. The episode shows that Crusoe's knowledge of Scripture is broad enough to convey to Friday "the same plain Instruction" that had earlier taught Crusoe "the great Work of sincere Repentance for my Sins, and . . . Obedience to all God's Commands" (221). He ultimately comes to admire Friday as a "much better [Christian] than I" (220). For instance, Friday speaks of returning to his own land (along with Crusoe) to teach his people to "know God, pray God, and live new Life" (226). This relationship, like the previous climactic incidents in the book—Crusoe's shipwreck, illness, and discovery of the footprint—push Crusoe to a new level of trust in and understanding of his life in biblical perspective.

From this point on, Crusoe experiences few inner conflicts. Nor are there any more incidents that cause significant growth in his life. The narratives of Scripture diminish in importance. The end of the novel, like the first sequel, reads more like an adventure tale with a Christian character rather than the tale of a man whose character is being fashioned in mysterious harmony with biblical narratives.

There is quite as much "religious" matter in volume two, Farther Adventures of Robinson Crusoe, but Crusoe has nothing to learn in this later book. This is not to say the religious material is uninteresting: Crusoe has significant ecumenical discussions with a Catholic priest; the priest wishes to perform marriages for the men and women who live together on Crusoe's old island; the crew on Crusoe's vessel later sack and massacre a village in Madagascar; and Crusoe's constant preaching on "the Massacre of Madagascar" ultimately leads to his being discharged from the ship at Bengal, where his adventures continue.

The most significant treatment of religion in the second volume is the lengthy conversion of Will Atkins and his wife, Mary, a native woman (140-63). This set of scenes is rather disconnected. Defoe's interest in the first part seems to be the Catholic priest's insistence that, prior to marrying them, Will and Mary profess Christian faith. Defoe then turns to the oddity of this priest participating in a Protestant conversion. Will Atkins's relationship with his father, a reprise of Crusoe's own, comes next. Finally, Defoe concludes with a catechetical dialogue between Will and Mary, similar to the conversations in Defoe's earlier work, The Family Instructor (1715). There is no narrative connection among these scenes that can compare with Crusoe's struggle to learn how to trust in God. Significant religious issues arise, but they arise more in the form of argument than narrative. Unlike the reader's experience in Robinson Crusoe, the reader has not sufficiently participated in the life of Will or Mary Atkins to see how their new Scriptural perspective collides with that of their former life.

Later in the second volume, Crusoe visits the Chinese port city of Quinchang, where he makes critical observations on Catholic missionary activity. Crusoe afterwards embarks on a bizarre, religious holy war against some pagans of the Russian plains, destroying an idol and proposing the slaughter of an entire village as vengeance for a Russian who was sacrificed to the idol. (The difference between the heathens of Madagascar and the pagans of Russia seems to be that the pagans are actively engaged in idol worship.) Defoe returns to this theme in Serious Reflections, in which he has Crusoe propose a bloody "crusado" against the Muslims and Chinese (who administer "the kingdom of the devil") "for Gospel labourers to enter upon the harvest" (240).

It is almost as if, by the third volume, Defoe has forgotten the narrative use of Scripture. Serious Reflections, in fact, is a series of essays (on solitude, honesty, providence, etc.) and not a tale at all. Scripture has become merely a set of doctrines or illustrative examples. The doctrines, however edifying or meaningful, make few demands on Crusoe. Perhaps this is because their edifying material is divorced from the historical truth of the biblical narratives, and the narrator of the later volumes no longer believes he can discover the truth through fictional material. There is no fruitful clash between Crusoe's story and the scriptural narratives that had earlier formed the basis for his identity. When Crusoe refers to Scripture at all, it merely confirms what he already "knows." For instance, in the discussion of the "crusado" in Serious Reflections, Crusoe refers to the Israelites' conquest of Canaan to justify military operations against pagans (224). But in Robinson Crusoe, Scripture did not justify Crusoe: it showed his shortcomings and pointed to the need for transformation. Scripture is discussed and applied to life in this volume, but it is not the primary means for interpreting one's life. It is not "the real world" anymore. By the time of Serious Reflections, Defoe has abstracted the fictional narrative of the book from its "meaning." The book's very structure—true, non-fiction essays as opposed to false, fictional narrative—illustrates the hermeneutical shift that was taking place.

Narrative theologians have encouraged us to recover a "second naivete" that restores the full meaning of Scripture by understanding the life of the believer within the narratives of the Bible. This approach to Scripture is different from an exclusive reliance upon the modern hermeneutics of higher criticism or upon the postmodern hermeneutics of suspicion. Robinson Crusoe shows us how a fictional character enters that "second naivete." When he begins to see that the world he encounters in Scripture is the real world, his entire life begins to make sense for the first time. The language of this world, biblical language, merges with that of his own narrative. Crusoe finds that the truths of biblical narratives are validated in his own narrative. But when Defoe begins to hesitate over the validity of Crusoe's fictional narrative, he is mirroring a larger hermeneutical change. In the emerging hermeneutics of the Enlightenment, an unverifiable narrative like Crusoe's cannot lead to truth, although the meaning that one detaches from that narrative may be valid. Narrative theology has recently begun to suggest ways for us to recombine narrative and meaning. Both Defoe's first volume of Robinson Crusoe and his later hesitations may have wider significance than we have yet realized for the way modern readers recognize the truth of fictional narratives.

NOTES

1. Following the original printings of these books, the first sequel (*Farther Adventures of Robinson Crusoe*, 1719) is usually designated "volume two" and Serious Reflections

"volume three" of the series. I have used this designation as well, reserving Robinson Crusoe to refer, as usual, to the famous volume one, *The Life and Strange Surprizing Adventures of Robinson Crusoe.*

2. These three readings come, respectively, from John Bender, Carol Flynn, and Michael McKeon.
3. Frei's major work, for instance, was reviewed in only three journals that keep abreast of literary studies, *TLS*, *Yale Review*, and *Philosophy and Literature*. See the bibliography in Green (200-01).

REFERENCES

Auerbach, Erich. *Mimesis: The Representation of Reality in Western Literature*. Trans. Willard Trask. Garden City, NY: Doubleday-Anchor, 1957.

Backscheider, Paula. *Daniel Defoe: His Life*. Baltimore: Johns Hopkins UP, 1989.

Bender, John. *Imagining the Penitentiary: Fiction and the Architecture of Mind in Eighteenth-Century England*. Chicago: U of Chicago P, 1987.

Crites, Stephen. "The Narrative Quality of Experience." *Journal of the American Academy of Religion* 39 (1971): 291-311.

Defoe, Daniel. *Farther Adventures of Robinson Crusoe*. Vol. I of *The Works of Daniel Defoe*. 16 vols. Philadelphia: John D. Morris, 1903.

——. *The Life and Strange Surprizing Adventures of Robinson Crusoe*. Ed. J. Donald Crowley. London: Oxford UP, 1972.

——. *Serious Reflections During the Life and Surprising Adventures of Robinson Crusoe*. Vol. 2 of *The Works of Daniel Defoe*. 16 vols. Philadelphia: John D. Morris, 1903.

Flynn, Carol Houlihan. *The Body in Swift and Defoe*. Cambridge: Cambridge UP, 1990.

Frei, Hans W. *The Eclipse of Biblical Narrative: A Study in Eighteenth and Nineteenth Century Hermeneutics*. New Haven: Yale UP, 1974.

——. *Theology and Narrative: Selected Essays*. Eds. William C. Placher and George Hunsinger. New York: Oxford UP. 1993.

Green, Garrett. 'The Bible As . . .': Fictional Narrative and Scriptural Truth. *Scriptural Authority and Narrative Interpretation*. Ed. Garrett Green. Philadelphia: Fortress, 1987. 79-96.

Hunter, J. Paul. *The Reluctant Pilgrim: Defoe's Emblematic Method and Quest for Form in Robinson Crusoe*. Baltimore: Johns Hopkins UP, 1966.

McKeon, Michael. *The Origins of the English Novel, 1600-1740*. Baltimore: Johns Hopkins UP, 1987.

Placher, William C. Introduction. *Theology and Narrative: Selected Essays*. By Hans W. Frei. Eds. William C. Placher and George Hunsinger. New York: Oxford UP. 1993. 3-25.

Rogers, Pat, ed. *Defoe: The Critical Heritage*. London: Routledge, 1972.

Starr, G.A. *Defoe and Spiritual Autobiography*. Princeton: Princeton UP, 1965.

Stroup, George W. *The Promise of Narrative Theology: Recovering the Gospel in the Church*. Atlanta: John Knox, 1981.

Watt, Ian. "Robinson Crusoe as a Myth." *Essays in Criticism* (April 1951): 95-119.

6

Expanding Empires, Expanding Selves: Colonialism, the Novel and Robinson Crusoe

—Brett C. McInelly

Featuring a British trader as its hero and set on a distant Caribbean island, Robinson Crusoe cries out for study in its colonial contexts. Indeed, British colonialism informs nearly every feature of Daniel Defoe's first novel. Spatially, Robinson Crusoe illustrates that the vastness of the globe can bring a corresponding enlargement, rather than shrinking, of the venturing self and can produce close self-reflection of a kind not easy to achieve in "civilized" society. Religiously, the novel demonstrates that a spiritual awakening can take place in isolation from society and can be crystallized when an Englishman subordinates and converts a non-European Other. Economically, Defoe's novel functions as an argument for the expansion of trade. And psychologically, Robinson Crusoe shows that relations with an alien Other can hone an ego that can master both its own selfhood and the destiny of others. In short, Robinson Crusoe owes many of its most characteristic traits to the colonial context.

Not surprisingly, contemporary readers commonly regard Defoe's novel as the prototypical colonial novel[1] of the eighteenth century, if not in all of English literature. Yet, the colonial elements of Robinson Crusoe have not been as thoroughly treated as we might expect in either eighteenth-century studies or postcolonial theory and criticism. Curiously, some of the more provocative postcolonial analyses of Defoe's novel appear not in criticism but in postcolonial literature such as Derek Wolcott's Pantomime and J.M. Coetzee's Foe, works that "write back" to Defoe's "master" narrative of empire. Even more numerous are the frequent allusions to Robinson Crusoe, particularly the Crusoe-Friday relationship, in postcolonial theoretical discourse. The mere mention of Defoe's novel, or his protagonist's relationship to Friday, seems to encapsulate the colonial myth and the dynamics of colonial relationships in general. Edward Said, for example, alludes to Robinson Crusoe as "a work whose protagonist is the founder of a new world, which he rules and reclaims for Christianity and England" (70). References like Said's are common, yet there seems to be an odd attempt to avoid engaging the colonial elements of the text in a sustained way. The novel's status as the prototypical colonial novel, I suspect, helps to account for this neglect, seemingly making such analyses unnecessary. Of those studies that engage colonial themes and issues directly and at length, many, if not the majority, tend to focus on the Crusoe-Friday relationship or related matters, such as cannibalism—Peter Hulme's Colonial Encounters: Europe and the Native Caribbean, 1492-1797 being a case in point. Martin Green's reading of the novel as a modern adventure tale illustrates another tendency in Defoe scholarship to reduce the essence of Robinson Crusoe to an expression of a colonial myth or fantasy. The issue of colonial trade has likewise been explored, most notably by Maximillian E. Novak.[2]

In this essay, I attempt to demonstrate the extent to which colonialism shapes Defoe's novel both formally and thematically, and I suggest that Robinson Crusoe indicates ways in which British colonial history made the genre of the novel possible. Specifically, I trace the influence of empire on the novel to the most elemental of novelistic conventions, namely, its attention to individual character, the starting point of Ian Watt's landmark study, The Rise of the Novel. Watt distills the essence of the novel to its "formal realism"—the "narrative method" by which novelists represent a "circumstantial view" of an individual life (32)—and he identifies Robinson Crusoe as the first novel precisely because of the detailed attention Defoe gives an "ordinary" individual.[3] Watt, however, fails to consider just how contingent Crusoe's self-image is on the colonial setting of the novel. Though his journey toward selfhood begins on precarious grounds—he is nearly swallowed by a storm, enslaved by Moors, and shipwrecked on an uninhabited island frequented by cannibals and located in the middle of the Spanish Empire—Crusoe gradually learns how to assert himself over land and people. In short, the colonial setting facilitates Crusoe's individualism as he comes to recognize the unique place he occupies as a British Protestant in a world in which he is surrounded by religious and cultural Others.

In assessing the influence of colonialism on Crusoe's individualism, we should acknowledge that we are dealing with an imagined colonialism. Terms such as "colonial context" and "influence of empire" sound as if I will ground my discussion in the actual practices of colonialism, but this implication is only partly true. Just as some readers of Robinson Crusoe protested that its author had wholly invented an individual's sacred experience, and Defoe responded that the narrative still was true in an allegorical sense, we must factor into any discussion of the novel's engagement in colonialism the fact that the engagement is wholly fictional. Robinson Crusoe stands as an allegory or figure of colonialism, not an exhibit of it. Defoe had no direct experience with plantations, South American coastal peoples, oceanic voyages, the slave trade, or a colonial economy. What he "knew" came through the play of his imagination on information from travel narratives, trade, geographies, etc. The actualism of his novel functions as an effective mode of deception, serving to engage the reader in a mental journey that merely resembles the experience of colonialism.

Defoe, himself, likely acknowledged the distance between the reality of Britain's colonial endeavors and his representation. Prose fiction provided him a medium of depicting reality that, as Novak argues, "could be turned to useful ends." Novak, who traces the influence of Dutch realist painting on Defoe's fiction, suggests that Defoe's "interest [in painting] was not so much in getting at `the thing itself,' something any writer and artist has to know to be impossible, but in the methods of deceiving the eye and the mind into accepting the presence of the representation as something that might have existed" ("Picturing" 2). Novak concludes that Defoe eventually learned that "he was working in a medium that was even more powerful—more vivid—than painting" (15). In Robinson Crusoe, Defoe transforms colonialism through the power of fictional representation into the adventures of a single man who masters an island, his native companion, and himself. His formal realism works to enfold the myths of psychological and economic self-sufficiency in a texture of convincing detail. The highly imaginative nature of Defoe's colonialism is acutely illustrated in a passage from The Complete English Gentleman. There, Defoe essentially claims that the English Gentleman can take possession of the world through reading:

> [The English gentleman can] make the tour of the world in books, he may make himself master of the geography of the Universe in the maps, attlasses

> and measurements of our mathematicians . . . He may go round the globe with Dampier and Rogers . . . He may make all distant places near to him in his reviewing the voiages of those that saw them . . . with this difference, too, in his knowledge, and infinitely to his advantage, viz. That those travellers, voiagers, surveyors . . . etc., kno' but every man his share . . . But he recievs the idea of the whole at one view. (225-26)

The point of view of the English gentleman while "making the tour of the world in books" is not unlike Crusoe's as he overlooks his island home, master of all he surveys. Authority in both instances is primarily imagined, preceding, in Crusoe's case, his actual control over the island and shaping colonial attitudes and assumptions of the English gentleman. We must also recognize that any distinction between real and imagined colonialisms, imperialisms, and other practices quickly surrenders to the view that such institutions are themselves, to a large extent, imaginary constructs, which in turn influence the concrete practices and policies that help govern and regulate political, social, and economic relations with other peoples. Defoe's debt to the colonial context takes place at the level of representing anticipations and premonitions of colonialism. Any influence he had on the colonial mentality is much more precisely that—a mentality—than a practice conducted by actual agents in history. And the contribution of the colonial context to the history of the novel takes place in a similar vein. By imagining a solitary escapee on a far island, Defoe creates the conditions that will be crucial to the development of the novel: fully realized characters who internalize experience within a setting that resembles real life.

Crusoe's individualism represents one of the more peculiar features of Robinson Crusoe. Despite his insignificant origins—"mine was the middle State, or what might be called the upper Station of Low Life" (4)—Crusoe, by the end of his adventures, is filled with a sense of his own self-importance. At least part of the significance of Defoe's hero, particularly as that significance relates to the origins and development of the novel, is the appearance of a character who sees himself and his experiences as being of immense consequence; in Robinson Crusoe we get, perhaps for the first time in English prose fiction, a work that asserts the primacy of the individual human subject.

Watt, of course, attributes such individualism to the rise of capitalism and the spread of Protestantism. While Watt's thesis remains convincing, Said and other postcolonial critics have shown the profound influence of imperialism on Western culture and its artifacts, and Watt's argument merits reassessment in light of the overarching implications of Britain's colonial history. Implicit in Watt's argument is the idea that the kind of individualism we see in Robinson Crusoe could have only arisen in eighteenth-century England, a stronghold of Protestantism and material capitalism. Watt mentions the debt Robinson Crusoe owes seventeenth- and eighteenth-century travel literature, and he suggests that colonialism helped to "assist" the "development of capitalism" (67), but his study goes no further in examining the influences of colonialism on the early novel. Studies of the novel since Watt, while otherwise thorough in tracing the social and cultural influences that gave rise to the novel, have similarly paid little attention to colonialism as a shaping force.

The movement of Defoe's narrative from the colonial center to the periphery facilitates Crusoe's development as a character. The sheer expanse of the globe through which Crusoe wanders has a paradoxical effect on him: rather than being overwhelmed by the vastness of his environment and dwindling under feelings of insignificance, Crusoe's self-image enlarges the farther he travels from

England. This double movement—what I refer to in my title as expanding empires, expanding selves—serves to position Crusoe at the center of both the world he inhabits and Defoe's novel. Crusoe takes on significance as a character because he stands as a seemingly stable and coherent subject in the wake of, what is for him, an expanding empire. This is precisely the type of mindset that colonialism would require, and Crusoe certainly is not the first fictional character to show British self-assurance among a people or in a landscape that could easily overpower him (e.g., Shakespeare's Prospero). Voyage accounts by Raleigh, Dampier, and others provide further evidence that such self-assurance was already firmly embedded in the British outlook, but Crusoe is the most notable because of his long solitude and growing control of his imagination.

The enlarging self that typifies Crusoe's response to his experiences compensates in many ways for the actual precariousness of his situation. Particularly while on the island, Crusoe constantly faces physical peril, both real and imagined. He finds himself stranded in the middle of the Spanish Empire on an island beset by cannibals. While Crusoe' s situation should (and at times does) impress upon him a sense of his own smallness in the world, Crusoe responds by finding confirmation of his self-importance. Surveying his circumstances on the island, Crusoe imagines himself "Lord of the whole Mannor; or if I pleas'd, I might call my self King, or Emperor over the whole Country which I had possession of" (128). The seeming unflinching confidence with which Crusoe asserts himself over the island derives largely from the nature of his predicament: the only inhabitant on the island, he might just as well shrink in terror. Instead, he imagines himself in grandiose terms (i.e., as a "King, or Emperor").

As Defoe transforms colonialism through representation, Crusoe refashions himself and the island, in part, through the imagination and language. As Novak argues in "Friday: or, the Power of Naming," Crusoe "transforms his island world through the agency of language, and particularly ... through a creative process of naming" (110). In making laws and giving names to places and things on the island, including himself, Crusoe both creates and assumes control over his island home. "By renaming [Friday]," Novak states, "Crusoe assumes possession of him in the same way that Columbus assumed possession of the land by his namings" (117). Like Defoe's novel, Crusoe's tendency to imagine and create through language his own reality reveals something of the nature of colonialism in general, namely, that it involves an assembly of images and cultural constructs, as well as material practices and circumstances.

Crusoe's tendency to imagine himself in grandiose terms replicates something of what was occurring in the culture at large in the early eighteenth century: "From 1688 on," Green explains, "England had been expanding, and the pride of Englishness had been swelling, particularly with reference to the country's overseas possessions" (4). Imperialism began to influence English national identity as early as the mid-seventeenth century, and the English continued to associate their national prominence with their colonial activities, whether trade or the acquisition of foreign territories, throughout the eighteenth century. Nonetheless, Great Britain experienced its share of anxieties on the road to imperial greatness, both in its dealings with other European powers and its native subjects, and the British people's proclivity to view themselves and their international achievements with intense pride helped to neutralize those anxieties in much the same way Crusoe's imagined responses to potential dangers ease his fears. The English further alleviated their concerns regarding their international status by becoming an increasingly self-referential society, seeing more of themselves in spite of their increasing contact with a diverse range of cultures; or, we might more accurately say, seeing more of themselves through their contact with colonized peoples. Crusoe's character illustrates the point perfectly, in that no experience, except perhaps that with his God, validates his self-image and culture more than his relationship with Friday (a point I address in detail later in this essay).

Given the reach of Britain's trading and territorial empire during the eighteenth century and the resulting effects on British subjectivity, it is not surprising that Robinson Crusoe, with its bold assertion of colonial authority by means of a single individual, emerged in England when it did. At a time when the British were struggling to establish a trading empire and competing with other European powers for territory and market's abroad, Robinson Crusoe effectively defused insecurities relating to Britain's colonial endeavors by affirming, through Crusoe's character, the exceptional nature of the English subject.

By placing Crusoe outside of human society for nearly two decades, Defoe grants his protagonist the opportunity never afforded in actual experience. Crusoe has the luxury of working out the political ramifications of colonialism before the economic. While it may seem odd to speak of political implications of an individual dwelling in solitude, Crusoe's mental work for nearly twenty years is essentially political. Crusoe's mastery of himself and his creation of an imaginary kingdom prepare him for his reencounter with human beings of an alien (to him) culture and eventually for the recovery of his property and revenues and his renewed trading ventures. The trajectory of Crusoe's colonial experience, then, is clear: master yourself and you master your destiny; master your destiny and you master others; master these and you master the economic contingencies of life.

In Britons: Forging the Nation 1707-1837, Linda Colley suggests that the British developed a sense of national identity as a result of anxieties relating to their international status. Although marked by a myriad of local and regional differences, Colley contends that the Welsh, Scots, and English defined themselves as Britons because they came to see themselves as a people apart and distinct from other nations and peoples: "Britishness was superimposed over an array of internal differences in response to contact with the Other, and above all in response to conflict with the Other" (6). Specifically, Colley refers to the French and other Catholic nations of Europe, from whom the British, because of their common commitment to Protestantism and their market economy, distinguished themselves. Protestantism, in particular, served as a unifying agent during the eighteenth-century conflicts with these other nations (18), which often involved colonial possessions and trade routes throughout the non-European world.[4]

Naturally, Colley acknowledges the rivalries among competing Protestant denominations, but she contends that "the gulf between Protestant and Catholic" was "still the most striking feature in the religious landscape" of the eighteenth century (19). The constant threat of a Catholic monarchy being restored by force (which could only have come about with the aid of France or Spain) and the persecution of Protestants throughout Europe heightened the English, Welsh, and Scots' sense of separateness from other European nations. Due to the military victories against such adversaries, Protestant Britons came to see themselves as God's chosen people and in his divine care. This is not to suggest that the British were necessarily an extremely pious people. The Protestant worldview, however, was such an elemental aspect of their culture that it informed their thinking and identity, even if regular church attendance was not a priority (31).

While the sincerity of Crusoe's conversion and his religious commitment have been debated by critics since Defoe's novel was first published, Defoe does fashion in Crusoe a Protestant viewpoint that is close to his own and crucial to the colonial possibilities as he envisioned them in the novel. He creates a Protestant who is tolerant, committed to essential practices rather than doctrinal controversy, keenly evaluative of his own behavior in relation to his religion, intensely personal in his encounter with God, and committed through acts of interpretation to seeing God's hand in everything from the grand outlines to the daily details of his life.

Crusoe's religious views are especially crucial if we see him as a British Protestant competing for territory with Catholic French and Spanish colonials. As Jack P. Greene observes, "The English overseas Empire, from the beginning, defined itself in opposition to the Catholic empire of Spain" (213). Boyd Stanley Schlenther similarly claims that Protestantism served "as a handmaid to Empire in the context of renewed rivalry with Roman Catholic France and Spain" (131). The British saw themselves as saving native peoples from Catholicism as well as from their own "savage" ways, a historical fact that helps elucidate the geopolitical implications of the Crusoe-Friday relationship. In addition, the British tended to view their empire as a trading empire during the first half of the eighteenth century,[5] significantly different from the Spanish Empire, which, from the point of view of the British, was raised through conquest and territorial rule (a distinction I discuss in more detail later in this essay).

By isolating his protagonist on a deserted island, Defoe effectively establishes Crusoe as a character apart and distinct from other human beings. Most important, Crusoe comes to view his isolation as the result of a divine will; that is, God is both aware of and responsible for his isolation. Reflecting on his deliverance and the fate of his comrades, Crusoe wonders "that there should not be one Soul sav'd but my self" (46). He later asks himself, "Why were you singled out?" (63). Eventually believing that "nothing happens without [God's] knowledge," Crusoe assuredly claims that God "knows that I am here"; and Crusoe declares he "was brought to this miserable Circumstance by [God's] Direction" as a form of punishment for a "dreadful misspent Life" (92). Crusoe's isolation thus serves to both magnify and render significant his existence in the world; he, unlike the rest of the crew, was "singled out" by God. The Spanish shipwreck Crusoe discovers off the coast of the island reinforces this interpretation of his experience: "of two Ships Companies who were now cast away upon this part of the World, not one Life should be spar'd but mine" (187). Notably, the second of the shipwrecked crews is Spanish; Crusoe's own ship is en route from Brazil, a Portuguese colony, to Africa, when it founders on the rocky coastline that surrounds the island. As far as we know, then, Crusoe is the only English Protestant among either crew.

Crusoe's Protestantism, which develops and is refined through his island experience, and the fate of the other crew members might seem a minor point were it not for a number of anti-Catholic references scattered throughout the novel. Referring to the "Priestcraft" Friday describes among his people, Crusoe observes that "the Policy of making a secret Religion, in order to preserve the Veneration of the People to the Clergy, is not only to be found in the Roman, but perhaps among all Religions in the World, even among the most brutish and barbarous Savages" (217). While Crusoe associates "Priestcraft" with "all Religions in the World," he is generally more conscientious in distinguishing his faith from Catholicism: in explaining his apprehensions toward rescuing the Spanish crew on the mainland, Crusoe suggests "that they should afterwards make me their Prisoner in New Spain, where an English Man was certain to be made a Sacrifice

. . . I had rather be deliver'd up to the Savages, and be devour'd alive, than fall into the merciless Claws of the Priests, and be carry'd into the Inquisition" (244). The claim that an "English Man" would be made a martyr in New Spain indicates the interrelated nature of religion and national identity for Defoe and many eighteenth-century Britons.

Further, the reference to the Inquisition would have had particular resonance for Defoe's audience, since the Inquisition persisted throughout the eighteenth century. The Inquisition, of course, helped to solidify anti-Catholic sentiment and reinforced the idea that British Protestants were a chosen people. Crusoe, who before his conversion on the island has no reservations about living among Catholics in Brazil, explains:

> I had entertain'd some Doubts about the Roman Religion, even while I was abroad, especially in my State of Solitude; so I knew there was no going to the Brasils for me, much less going to settle there, unless I resolv'd to embrace the Roman Catholic Religion, without Reserve; unless on the other hand, I resolv'd to be a Sacrifice to my Principles, be a Martyr for Religion, and die in the Inquisition; so I resolv'd to stay at Home, and if I could find the Means for it, to dispose of my Plantation. (303)

Crusoe's island experience establishes in his mind religious, and hence, national boundaries; once he has been literally singled out and separated from the European world by God, Crusoe, on reentering that world, is assured of his place in it. Crusoe comes to see the unique place he occupies in the world as an English Protestant. This is not to say that Crusoe becomes a religious bigot. As a Dissenter who experienced religious prejudice himself, Defoe was an advocate for religious freedom, and much of his antagonism toward Catholicism naturally derived, as it did for many of his contemporaries, from the perceived intolerance on the part of Catholics toward non-Catholics, hence Defoe's references to the Inquisition. During the short reign of James II, Defoe openly distrusted Catholic offers of toleration, a distrust that remained with Defoe throughout his life. Defoe's animosity was not, of course, directed exclusively toward the Catholic Church, and Defoe likewise openly criticized the Anglican Church's efforts to deny religious freedom to non-Anglicans: "I DISSENT," he writes, "believing every Christian to be obliged to worship God in that manner of form he finds most agreeable to the will of God declared in the Scriptures, and to join in Communion with those that he thinks do so—and upon these reasons I SEPARATE" (qtd. in West 151). Although clearly unhappy with the religious persecution prevalent in his own culture, Defoe and many eighteenth-century Britons believed that the Inquisition embodied an extreme form of religious intolerance that allowed them to see, by comparison, Great Britain as a nation founded on constitutional and religious liberties, in spite of widespread prejudice among Protestants and government legislation designed to deny non-Anglicans fundamental rights (e.g., the Test Act). Defoe's sense of being a Protestant Dissenter among a Protestant majority may, in fact, have suggested Crusoe's isolation on his island.

Defoe's commitment to the cause of religious freedom informs the nature of the colony Crusoe creates on his island, and the image of Crusoe surrounded by his island subjects is a pointed illustration of what was, for Defoe, an ideal nation and colony: "It was remarkable too, we had but three Subjects, and they were of three different Religions. My Man Friday was a Protestant, his Father was a Pagan and a Cannibal, and the Spaniard was a Papist: However, I allow'd Liberty of Conscience throughout my Dominions" (241). Crusoe's colony, then, is implicitly contrasted with Brazil, since "Liberty of Conscience"—

expressly associated with Crusoe's island colony—seems outside the ideological bounds of a predominantly Catholic colony.

Though critical of Catholic intolerance toward non-Catholics, Defoe is simultaneously gracious in his portrayal of his Catholic characters, particularly the Spanish Captain, who, along with the British mutineers, succeeds Crusoe on the island. Interestingly, the British mutineers initially prove to be the most degenerate of Crusoe's island subjects, and the Spanish castaways are the better colonists (although this statement must be qualified, since the Spanish Captain is essentially schooled by Crusoe in the art of running a productive colony in much the same way Friday is schooled in Western culture and Christianity). Defoe's characterization of Crusoe's successors on the island consequently seems to blur the national distinctions that I have argued are fundamental to the formation of Crusoe's character. Defoe was not so simple in his thinking as to discriminate merely on the basis of one's national origins or religious affiliations, and although he is outwardly critical of Catholicism in general, he likewise acknowledges individual humanity (and inhumanity) on a case-by-case basis. Defoe's portrayal of the Catholic Priest who accompanies Crusoe on his return visit to the island—recounted in The Farther Adventures—illustrates this point. Crusoe admires the Priest for his relatively liberal religious views, and he even leaves him on the island to convert his pagan subjects to "the Faith of Christ" (27). The Priest, in seemingly atypical fashion, espouses a generalized Christianity over adherence to a particular denomination, which accounts for Crusoe's admiration and qualifies him to act as a spiritual advisor on the island. Shaking hands with the Priest, Crusoe proclaims, "I wish all the Clergy of the Roman Church were blest with such Moderation, . . . but I must tell you, that if you should preach such Doctrine in Spain or Italy, they would put you into the Inquisition" (42). While together on the island, the two men share religious authority, and they concur that there should be no "Differences or Disputes . . . about Religion" among Crusoe's English and Spanish subjects (61).

Certainly, Crusoe's attitude toward Catholics is tempered as a result of his contact with the Spanish Captain and the Priest; yet Crusoe's attitude toward Catholicism in general remains intact and integral to both the formation of his identity as a British Protestant and the kind of colony he establishes on the island. While Defoe surely intended to criticize the intolerance he perceived in his own culture through his representation of Crusoe's island, the distance between Protestant and Catholic still remains the dominant feature throughout the novel, despite Defoe's relatively favorable portrayal of the Catholic characters with whom Crusoe comes in contact. Further, the island—a place where mutual respect and tolerance between Protestant and Catholic flourish—is ultimately Crusoe's creation and represents a distinctly English colony, deliberately contrasted with those of Crusoe's "more typical" Catholic competitors. Just before leaving his island for the last time, Crusoe, in a distinctly Protestant-like gesture, leaves a Bible with his island subjects, thereby recalling the instrumental role the Bible plays in Crusoe's own conversion and intimating the role the Bible will play in the spiritual lives of his island subjects.

The religious overtones of Defoe's text thus provide a blueprint for a religiously "sound" colonial policy. Since colonialism brings colonizing peoples into contact with individuals of competing Christian creeds as well as non-Christians, colonialism must, as does Crusoe, establish a strong, liberal, and principled policy on religion. Sectarian disputes are to be abandoned in favor of central truths and essential points of ethical behavior. Native populations are to be gently encouraged, not compelled, to accept Christianity.

As Colley contends, British national identity was further solidified by the economic prosperity the country experienced during the eighteenth century. A chapter on "Trade" in the 1718 issue of The Present State of Great Britain begins: "Next to the purity of our religion we are the most considerable of any nation in the world for the vastness and extensiveness of our trade" (qtd. in Colley 59). Defoe himself associated global trade with national prominence, writing in 1726, "We are not only a trading country, but the greatest trading country in the world" (English Tradesman 212). Defoe saw the colonies as integral to the nation's commercial success, and the importance of colonial markets to the local economy was evident throughout the century: "Of all the branches of our Commerce," George Lyttelton wrote in 1739, "that to our colonies is the most valuable . . . it is by that alone we are enbled to carry out the rest" (qtd. in Wilson 154). Thus, Crusoe's successes as a trader and colonizer make a powerful political statement. Crusoe, the quintessential colonizer, is an English colonizer, and Defoe distinguishes between Crusoe's particular brand of colonialism and that of his European competitors. His brand involves free trade and the "improvement" and upkeep of his colonial possessions, in addition to freedom of conscience.

Defoe, who envied Spain's control of Central and South America, portrays Spain' s involvement in the Americas as nothing more than a ruthless conquest for riches. "It could not be just for me to fall upon them," Crusoe explains as he considers attacking a group of cannibals, "This would justify the Conduct of the Spaniards in all their Barbarities practis'd in America" (171). In conversing with Friday, Crusoe learns that the "Cruelties" of the Spanish in America have "spread over the whole Countries, and [were] remembr'd by all the Nations from Father to Son" (215).

The Spanish shipwreck that Crusoe discovers indicates the motive for Spain's "barbarities": "I had room to suppose, the Ship had a great deal of Wealth on board; and if I may guess by the Course she steer'd, she must have been bound from the Buenos Ayres, or the Rio de la Plata . . . to Havana, in the Gulph of Mexico, and so perhaps to Spain: She had no doubt a great Treasure in her" (192).

Hulme, who suggests that Defoe's novel attempts to reconfigure the colonial experience by denying the harsh reality of colonial relationships and the similarities between "civilized" and "savage" cultures, contends that Defoe's portrayal of the Spanish allows Defoe to distance his English hero from the native cannibals and their supposedly savage practices. "The Spaniards," Hulme explains, "are allowed to be like Crusoe—only not as efficient; and they are chosen to bear the brunt of the undeniable similarities between European and Carib" (200). When Crusoe entertains thoughts that the Spanish castaways may have resorted to cannibalism in order to survive, Hulme argues that the supposed gulf between civilized and savage societies remains intact, since the castaways are Spanish, not English. Moreover, Crusoe's self-sufficiency contrasts strikingly with the dependence of his Spanish counterparts on the native Caribs, thus validating the preeminence of Western civilization on a distinctly English model (200).

Though perceptive, Hulme's reading presents at least two problems: first, Robinson Crusoe and Defoe's other writings, particularly The Further Adventures, indicate that Defoe accepted cannibalism as a necessary human behavior in severe situations, even for an Englishman; second and more germane to my argument, Hulme does not address the fact that Defoe affirms through Crusoe's character proper colonial policies, in addition to the superiority of European civilization. Just as the natives are depicted as cultural savages, the Spanish are portrayed as ruthless colonizers. Contrary to Spain's acts of aggression against the natives, Crusoe's attacks on the cannibals are justified on "higher" moral grounds, namely, "Self-preservation" and to save the life of a "poor Christian" (199, 233); and Crusoe's efforts to "improve" the island and bring it into the world of commerce and trade stand as an indictment of Spain's conquistador approach to the Americas. As Novak states, "Defoe was thoroughly familiar with the black legend of Spanish cruelty toward the Indians, . . . but the story he wants to tell is not that of conquest but that of colonialism, of the advantages of exploiting foreign lands and of a good relationship between colonizer and indigenous population" ("Friday" 114). Indeed, Defoe viewed colonial populations, including natives, as potential consumers of English goods. Crusoe's rescue and subsequent return to his island colony fulfill Defoe's colonial vision by connecting the island to England and the commercial world through trade.

Like the majority of his contemporaries, Defoe believed that Britain's colonial activities were carried on relatively peacefully. Seven years after the publication of his first novel, Defoe, writing in The Complete English Tradesman, claimed:

> We have not increased our power . . . by subduing the nations which possessed those countries, and incorporating them into our own, but have entirely planted our colonies, and peopled the countries with our own subjects, natives of this island; and, excepting the negroes, which we have transported from Africa to America, as slaves to work in the sugar and tobacco plantations, all our colonies . . . are entirely peopled from Great Britain and Ireland . . . the natives having either removed farther up into the country, or by their own folly and treachery raising war against us, been destroyed and cut off. (219-20)

Of course, the casual dismissal of the African slaves and the native inhabitants of the Americas in Defoe's claim for a peaceful colonialism seriously compromises the validity of his assertion. Nonetheless, Defoe's comments reflect the attitudes of many Britons who associated British prosperity with a relatively peaceful empire based on free trade, or what T. H. Breen has termed an "empire of goods" (468), not territorial conquest and domination, which they associated with Spain and its empire. That Crusoe's island is uninhabited and later peopled by Europeans—the British mutineers and the Spanish Castaways—and a handful of "converted" natives is thus a convenient way for Defoe to present Crusoe's activities as a relatively nonviolent enterprise. Initially a blank space awaiting Crusoe's arrival, the island represents the quintessential pure English colony Defoe articulates in The Complete English Tradesman. Playing off of Novak's observation that Crusoe does not grow wealthy as a result of his incessant desire to travel the globe (see Economics 32-48), Alan Downie points out, quite accurately I think, that Crusoe gains wealth by his plantation in Brazil and the dutifulness of his benefactors, the widow and the Portuguese Captain (20). In other words, Crusoe's island experience does not translate into material prosperity. While on the island, however, Crusoe solves the personal challenges of foreign residence and survival, and his development, in turn, prepares him to face and resolve properly the political constituents of colonialism: authority over peoples of different beliefs and customs, with some customs being intolerable to a Christian, and authority in competition with other foreign nationals whose methods descend to the level of barbarity shown by the savages over whom they exert control. When these problems have been solved—and they are the core problems of colonialism and can be solved this way only in fiction—the subject is ready to tackle the less problematic realm of economics and commerce. Trade and commerce, Defoe seems to be saying, are the primary means of gaining wealth and increasing the power of the nation, but even though they are among the driving incentives for venturing abroad, individual mental states and political attitudes must lay a proper foundation for them.

Another advantage of the island setting is that it provides the ideal conditions for Crusoe to make himself the object of his own reflections, a process that teaches Crusoe how to master himself and prepares him to master his native companion, Friday. The farther Crusoe wanders into the world, the more he comes to see of himself; he becomes a narcissistic, inward-gazing character. The longest section of the novel—nearly 180 pages—takes place on the island while Crusoe is alone. His self-meditations (and his authority) go virtually unchecked and are almost without interruption. During his time on the island, Crusoe meticulously keeps a journal—at least until his ink runs dry—in which he makes his daily reflections and activities the focus of his own attention. Crusoe's isolation, then, heightens his self-consciousness and fixes him as not only the exclusive focus of Defoe's novel, but also the sole focus of his own musings; and he acquires, through sustained self-reflection, the psychological equipment needed to convert an imagined authority into a reality. While alone on the island, Crusoe himself realizes that his authority is the result of his isolation: "I had no Competitor, none to dispute Sovereignty or Command with me" (128). Once internalized, however, Crusoe eventually transforms that authority into a means of gaining sociopolitical power, first, over Friday, and then, over the British mutineers. Crusoe's self-involvement revises itself into grandiose possession and legitimate authority.

Michael McKeon makes a similar claim when he suggests that Crusoe's social mobility depends on his ability to first internalize his authority. Unlike Watt, McKeon sees the "religious element" as "crucial and complementary" to the economic (326); and he contends that before Crusoe can improve his standing in society, he must first develop the capacity to "spiritualize" his experience on the island, that is, to acknowledge a divine presence operating in his life. Once Crusoe detects god's directing influence, he is then able to "spiritualize" his advancement in society as being the will of God. Moreover, the relationship between God and Crusoe—i.e., savior and saved—is eventually "literalized" in the Crusoe-Friday relationship. At the moment of Friday's deliverance from cannibals, Crusoe's authority on the island is no longer merely "figurative," since, as McKeon puts it, "the necessarily metaphorical relationship of creator to creature [is] quickly literalized into one of sociopolitical subordination" (332). Eventually, Crusoe develops the mental capacities needed to assert himself in English society and to advance beyond his original social class (334).

While McKeon implies that religion provides a legitimating narrative context for Crusoe's colonial activities, he does not pursue the colonial thread that he introduces into his reading of Robinson Crusoe, choosing instead to focus on Crusoe's island experience as a proving ground for his seemingly more consequential reentry into English society. Nonetheless, Robinson Crusoe is clearly concerned with expansionist politics, and Crusoe's island home is much more than a benign environment in which Crusoe learns how to be economically and spiritually successful in English society. Not insignificantly, the justification of authority within the colonial context disguises both the ugliness and possible malignity of grandiose possession. Once Crusoe learns to interpret his life as a divinely sanctioned event, his authority on the island is naturalized. As Crusoe comes to believe that God is intimately aware of him and his circumstances, he readily accepts the notion that Friday, like the island, is delivered into his hands, and questioning the legitimacy of his authority would require a questioning of God himself.

Though the model of colonial rule Defoe articulates in Robinson Crusoe may appear egocentric to the modern reader, it is largely informed by Defoe's political thought. Manuel Shonhorn, who reads Defoe's novel as "a political fable that emanated from an imagination that had been actively engaged in the most intense political debates in modern English history" (141), argues that Crusoe's island experience reveals Defoe's faith in a monarchical system of government, in which divinely appointed kings rule submissive subjects according to God's will. Fearing that growing parliamentary control actually impinged on the liberties of the people, Defoe believed that royal absolutism represented the surest means of ensuring political stability. At odds with Whig philosophy that suggested that "God's power passed to the king through the medium of popular choice or popular covenant," Defoe, Shonhorn states, looks "back to an earlier mode, in which covenants are initiated between the deity and his chosen kings," thereby allowing them "to perform a godly service with godly assistance" (151). In taking possession of the island and Friday, Crusoe merely takes what God gives him. While Schonhorn is relatively uninterested in British expansionism, his efforts to recuperate Defoe's political philosophy suggest how a monarchical system of government fully legitimizes Crusoe's authority on the island and, by extension, Britain's involvement in the colonial world. Again, what better way to validate the ugliness of grandiose possession than to construe it as being authorized by God?

Coupled with God's blessing, the colonial world Defoe creates affords a context wherein a common Englishman can become, in a limited capacity, a master, a king, and an emperor. Even more so than the national context, in which it was also occurring, the colonial sphere offers the "private man" a setting in which he can become extraordinary and powerful; and Friday, a cultural inferior, (6) is the perfect companion to advance the self-image of a character who, in English society, would have been a nobody. As Albert Memmi contends, "Even the poorest colonizer thought himself to be ... superior to the colonized" (xii).

Crusoe, in venturing out into the world, discovers perhaps the most essential element of his self-image, namely, a mirror, someone to reflect a self-validating image of himself. Shortly after rescuing Friday, Crusoe explains: "I made him know his Name should be Friday, which was the Day I sav'd his Life . . . I likewise taught him to say Master, and then let him know, that was to be my Name." As cited earlier in this essay, Novak sees the act of naming as a means of taking possession of Friday. Hulme similarly observes Crusoe's shrewd use of language: "By naming him Friday . . . Crusoe underlines to him that his previous life has been forfeited, providing a weekly mnemonic to remind him who was responsible for giving him that second life" (206). I would add that nullifying Friday's identity and history through the imposition of the name Friday also begins a process of transforming Crusoe's native companion into an image of Crusoe himself. Friday's transformation is achieved in large part through education, which includes instruction "in the true Knowledge of Religion," "Europe, and particularly England," and "how [they] traded in Ships to all Parts of the World" (220-22). Friday becomes, in many ways, a carbon copy of his white savior: "and thus he was cloath'd for the present, tollerably well; and was mighty well pleas'd to see himself almost as well cloath'd as his Master" (208).

Ironically, Crusoe's desire for a companion/servant is simultaneously another manifestation of his narcissism. In (re)creating Friday, Crusoe actually prolongs his isolation on the island: Friday speaks Crusoe's words and imitates his actions; he is a mere extension of Crusoe himself. In this regard, Friday is not unlike Crusoe's pet parrot, who learns to repeat Crusoe's words and even parrots back his own thoughts: "Poor Robin Crusoe, Where are you? Where have you been? How come you here?" (143). Of course, no matter how Anglicized he becomes, Friday is always Other, and Crusoe maintains the master-slave paradigm that underlies their relationship. Friday is thus the perfect companion for Crusoe: he provides a mirror image of Crusoe's character while simultaneously reinforcing his authority.

In this respect, the Crusoe-Friday relationship[7] exemplifies what Homi Bhabha means by colonial mimicry and ambivalence. "Colonial mimicry," Bhabha explains, "is the desire for a reformed, recognizable Other, as a subject of a difference that is almost the same, but not quite. Which is to say, that the discourse of mimicry is constructed around an ambivalence; in order to be effective, mimicry must continually produce its slippage, its excess, its difference" (86). A "double articulation" is built into the discursive field that produces Crusoe's authority, a doubling that "fixes" the colonized subject as a "partial presence." Again, no matter how well Friday imitates his master, he is always Other. In this regard, Bhabha postulates that colonial mimicry helps to establish and regulate the power structures that underlie colonial relationships. But Bhabha also sees mimicry as a potentially disruptive force, capable of resisting and undermining colonial authority: "The menace of mimicry is its double vision which in disclosing the ambivalence of colonial discourse also disrupts its authority" (88). Essentially, the "partial presence" of the colonized subject produces a fragmentary vision of the colonist's own identity, thereby undercutting notions of a homogeneous and stable subjectivity; that is, colonial mimicry does not reproduce a faithful image of the colonizer, but instead distorts the colonizer's self-image by casting back an unfamiliar and, at times, unidentifiable image.

The extent to which Crusoe's identity depends on his relationship to Friday illustrates the "menace" of colonial mimicry by exposing the delicate and precarious nature of Crusoe's self-image. Friday, for example, is introduced into the novel after Crusoe's encounter with the footprint, which completely unsettles Crusoe's self-perception: "I stood like one Thunderstruck, or as if I had seen an Apparition" (153). After eleven years of solitude, during which time Crusoe plays the part of "Prince and Lord of the whole Island" (148), the footprint represents the first challenge to his personal safety and authority. Moreover, Crusoe's narcissism is colored by a neurotic paranoia as a result of his encounter with the footprint. Crusoe experiences recurrent nightmares; anxiety continually afflicts his mind; and every unusual sound startles the shipwrecked hero. Crusoe explains: "I say, that I should now tremble at the very Apprehensions of seeing a Man, and was ready to sink into the Ground at but the Shadow or silent Appearance of a Man's having set his Foot in the island" (156). Crusoe's authority—indeed, his internalized image of himself—is threatened by the mere prospects of an encounter with the Other.

Crusoe's reaction to the footprint thus reveals how the ambivalence of colonial discourse, by fixing the colonized subject as a partial presence, can be inherently subversive. The footprint represents, quite literally, both a presence and an absence. For the first time since arriving on the island, Crusoe faces the possibility of encountering someone other than himself, the prospect of which unsettles Crusoe's solipsistic state. Prior to this event, Crusoe has virtually no reason to reflect at length on anyone but himself, and the footprint forces him, for the first time, to contend with an image other and different from his own.

What, then, serves to solidify Crusoe's character after his encounter with the footprint? Hulme states that the encounter blurs for Crusoe the boundaries between self and Other—Crusoe imagines for a moment that the print is his own—and he suggests that the remains of the cannibal feast enable him to recompose himself: "that paradigmatic manifestation of cannibalism finally allows Crusoe to clearly distinguish himself from others" (198). While Crusoe's firsthand experience among the cannibal remains redraws for Crusoe the boundaries between self and Other, the remains, I suggest, actually further discompose Crusoe's character. The fear of an encounter with the Other, cultivated by the footprint, intensifies when that Other is identified as a cannibal. Crusoe's self-composition, accordingly, hinges on more than a distinction between a "civilized" self and a "savage" Other; mastering the self requires mastering the Other. It is not until Friday is introduced into the narrative and his subsequent relationship with Crusoe that Crusoe is able to compose himself as "master," in control of himself as well as the native Other.

In Crusoe's relationship with Friday, Defoe circumvents the menace of mimicry by imagining a native subject who mimics his master but is not inclined to assert his difference or independence in a way an actual colonial subject might. Friday willingly submits to his white savior—he makes "all the Signs . . . of Subjection, Servitude, and Submission" (206)—and he changes himself into a copy of his master. His almost flawless mimicry of Crusoe reinforces Crusoe's belief in the superiority of his religion, culture, and social and political values. Moreover, Friday reflects back to Crusoe the image of a benevolent colonizer, thus firmly establishing Crusoe's authority on the island. When his authority is later challenged by potential rivals—specifically the British mutineers—Crusoe, without flinching, assumes the title of governor and is even mistaken for God on one occasion (254). At the end of his sojourn on the island, Crusoe goes from a man saved by God to one who is a savior appointed by God: "And where, Sir," Crusoe asks the Captain of the English ship, "is your Belief of my being preserv'd here on purpose to save your Life?" (260).

Crusoe's proclamation suggests how self-composed he has become as a result of his experience on the island.

Ultimately, Crusoe's images of himself and his culture are, as I have shown, essentially projections onto a complex and threatening reality. In mastering his own selfhood, Crusoe simultaneously masters his environment and (re)creates a world to his liking—a decisively colonial act. Crusoe reenters British society having acquired a radically heightened sense of self, and the detailing of an otherwise ordinary man's life is validated by the highly politicized context in which the action of the novel occurs, from Defoe's criticism of Spain's colonial practices to the Anglicization of Friday.

The entire process of isolating the personal, religious, political, and even economic facets of a fictional subject's life within an imagined colonial setting contributed directly to the features we now associate with the early novel: attention to individual character and the particulars of day-to-day experience, and an intense exploration of the dynamics of selfhood. As J. Paul Hunter observes, "The subjectivity of the novel involves not just a raised status for the individual self but an intensified consciousness, individual by individual, of what selfhood means" (24). While later novels—such as Pamela and Tom Jones—are not directly associated with the colonies, their protagonists can be the focus of a literary work because an individual (British) subject, as Robinson Crusoe so keenly illustrates, occupies a unique place in a widening world. I do not want to suggest that imperialism gave rise to the novel; rather, imperialism contributed significantly to the construction of the focal point of the novel's attention, namely, the individual (British) subject. Eventually, the colonial backdrop against which the British defined themselves became so naturalized that it is merely assumed in later novels. With relatively few exceptions, colonial space and the colonized Other are relegated to the periphery of most British novels until the end of the nineteenth century. This does not suggest, however, that the colonized world did not have a profound impact on British consciousness and later novels. The absence of that world and its inhabitants from the novel suggests how self-referential British society became in the wake of an expanding empire. Clearly, for a country on its way to controlling over a quarter of the globe, such an enlarged sense of self was crucial to obtaining and maintaining the Empire. In this sense, the novel and imperialism have a reciprocal relationship, the rise of each paralleling and reinforcing the other.

NOTES

1. Martin Green touts Robinson Crusoe as "the prototype of literary imperialism" (5).
2. See Novak's chapters on Robinson Crusoe in *Economics and the Fiction of Daniel Defoe*.
3. While critics like Michael McKeon have shown "Watt's vulnerability in delimiting the formal characteristics of the novel" (3) and have challenged his claim for Crusoe as the first novel, most regard the preoccupation with individual character as among the novel's defining characteristics (see Hunter 24).
4. Following the War of Spanish Succession in 1713, the British acquired Minorca, Nova Scotia, Newfoundland, and St. Kitts as a result of the Treaty of Utrecht. More important to Britain's economy, they likewise acquired the slave Asiento for Spanish America as a result of the treaty. The War of Jenkins' Ear (1739) and the Seven Years War (1754) further illustrate the extent to which Britain's intra-European conflicts involved colonial issues and possessions during the eighteenth century.
5. It was not until the end of the Seven Years' War when the British seized control of France's North American, West Indian, and East Indian colonial possessions that the British began to view their empire as a territorial empire.

6. As critics frequently observe, Friday is presented as an exceptional Other, and contrasted with his English master, Friday possesses, in many respects, superior physical and moral attributes. Moreover, Crusoe, in a paradoxical reversal, is "improved" as a result of his contact with Friday. Crusoe, for example, comes to recognize their common humanity and becomes a better Christian through their relationship. Novak suggests that the set physical descriptions of Crusoe and Friday-Defoe "makes his colonizer grotesque and his savage handsome, generous and affectionate"—is Defoe's way of "making a statement about the imperial spirit" ("Picturing" 13-14). While Crusoe is, of course, not without his faults and Friday exceptional in his way, there is, in my opinion, no question in the novel as to the intended superiority of Crusoe's culture and, consequently, the legitimacy of Crusoe's efforts to Anglicize Friday. Notably, Friday is admirable precisely because he embodies traits—generosity, gratefulness, fidelity, and a desire to do good—which should, according to Defoe, be characteristic of his own culture; that is, Friday is admirable because he is, in many ways, as the British should be.

7. Parallels can be drawn here between the Crusoe-Friday relationship and the British-Spanish dichotomy discussed earlier in this article. The articulation of difference in regard to divergent colonial and religious practices authorizes Crusoe's colonizing activities in much the same way that a partially reformed Friday legitimizes the supremacy of Western culture. What ultimately counts in Robinson Crusoe is not the similarities between Crusoe and his Spanish counterparts or Friday, but the subtle and persistent differences that distinguish the former from the later.

REFERENCES

Bhabha, Homi K. *The Location of Culture*. London: Routledge, 1994.

Breen, T.H. "An Empire of Goods: The Anglicization of Colonial America, 1690-1776." *Journal of British Studies* 25 (October 1986): 467-99.

Colley, Linda. *Britons: Forging the Nation 1707-1837.* New Haven: Yale UP, 1992.

Defoe, Daniel. *The Complete English Gentleman.* Ed. Karl D. Bulbring. London: David Nutt, 1890.

——. *The Complete English Tradesman.* Gloucester, UK: Alan Sutton, 1987.

——. *The Farther Adventures of Robinson Crusoe.* Vol. 3. Oxford: Basil Blackwell, 1927.

——. *Robinson Crusoe.* Ed. J. Donald Crowley. Oxford: Oxford UP, 1972.

Downie, Alan. "Robinson Crusoe's Eighteenth-Century Contexts." *"Robinson Crusoe": Myths and Metamorphoses.* Eds. Lieve Spaas and Brian Stimpson. New York: St. Martin's, 1996. 13-27.

Green, Martin Burgess. *Dreams of Adventure, Deeds of Empire.* New York: Basic Books, 1979.

Greene, Jack P. "Empire and Identity from the Glorious Revolution to the American Revolution." *Marshall* 208-30.

Hulme, Peter. *Colonial Encounters: Europe and the Native Caribbean, 1492-1797.* London: Methuen, 1986.

Hunter, J. Paul. *Before Novels: The Cultural Contexts of Eighteenth-Century English Fiction.* New York: Norton, 1990.

Marshall, P.J., ed. *The Oxford History of the British Empire.* Vol. 2. Oxford: Oxford UP, 1998.

McKeon, Michael. *The Origins of the English Novel, 1600-1740.* Baltimore: The Johns Hopkins UP, 1987.

Memmi, Albert. *The Colonizer and the Colonized.* New York: Orion Press, 1965.

Novak, Maximillian E. *Economics and the Fiction of Daniel Defoe.* New York: Russell & Russell, 1976.

——. "Friday: or, the Power of Naming." *Augustan Subjects: Essays in Honor of Martin C. Battestin.* Ed. Albert J. Rivero. Newark: U of Delaware P, 1997. 110-22.

——. "Picturing the Thing Itself, or Not: Defoe, Painting, Prose Fiction, and the Arts of Describing." *Eighteenth-Century Fiction* 9.1 (Oct. 1996): 1-20.

Said, Edward W. *Culture and Imperialism.* New York: Knopf, 1993.

Schlenther, Boyd Stanley. "Religious Faith and Commercial Empire." *Marshall* 128-50.

Schonhorn, Manuel. *Defoe's Politics: Parliament, Power, Kingship, and "Robinson Crusoe".* Cambridge: Cambridge UP, 1991.

Watt, Ian. *The Rise of the Novel.* Berkeley: U of California P, 1957.

West, Richard. *Daniel Defoe: The Life & Strange, Surprising Adventures.* New York: Carroll and Graf, 1998.

Wilson, Kathleen. *The Sense of the People: Politics, Culture and Imperialism in England, 1715-1785.* Cambridge: Cambridge UP, 1995.

7

Commercial Paper, Commercial Fiction: 'The Compleat English Tradesman' and Defoe's Reluctant Novels

—Sandra Sherman

Students of Daniel Defoe have always read The Compleat English Tradesman (1725-27) as illuminating the tropes of his novels, their ethos, or more generally their implication in an emergent market capitalism.[1] But no one has suggested that the long excurses on the Tradesman's accounts (his "books") have much to say regarding the novels' generic self-conception, their coy reluctance to avow themselves as fiction or truth. The rhetorical agility of such reluctance is a commonplace of Defoe scholarship, indeed of histories of the Novel, and has been parsed by Lennard Davis, Michael McKeon, and most recently Joseph Bartolameo.[2] None of these critics, however, sees the novels' failure to account for themselves as related to their status as commodities, objects for sale in a market still resistant to avowed fiction.[3] In commercial terms, the novels' coyness operates to frustrate suspicion and excite interest without over-promising. If the texts purport neither to lie nor tell the truth, then the "author" (Crusoe, Moll, Roxana) and hence the author (Defoe) cannot be held to account for misrepresentation (if the reader senses any or the text is exposed).[4] The author remains in the market generating more texts. His own accounts (his finances) remain secure.

The novels thus position themselves-alongside other types of "commercial paper," circulating in a market where the voracity of such paper is a major concern. The novels' ambivalent truth-claims therefore jibe with tropes of other texts—bills of exchange, promissory notes—that configure a commercial episteme where determinate knowledge is itself problematic.[5] The novels' generic opacity reifies the dissonance of market-generated texts, the L.O.U.'s, bills, and notes whose uncertain promises disrupt the clarifying assurances of the accountant's ledger. Defoe's non-committal generic posture, constructing an escape from accountability, capitalizes on a complex discourse of emergent market capitalism, in which the veracity of texts, always being assessed, cannot always be determined. In The Compleat English Tradesman, the Tradesman's affairs are radically indeterminate, controlled by texts that operate outside the sphere of his volition, even as he tries to assert that violition, inscribing accounts that purport to rationalize every contingency. The texts of credit-calculated lies, desperate shifts, mere promises of future performance—challenge the texts of accounting, written "to the moment," claiming transparecy, asserting Truth. The ethos of credit is roguish, like Moll Flanders slipping past pursuers (including creditors).[6]

In this article, I argue that the impenetrable truth-claims characterizing Defoe's novels, are logically consistent with the unstable credit—based textuality portrayed in The Compleat English Trademan. Defoe's novels exploit the disjunction in market-place texts: the Tradesman commits his affairs to "definitive" accounts, but he transacts his affairs through texts that are contingent. In the narrative of The Compleat English Tradesman, credit infects accounting, so that market-generated texts elude effective monitoring. The resultant impenetrable textual formations underlie the logic of a credit/fiction crux in emergent capitalism—the shared, impenetrable truth claims of Defoean fiction anti instruments of commercial credit.

I argue further that The Compleat English Tradesman does not merely manifest a market discourse whose logic inhabits Defoe's fictions. It intervenes in that discourse, attempting to destabilize the growing promotion of accounting. The Compleat English Tradesman teaches the instability of marketplace knowledge. It becomes self-reflexive, a meditation on Defoe's own fiction ("compleat" by 1724) that attempts to break down the nation that any text affiliated with the market (even accounting texts) can ever represent phenomena with integrity.[7] The reader in the market is left in a triple bind. Not only are the texts of credit uncertain representations of their authors' intent; not only do the texts of accounting and credit discredit each other's version of textual credibility; but accounting texts themselves are uncertain—they are like credit. If at every level texts in the market are contingent, shielding authors from accountability, then Crusoe, Moll Flanders, Roxana and the others can be held to no higher standard of generic certitude. The reader is daunted in attempting to sort out fiction and truth.

I begin my argument by sketching the environment of credit evoked in The Compleat English Tradesman. I then examine the discourse of accounting as it developed in the eighteenth century and as Defoe may be said to have unsettled it. I conclude by suggesting that Defoe's anomalous version of accounting was a brilliant inversion of its ethos: established as a means of organizing credit, accounting is recast as itself disorganized, instantiating credit. My point is to show that Defoe casts "literary" texts and "commercial" context into a single discursive practice; he disperses authorship into marketplace discourse, delivering unaccountable accounts.

The Compleat English Tradesman is an author, generating credit instruments inevitably inflected wIth the discrediting discourse of the market. Defoe observes that as a means-of postponing debt, tradesmen endorse inland bills for their creditors, ramifying obligation into a mutual house of cards:

> . . . if he cannot get a particular friend to endorse the Bill for him, or a debtor, then he comes into a fatal confederacy with another Tradesman in like circumstance with himself, and he having endors'd for the weaver, the weaver does the like for him. and so they change endorsements; blending in a word, not their credit only, but even their fortunes together, till at last he finds himself insensibly involv'd, and 'tis ten to one but a disaster follows, nay, 'tis much if they do not fall together.[8]

The credibility of the credit instrument is not represented by its face value, since value is disseminated, contingent on events remote in time and space from the instrument's production. If the recipient of a Bill cannot read it with assurance, neither can the Tradesman, since he is himself recipient of a Bill he cannot read with assurance. Endorsement is a Mobius strip of irony: the Tradesman's credit is supported by others, while he becomes responsible for theirs. If their credit fails; if the Tradesman cannot cover them; they will be unable to cover him; his credit fails as well. Thus even as the Tradesman is an author, he is a reader unable to read what he authors with a sense of whether it is true—a fair representation of a promise to pay—or a fiction. In fact it is both, an elusive, ramifying intertext of mutually disorganizing promises, remote from an author and resistant to readers.

In Robinson Crusoe, Moll Flanders, and Roxana, a bustle of personages share unspecified influence on the text.[9] Such mutual (ir)responsibility is consistent with a discursive practice that inhibits verification of marketplace texts. The endorsement of bills is intended to lend credibility, but may have just the opposite effect. The multiplication of Defoean voices purports to anchor the text in the facts of its production, but disperses its facticity in noise.

The trope of such a market is irony, which precipitates in Defoe's "account" of the market. Bivalent commercial paper, its face-value devalued by side-deals, its integrity supported by form, descends towards fiction, its readers unable to establish its worth. Describing the "most fatal article of Discount," in which successive endorsements of numerous bills thrive upon percentages pledged to "the money'd men," Defoe observes that at first no one saw the depreciation, but "when one [endorser] fail'd, he shook the rest, so that few of them could stand after him, and not one of them above a year, or thereabouts."[10] Credit encourages disregard of common sense in favor of potential payoff.

Defoe leaves no doubt about whom the Tradesman can fault:

> . . . in this affair of Discounting he sees no fraud, no deceit, neither is there any fraud but to himself; he is only his own deceiver, acts to his own loss and wine, and heals his present wounds at the expence of his own foundation; for indeed he undermines himself and destroys himself by the very means which he uses to preserve himself.[11]

As a reader, the Tradesman must negotiate texts that are not transparent, while he has no one to blame but himself if he reads incorrectly. As a source of meaning, the author is diffused by a permitted ("no fraud, no deceit") discursive praxis of multiple derogating signatures. Representational integrity dissolves along with an integral author responsible for discourse.

The market's capacity to diffuse authorial responsibility is exploited by Moll Flanders, when she and a fortune-hunting suitor joust with texts. Moll tells the truth about her poverty ("I'm Poor: Let's see how kind you'll prove"), yet there is in the air a rumor that she's rich; her claim may therefore be a "jest." Moll is banking on the common knowledge that marketplace language is ambivalent. From the suitor's point of view, such language has a literal sense, but also a hyper-literal meaning informed by rumors (which he hopes may be truer). The suitor appears to disavow the hyper-literal valence ("Be mine with all your Poverty"). But Moll reads his own text against the literal ("Yet secretly you hope I Lye"), since as a practiced maker of marketplace fictions she is suspicious of texts.[12]

In Moll's representation ("I'm Poor"), there is no lie. However, she has been complicit in confusing her suitor's misperception by allowing the market to proliferate fictions around her. Thus while she has never explicitly claimed to be rich, she has promoted the versimilitude of such fictions: "I pretended on all Occasions to doubt his Sincerity, and told him, perhaps he only courted me for my Fortune" (I, 79). By allowing market-place noise into her own text, Moll dislocates the source of misrepresentation, relying on her reader to be confused (and to follow the noise). Not having provided a univalent lying text, Moll escapes culpability:

> He has fore closed all manner of Objection, seeing, whether he was in jest or in earnest, he had declared he took me without any regard to my portion and, whether I was in jest or earnest, I had declar'd he took me without any Regard to my Portion, and,

> whether I was in jest or earnest, I had declar'd my self to be very Poor, so that, in a Word, I had him fast both ways; and tho' he might say afterwards he was cheated, yet he could never say that I cheated him. (I, 81).

Since Moll has not lied, and her suitor has acquiesced, the contract is enforcible. Moreover, by a "jest" in "earnest," Moll dissipates any objective determination of intent, leaving only the penumbra of negotiation—the market—in which to search for the cheat.

The incident enacts the ambiguity of credit-based texts that Defoe describes in The Compleat English Tradesman. What should be an intimate transaction between author and reader, is inflected—infected—by currents in the market. The suitor/reader is left with no recourse while Moll remains to dissemble again. Her strategy is like Defoe's. As Joseph Bartolomeo observes, "A reception-oriented aesthetic dominates the preface to Moll Flanders, with multiple references to types of readers and ways of reading . . . Defoe, in the preface, has artfully left the question of literal truth up to the reader."[13]

That the market forces authors to create impressions they might otherwise disallow ('Defoe must pretend to truth in response to-Gildon, Moll must pretend to wealth since "Money only made a Woman agreeable" [I, 67]), is suggested by Defoe's inculpation of coercive creditors:

> [M]en in trade, I say, are under this unhappy necessity, they are forced to make them [absolute promises], and they are forced to break them; the violent pressing and dunning, and perhaps threatning too, when the poor shop-keeper cannot comply with his demand, forces him to promise . . . and the poor shop-keeper almost worried, and perhaps a little terrified to [sic], and afraid of [the

> creditor] is glad to do any thing to pacify him, and this extorts a promise, which when the time comes, he is no more able to perform than he was before; and this multiplies promises, and consequently breaches . . .[14]

While Defoe does not absolve the Tradesman for multiplying unrealizable promises, he argues that the misrepresentation is nonvolitional (an "unhappy necessity"). It emanates from a paradox of the market, which disorganizes representation with noise, but demands that respresentation be noiseless, free from qualification. Such demands are irrational. The coercive creditor/reader receives primary blame, precipitating his own misreadings, yielding to a credit ethos which encourages the hope that shaky promises might pay off. Once again, the text emanates from a transaction which dissipates the "author" as the source of meaning. The Compleat English Tradesman posits a discursively "incompleat" Tradesman, a maker of fictions which should not, cannot be cited to him. Thus within the discourse of credit, Defoe articulates a logic of fiction, producing an author whose "credit" cannot be impugned since authorship is of "necessity" pre-empted. The credibility of textuality becomes unclear; lying loses its conventional meaning, becoming an ever-present potential of market-place texts. The Compleat English Tradesman softens the category of fiction; the market purveys only "texts" of uncertain genre. We give them the benefit of the doubt because we must if a credit-based market is to be sustained. Textual uncertainty is the "bottom line" towards which The Compleat English Tradesman drives. It demonstrates that there is no point interrogating texts in the market, and if we do, no author is accountable. Defoean "fiction" is just like commercial paper: opaque.

The crux in Defoe's logic is that commercial culture held that textual veracity was possible, that contingencies of the market could be kept at bay in the construction of texts. The texts produced by accounting were the opposite of credit-based texts: fixed, certain, "readable" in the sense that what you see is what you get. The reader/accountant, and indeed any reader, could "fix" receivables and payables, establishing an accurate credit position. Thus accounting opposes notions of textual production that deny generic integrity. Accounting encourages readers to think that representation of market phenomena is possible; that a discrete author is responsible for a text; that he is subject to rules which expel uncertainty. It posits a regime where authority ensures transparency. In this section I shall discuss accounting theory, demonstrating the potent nature of its threat to Defoe's logic of unaccountability. I shall then discuss Defoe's brilliant deconstruction of accounting, returning The Compleat English Tradesman to a regime of credit-based uncertainty. My point is to show that Defoe consistently develops a theory of "unaccountable" fiction within a discourse of commerciality, spanning both credit and its monitory apparatus. Defoe's accounting texts are not "untrue," but like the Tradesman's bills and notes, mere shaky representations of potential pay-offs.

In The Gentleman Accomptant (1715), Roger North described accounting as "an Act of the Mind, intent upon the Nature of the Truth of Things."[15] Like art, its production requires "the Solitude of a Compting-House, or Retirement from all Manner of Interruption . . . [R]ather than leave Defect, Impropriety, Doubts, or Ambiguity of Expression, whereby the very Truth is-obfuscated, the Accomptant is not to grutch his pains" (23). This sense of the mind acting on the world to describe it, of a world amenable to such description, is basic to accounting. It is reflected in North's obvious reference to the ideology of empiricism espoused by the Royal Society: "Accompts are kept in a certain Method . . . which Method is so comprehensive and perfect, as make it worthy to be put among the Sciences, and to be understood by all Virtuosi" (1). En A New Treatise of

Arithmetic and Book-keeping (1718), Alexander Malcolm makes the same point, arguing that accounting evinces the ability of the mind to dispel disorder, to refine phenomena into categories that permit intelligibility:

> As Regularity and Order are the Product of Reason, they serve to distinguish the Rational, from the irrational World: Reason is not only the Glory of our Nature, but to exercise it with utmost Advantage, is certainly the Interest of our Being; its Functions are not confined to one Sort of Actions, they extend to every Thing transacted among Men, in so much, wherever we find the Effect of Counsel, Contrivance and Design, there we acknowledge Reason.[16]

The premises of accounting directly challenge the ambivalence of market-generated texts. In their eighteenth-century articulation, they are absorbed into an empiricist counter-current that privileges sense perception, and presumes that rational and irrational can be segregated.[17]

The first accounting text in English was published in 1543.[18] During the seventeenth century, a vast number of treatises on accounting ("double-entry book-keeping") were in circulation, maintaining a remarkable level of technical uniformity.[19] By 1718, Malcolm acknowledged "the great . . . Cloud of authors in my Way" (Preface), and by the 1720's Defoe had as models Malcolm, North, and a host of predecessors. Since he adopts much of their standard apparatus, such as sample accounts, as well as much of their standard rhetoric, such as warning against the perils of ignoring accounts, he must at least have examined such texts, even if he did not learn his accounting from them.[20]

Though accounting was highly evolved by the early eighteenth century, differing only over minor theoretical matters and pedagogical modes, my concern is not with its formal intricacies. Rather, I wish to examine the structural basis for its extraordinary claims to truth and stability, its assertion of perfect transparency notwithstanding the uncertainties of a business enterprise. Alexander Malcolm poses the issue precisely:

> Now, Words or Writing, are the Picture or Representation of a Thing, and in the present Case, I conceive the Merchants Books of Accompts, which being a Thing subject to Alterations according to the various Additions, Subtractions, and other Changes, the Course of his Negotiations brings it to, to have always the true Picture, it must suffer the same Changes with the original, i.e. since every Transaction by the Merchant, or his Doers, makes some Alteration, if not in the Value, at least in the Posture of his Affairs: Therefore; a faithful record ought to be made of every Thing that any way concerns a Man's Business. (124)

The characteristic premise of accounting is its assertion that a "true Picture" in "Words or Writing" can accommodate "Changes" in one's affairs; it elides any challenge from phenomena that would distort true pictures.[21] It assumes that a "faithful record" can be maintained in absolute representational clarity as each "faithful record" is assimilated into the whole. The accounting text is in dynamic equilibrium, conceptually opposite the radical disequilibrium of credit texts, where truth or fiction may precipitate with equal (un)certainty. Malcolm defines accounting in terms that emphasize its perpetual accuracy as "[t]he Art of recording the Transactions of a man's Affairs, in such exact and regular Order, that at any Time he may know the true and just State of any Particular Part of his Affairs, or of the whole, with the greatest Ease and Dispatch" (114).

The salient feature of accounting, which "accounts for" its representational fidelity, is that in its ultimate articulation in the Ledger it produces an anti-narrative. At every point in the continuing notation of one's affairs in that text, closure—that is, complete disclosure—is implicit. Openness to revision is always coincident with the text's amenability to collapsing sequentiality into an extended discursive present. There is no suspense, no necessity to "read" through data to locate the outcome. The outcome is always retrievable, waiting to be ascertained "with the greatest Ease and Dispatch." It is this perpetual availability of definitive knowledge, this constant purported correspondence between text and world, that assures absolute, certain truthfulness. In its anti-narrative figuration, accounting is the opposite of credit-based texts, whose promises to pay precipitate a narrative suspense in which genre itself (Truth or Fiction) is suspended. Roger North argues that the accounting text is as accurate to the moment as if it had actually been inscribed in that moment:

> For the Dr. and Cr. [Debtor and Creditor method of accounting] is pure and perfect right Reason, and contains the whole Material Truth and Justice of all-Dealing, and nothing else . . . And all this in a perpetual State; so as every Question that can be proposed concerning any Dealing, is answered almost as readily as demanded; and so no person can be injured, who takes his Accompt upon the stating of the Books, so far as it runs: And in all Times, even in After-Ages, the Transactions thus duly accompted, will be understood as well, as if the same had been inquisted at the very Instant of the Writing. (3)

This "perpetual State" of true (dis)closure is achieved through the conversion of temporal notation into an extensive spatial relationship among inter-related, always changing (but ultimately stabilized) accounts.

To appreciate this conversion, and Defoe's ultimate assault upon it, one must understand accounting technique as it was prescribed by North, Malcolm, and others. The first step was to inscribe each transaction in a "waste book" under a specific date: A sold B two yards of cloth. There might be ten transactions that day, some in which the tradesman himself buys cloth, some involving purchase and sale of other commodities, some on credit and some for cash. Already one has a plethora of customers and suppliers, varying lines of business: (e.g. cloth and nails), different modes of payment. How does one keep track of "accounts" with debtors and creditors, of the profitability of different commodities, and of one's business as a whole? There has to be a way of unifying these transactions. The next step is to transcribe each transaction into a Journal, so that each appears in the form of Debtor and Creditor: B is debtor to A for two yards of cloth. At this point the statement is analyzed, but it is still one unit. The next and critical step is to transfer each journal entry into the Ledger at least twice. Accounts are opened, each with a Debtor and Creditor side. For each entry under each account (on one side or the other), there must be a reciprocal entry in another account (again, on one side or the ether), cross-referenced in each case to its origin in the journal. Thus under B's "account" in the ledger would appear, under the debtor side: 2 shillings, the price of two yards of cloth. Under A's Accounts Receivable, would appear: two shillings, the price of two yards of cloth sold to B. If B had sold A a commodity, the notations would be reversed, with A's liability noted in Accounts Payable. As payments came in and went out, the reciprocal accounts would be adjusted, so that all Debtor entries and all Creditor entries would always be equal and opposite each other. One might also open accounts to measure how well cloth was doing in comparison to nails. Ultimately, the results of all transactions would be carried to an account for profit and loss. Once the ledger was posted (ideally every night), one could measure 3's performance (assuming the proprietor to be A), merely by balancing his particular account, so that it might appear that he is ten shillings in arrears, but on purchases so far this year of 100 Pounds. One could measure the profitability of cloth, and bring all one's accounts down to determine enterprise profit and loss.

What begins with sequential notation is ultimately apprehended as if synchronic, with a sector for each account. As entries are posted, each account remains an ostensibly exact representation of reality. Moreover, the system contains its own self-checking mechanism, which insures that reality has not been misrepresented: because each transaction is entered as both a debit and a credit, all the debits and all the credits will balance if added separately (a process known as "trial balance"). If they do not, then the ledger can be checked against the journal, and if need be against the waste book, until error is found. Narrative remains suppressed, except to the degree required to achieve transparency in an anti-narrative iteration, the ledger.

The integrity of the whole, its continual balance, is the basis of accounting theory. North remarks that:

> The Art of Regular Accompting depends wholly upon this Supposition, viz. That every thing negotiated comes out of something, and goes into something, having (as they say of Motion) its terminus a quo and ad quem. But Increase or Decrease of the Whole, or any Part in the Transition, there is a common Receptacle, or Place, which receives of furnisheth exactly the same. So that however spaciously the Books are branched out, there is conserved a perpetual Par, or Balance of the Whole. (8)

North's language invokes an organicism that is ultimately restrained, a steady-state reliability "conserved" in organized, internally consistent space. He uses the example of shifting contents from one drawer of a "Scritoire" to another, which "Alterations make no Disorder, but the Repertory of the whole is continually compleat" (17). Most importantly, he emphasizes hat intertextuality is the key to representational perfection:

> As the Accompts depend on one another, so all the Books and Papers belonging to the Business, are connected in the Accompt by References; for the Ledger calls on the Journal, That on the Waste-Book, That on the Subsidiary Books of all sorts . . . And an Alphabet of the Names, or Titles of the Accompts, always attends to Ledger; by Help of which you have ready Recourse to any Accompt there; and then you have the Thread that guides thro' all; which Disposition as to Consultation or Searches, is to all Intents perfect. (31)

The point is that the entire system is designed for the "perfect" retrieval of reality, with an internal discipline that enforces accuracy. By writing first in the waste book, transcribing to the journal and posting to the ledger, multiple restatements curtail the possibility of a careless or fraudulent posting with no back-up text to provide corrrection. Not only can fiction be caught, but right use of the system discourages pepetration of lies:

> And that other way [posting directly to the ledger] is also open to Frauds, as may be practiced at any time, by writing what you please in the Books; for perhaps there is not occasion to write a Line in an Accompt for three or four Years together; and in the last Year you may write with a Date two Years before; and what shall shew the falsity? If the parcel

> be entered in the Day, it is justified to be done at the Time, by the continual daily, and perhaps hourly Entries, that are made before and after it. So that an After-cheat, not designed, when the Books were carried on day by day, can afterwards foist nothing into the Books that is false, to give a Colour to it. (31)

Virtually all the pedagogical texts discuss the prevention and cure of accounting errors. North says flatly, "Errors are to be adjusted to Truth in the Books" (39). The ultimate point of avoiding Error is that not only do accounts display one's affairs, they regulate the self—the author—who is prior to the act of inscription. The tradesman diligently keeping his accounts is less inclined to interpolate an "After-cheat."

Accounting's claims to represent Truth, require that truth be a distinct discursive category, and that accounting texts be able to segregate fiction and truth. In other words, such texts must be the exact discursive opposite of credit texts described in The Compleat English Tradesman. How is this accomplished? In A New Treatise, Malcolm speaks of "Imaginary" accounts (122). In Principles of Book-keeping, explain'd, Alexander Maghie speaks of "fictitious accounts."[22] The terms sound paradoxical within a discourse of militant transparency, but in fact they make sense: events that must be represented but cannot be accommodated by accounting's representational conventions are given accounts of their own, so that convention remains uncompromised in rendering Truth. "Imaginary," "fictitious" events are reified as separate accounts consistent with the discursive project. The discourse of credit, in which "truth" and "fiction" are indeterminate, is superseded by a logic that maintains both categories in the same discursive space (the ledger), but as distinct.

Malcolm explains that in order to separate determinate and indeterminate, "some Accompts be used, which, for Distinction, I call Imaginary":

> Suppose I send Goods as Tobacco to Sea, consigned to my Factor at Amsterdam, the Creditor Side of the Accompt of Tobacco, must be made to show, how it is dispos'd of; a Creditor requires a Debtor, but there is no Person or Thing come in their Place to be made Debtor; for I cannot charge my Factor, till he advises me they are come to his Hand, therefore I erect an Accompt in my Leger by the Title of Voyage to Amsterdam, &c. which I charge, or make Debtor for the whole Cargo, and so it will stand till I am advised that they are Lost, or come safe to my Factor, and then the Accompt Voyage is discharged, i.e. made Creditor, to my Factor Debtor . . . (122-23)

The system requires creation of a "fiction," an imagined entity, that mediates among real entities (real accounts, representing real phenomena) if an outcome is unknown and therefore unrepresentable. Fiction signifies indeterminacy, and is segregated from other, determinate accounts. Malcolm describes a similar schematic where a debt is "due only upon Condition of a certain Event" (123), and Macghie requires a "fictitious" account when one receives but does not deliver in return (9-10). Thus the possibility of alternative outcomes is not permitted to interfere with the project of knowing the exact state of one's affairs. One knows when and in what particulars the text is uncertain, since contingency is not represented in the same discursive terms as the real; it is identified with fictivity.

The mode of production of accounting texts prohibits them from exhibitng ambiguity, for example, of Serious Reflections during the life and Surprizing Adventures of

Robinson Crusoe. Accounting is not a product of print culture, and is therefore off limits to Editors, Publishers, and other personae with authority to supervise (to revise?) texts sub silentio. The author is never forced to compromise his agency for reasons relating to the market (which demands that Moll's text be scoured, and which forces tradesmen to promise unconditionally). Rather, the author's agency is asserted, and if he observes accounting protocol, his honesty is prima facie a fact. In Idea Rationaria, or the perfect accomptant (1683), Robert Colinson argues that accounting induces reader confidence in the authorial persona:

> If he be unfortunate it satisfies the world of his just dealing, and is the fairest and best Apologie for his innocence and honesty to the World, and contributes exceedingly to the satisfaction of all his friends and well-wishers, and to the Confutation and silencing of all his malevolent and detracting Enemies, and often proves the great cause to bring him a most favorable Composition with his Creditors: whereas these that are ignorant of it, in such a Condition are censured by all, when they have nothing to show but bare words to vindicate themselves.[23]

The accounting text is credible to reader/creditors because it opens itself to investigation, confuting "malevolent and detracting Enemies." In The Compleat English Tradesman, credit texts that cannot bear investigation resist protocols that would permit, invite investigation. Against this disparity, Defoe has to discredit accounting's claims. He has to demonstrate that the accounting text, like the intertextual shell-games of credit, is a shaky version of the real.

In The Compleat English Tradesman, the accounting text is fragile. While still potentially defensive it is also potentially productive of irony, and more readily reinscribes the confusion it was intended to dispel. Defoe argues that "That Tradesman, who keeps no books, may depend upon it, he will e're long keep no trade, unless he resolves also to give no credit" (I, 268). He then suggests, however, that "He that does not keep his books exactly, and so as that he may depend on them for charging his Debtors, had better keep no books at all . . .; for as books well kept make business easy and certain, so books neglected turn all into confusion' and leave the Tradesman in a wood, which he can never get out of without damage and loss" (I, 271). Defoe's logic leads to paranoia. Inexact books are worse than no books; it is impossible to eschew books unless one gives no credit; yet "He that gives no trust . . . is not yet born, or if there was any such, they are all dead" (I, 268 In other words, if your books are inexact, you are out of business. The very texts supposed to safeguard the Tradesman can provoke his undoing.

Defoe suggests that the inept text proliferates hostile fictions around it:

> . . . if ever his dealers know that his books are ill-kept they play upon him, and impose horrid forgeries and falsities upon him; whatever he omits they catch at, and leave it out; whatever they put upon him, he is bound to yield to; so that in short, as books well kept are the security of the Tradesman's estate, and the ascertaining of his debts, so books ill kept will assist every knavish customer or chapman to cheat and decieve him. (I, 271)

The inexact text is vulnerable, yielding to "forgeries" that reconstruct the author as discreditable. No longer constrained by an abstracting protocol, the text is open to market-place noise, to opinion and irony. The vulnerability of the Tradesman's texts distinguishes them from those described by Colinson, North and Malcolm, which resisted "After-cheats." Defoe's version of accounting, which provides "the security of the Tradesman's estate" if well-inscribed, easily pitches into reverse.

The Compleat English Tradesman ambiguates the accounting evangelism so prominent in Defoe's predecessors. The difference is one of emphasis, of raising doubts. The point is not to discredit accounting, but to affiliate it with credit, so that commercial textuality becomes uncertain in all its iterations. Defoe's brilliance lies not in any sendup of accounting, but in his ability to blunt its knife-edged perfection.

The market can be depicted as particularly oppressive because the accounting procedures that Defoe recommends are not technically refined. There is no analysis of the transaction into Debtor and Creditor as in a formal journal entry. More significantly, transactions are recorded only once in the Ledger, under the debtor's account, rather than at least twice and potentially under multiple accounts. As a result, the theoretical justification of classic double-entry falls away: the ledger cannot be rationalzed, cannot be "ballanced" by applying the rule that for every Debtor in one account there is a Creditor in another. Errors are more likely to intrude, and a "trial balance" cannot be struck to determine whether a mistake has crept in.

Defoe's directions to the Tradesman for eradicating error suggest that accounting texts are inherently uncertain. Defoe proposes that accounts be wrenched into transparency by main force, by physically counting one's cash. Prior tracts describe a method that is self-correcting, indigenous to a regime of self-enclosed textuality. In order to "ballance" the Cash Book with the cash on hand, thereby achieving transparency, the Tradesman takes an inventory:

> What I call ballancing his Cash-book, is, first, the casting up, daily, or weekly, or monthly his receipts and payments, and then seeing what money is left on hand, or, as the usual expression of the Tradesman is, what money is in cash, secondly, the examining his money, telling it over, and seeing how much he has in his chest or bags, and then seeing if it agrees with the ballance of his book, that what is and what should be, correspond. (I, 276-77)

Defoe's notion of "ballance" is different from that of classic accounting. In classical theory, balance does not refer to what is actually in the cash chest, determined by physical counting, but to an agreement among discursive categories from which one can derive the state of one's cash. Classical accounting is autotelic, relying on the perfection of a self-referring ledger, annotated by subsidiary texts within a self-referring regime. Defoe's accounting is transgressive, denying the perfection of textuality, moving the ground of affirmation from Text to World. While Defoe states his theory in terms that resemble double-entry ("What is" in the cash chest and "what should be" in the Cash Book "correspond"), he interposes a physicality that denies the immediate correspondence characteristic of classical theory. The text loses the automatic presumption of veracity (though of course it may be true). While Defoe's method is likelier to yield an accurate "picture" than is double-entry, provided the Tradesman actually applies himself to the task, his approach makes concessions to the fragility of the text which double-entry does not. The text becomes contingent, a secondary notation of "what is," rather than a self-sufficient iteration constituting "what is." Since the Defoean text must always be-confirmed extra-textually, it hovers between "what is" and "what should be" with an incalculable margin of Error.

In a curious paradox, it is the very textual solipsism of classic double-entry, the mirror-images of the ledger reflecting the subsidiary images of anterior texts, which allows the system (in theory) to reflect the world, since fictional After-cheats are hard to disguise. The serenity of an encompassing, self-assured textuality differs from the anxiety projected onto the Tradesman, who as reader-accountant must anxiously interact with a world of fluctuating phenomena:

> The keeping a cash-book is one of the nicest parts of a Trasdesman's business, because there is always the bag and the book to be brought together, and if they do not exactly speak the same language, even to a farthing, there must be some omission; and how big or how little that omission may be, who knows? or how shall it be known, but by casting and re-casting up, telling, and telling over and over again the money? (I, 279)

By mandating a continual "casting and re-casting," Defoe denies the text's abstraction from the world, its ability to absorb flux and remain independent of any intervention (other than mere notation). The text becomes True only until the next transaction. It ceases to be a site for the generation of truth. The anxiety of credit is reintroduced.

At the empirical level, Defoe refocuses the reflecting mirrors of double-entry into a mise-en-abime, where "what is" and "what should be" become mutually unsettling dependent variables. Since the text loses its absolute integrity, one cannot be certain whether the text or one's counting house is in error, whether one's Books need reform or one's cash is deficient or unfairly in excess. In the most astounding irony, the first page of sample accounts m The Compleat English Tradesman displays a glaring arithmetical mistake: in a long column of figures, sixpence and sixpence are ad-deaf to make sixpence (I, Supp., 46). The error infects pages and pages of subsequent accounts, with no internal check sending the Tradesman back to his math. The Tradesman "telling" his cash might think he collected sixpence too much, and wonder who overpaid. If he does not "tell" his cash, he might think he has less than he does. Though I do not suggest that Defoe "planted" this error, I am suggesting that it reifies the fragility of the accounting text modelled in The Compleat English Tradesman.

By sub silentio eviscerating double-entry, Defoe permits the world of uncertainty to flow back into a text that ideally would keep it out. As a result, the confusion of credit occupies both the Tradesman's accounts and the account of those accounts in The Compleat English Tradesman. Defoe destabilizes the project of commercial culture to fix commercial phenomena into readable form. His reformulation of that project is itself unfixed; the exposition of market-place certainty ends in the bathos of school-boy mistake. Accounting, ostensibly a refuge from the impenetrability of texts, comes to exemplify it, becoming just another emblem of an ironic market.

Of all the major accounting tracts of the period, only Defoe's does not offer a proximate version of double-entry.[24] He offers instead a version that can be transparent, but that just as likely may not be. The bottom line is that the reader of The Compleat English Tradesman, having absorbed its ideology of credit, concludes that no text can challenge that ideology. No text certifies the transparency of texts. Texts in the market are radically unaccountable. Accounting is assimilated to this general unaccountability, rather than allowed to remain its foil. In answer to the question of whether the accounting text is true ("how shall it be known?"), Defoe directs the reader back to the world, with its own uncertainties.

In The Compleat English Tradesman, Defoe develops the didactic format so popular during the late seventeenth/early eighteenth century, into an anti-didactic subversion of marketplace knowledge.[25] The text reifies generic irony. While it inhabits the genre of updated Protestant guidebook, it misguides the Tradesman, offering a type of accounting that was susceptible to error, and that induced the assumption that fiction and truth were hard to keep apart. The Tradesman could, if he had the energy, trace down all the discrepancies between Text and World, but as a practical matter he learns that reading is fraught. Texts that he inscribes may not represent Truth, and adversarial readers are alert to impute fiction.

The Compleat English Tradesman is a primer in how texts resist disclosure. It constructs a theory of textual production in which potential diction proliferates fiction to hide its fictional potential. Its premises are articulated within the discourse of commercial "credit," which provides the logic for an epistemology of commercial fiction. The Compleat English Tradesman is not, therefoe, the landmark of Defoe's post-fictional career, the emblem of his inability to sustain the pressure of feigning.[26] To the contrary, it is Fiction By Other Means, a reflection upon Defoean novels that resist generic avowal. It evinces a commitment to producing fiction in a market that resists fiction, and it provides a theory of reading which frustrates such resistance.

The Compleat English Tradesman is a sustained argument carried on within a discourse of commerciality, bent on showing that texts circulating in the market—bills, notes, histories, memoirs—cannot be other than generically unfixed. It suggests that it would be a Category Mistake to demand anything more. As a consequence their authors are not liars in a conventional sense. If readers read at their peril, it is because reading is perilous.[27] The only alternative to abstention is to become inert. As Defoe observes: "He that gives no trust . . . is not yet born, or if there ever was any such, they are all dead."

NOTES

1. For example, see John Bender, *Imagining the Penitentiary: Fiction and the Architecture of the Mind in Eighteenth-Century England* (Chicago: university of Chicago Press, 1987), 51; Lincoln Faller, *Crime and Defoe: A New Kind of Narrative* (Cambridge: Cambridge University Press, 1993) 152-54; George Starr, *Defoe and Casuistry* (Princeton: Princeton University Press, 1971), Appendix: Of Mendacity; Bram Dijkstra, *Defoe and Economics: The Fortunes of Roxana in the History of Interpretation* (New York: St. Martin's Press, 1987).

2. In *Factual Fictions: the Origins of the English Novel* (New York: Columbia University Press, 1983), Davis demonstrates the techniques Defoe deploys to muddle his texts' affiliation with "fiction" or "truth." Davis remarks, for example, that "Crusoe is at once true and false; he is a fiction with a true existence and a true story with a fictional structure. As was the case with so many of the texts considered in this study, the distinction between fact an fiction is deliberately unclear" (157). In *The Origins of the Engish Novel* (Baltimore: Johns Hopkins University Press, 1987), McKeon observes that Defoe "doggedly pursued the problem of the false claim to historicity for the better part of two decades," making and justifying "claims to historicity, although with ambivalence and accompanied by a variety of uneasy extenuations" (120). Bartolomeo pursues this line of reasoning in A New Species of Criticism: Eighteenth-Century Discourse on the Novel (Newark: University of Delaware Press, 1994), 35-46.

3. See McKeon regarding standards of credibility applied to various genres, e.g. travel literature (Chapter 2). See also J. Paul Hunter, *Before Novels: The Cultural Contexts of Eighteenth Century English Fiction* (New York: Norton, 1990). Chapter 8 examines public interest in amazing but seemingly provable accounts. In *God's Plots and Man's Stories: Studies in the Fictional Imagination from Milton*

to Fielding (Chicago: University of Chicago Press, 1985), Leo Damrosch discusses Puritan objections to fiction stating that Defoe's effort "[t]o write novels . . . was a subversive innovation" (204). For an excellent review of Puritan hostility to fiction, see David Marshall, *The Figure of Theater: Shaftesbury, Defoe, Adam Smith, and George Eliot* (New York: Columbia University Press, 1986), Chapter 4 and accompanying citations. *The Life and Strange Surprizing Adventures of Mr. D . . . De F . . . of London*, Hosier (1719), launched Charles Gildon's famous attack on Robinson Crusoe as a fiction lacking sufficient moral purport to justify its fictionality. Crusoe issues his literally incredible riposte to Gildon in *Serious Reflections during the Life and Surprizing Adventures of Robinson Crusoe with His Vision of the Angelick World* (1720). See Davis, 156-61, analyzing the impossible metaphysics of Crusoe's response.

4. In *A New Species of Criticism*, Bartolomeo observes that "the author who never claimed responsiblity for his fiction used [the affective argument of knowing how to read Moll Flanders] primarily to avoid responsibility—for any number of reasons—for the moral ambiguity [in that text]" (45). The same logic applies to avoiding responsibility for a potential fiction, also morally suspect.

5. On the discourse of commercial paper (i.e. "credit") during the late seventeenth and early eighteenth centuries, see J.G.A. Pocock, *The Machiavellian Moment: Florentine Political Thought and the Atlantic Republican Tradition* (Baltimore: Johns Hopkins University Press, 1975), Chapter 13. Public credit, which financed the government, and private credit, the basis for trade among merchants, displayed the same characteristics: the likely payoff was speculative, appealing to the imagination. On the development of a metropolitan market linked through private credit, see Eric Kerridge, *Trade and Banking in Early Modern England* (Manchester: Manchester University Press, 1988). For a contemporary discussion of the various, highly sophisticated instruments of credit, see John Scarlett, *The Stile of Exchanges* (1680). The need for private credit and the lack of sufficient regulation is examined in B.L. Anderson, "Money and the Structure

of Credit in the Eighteenth Century," *Business History* 12 (1970), 85-101.

6. Moll's manipulation of a market defined by credit is discussed in Carol Kay, *Political Constructions: Defoe, Richardson, and Sterne in Relation to Hobbes, Flume, and Burke* (Ithaca: Cornell University Press, 1988), Chapter 2.

7. Defoe's novelistic fictions began with Robinson Crusoe in 1719, and ended with Roxana in 1724. The first volume of *The Compleat English Tradesman* followed the next year.

8. *The Compleat English Tradesman* (I, Supp., 26).

9. In the "Author's Preface" to the first volume of Robinson Crusoe, it is actually the "Editor" whose thoughts are revealed. Moll's voice is mediated by "The pen employ'd in finishing her Story." See *The Fortunes and Misfortunes of the Famous Moll Flanders* (Oxford: Blackwell's, 1927), I, vii. In Roxana, the "Relator," "Writer," and "I" pre-empt that of the "Author."

10. *The Compleat English Tradesman I,* Supp., 27, 28.

11. *Ibid.*, I, Supp., 29.

12. *The Fortunes and Misfortunes of the Famous Moll Flanders* I, 80.

13. *A New Species of Criticism*, 44-45.

14. *The Compleat English Tradesman* I, 235.

15. Roger North, *The Gentleman Accomptant: Or, An Essay to Unfold the Mystery of Accompts* (London, 1715), 9.

16. Alexander Malcolm, *A New treatise of Arithmetic and Book-keeping* (Edinburgh, 1718), 113.

17. According to the Royal Society, facts" could be constituted through witnessing their production in a public space; texts could recapitulate the production of facts, creating endless virtual witnesses" (readers) who confirm these facts. See Steven Shapin and Simon Schaffer, *Leviathan and the Air-Pump: Hobbes, Boyle, and the Experimental Life* (Princeton: Princeton University Press, 1985).

18. See Hugh Oldcastle, A Profitable Treatyce called the Instrument or Boke to learne to knowe the good order of the kepying of the famouse reconyge called in latyn, Dare and Habere, and in Englyshe, Debitor and Creditor (London: 1543). The first accounting text was published by a Milanese cleric, Fra Luca Pacioli, in 1494.

19. On the history of accounting, see James Winjum, *The Role of Accounting in the Economic Development of England: 1500-1750* (Urbana: University of Illinois, 1972); A.C. Littleton, *Accounting Evolution to 1900* (New York: American Institute Publishing Co., 1933); Basil Yamey, *Essays on the History of Accounting* (New York: Arno Press, 1978); A.C. Littleton and Basil Yamey, *Studies in the History of Accounting* (New York: Arno Press, 1978); Basil Yamey, et al., *Accounting in England and Scotland: 154-1800—Double-Entry in Exposition and Practice* (London: Sweet and Maxwell, 1963), which includes a bibliography of all accounting texts in English published during the period (including *The Compleat English Tradesman*). Winjum, 47-49, discusses the uniformity of technique from Pacioli to Oldcastle and into the eighteenth century.

20. Defoe would have used accounting in his early career as a hosier and pantile manufacturer and in 1695 was appointed accountant to one of the commissioners of the glass duty. He thought enough of his proficiency to mention it to Harley when seeking patronage. In a letter of May-June, 1704, Defoe states that "Matters of Accounts are my particular Element, what I have Allways been Master of." In a letter of June 19, 1707, he suggests work such as "Accompta or Comptr of the Accounts, things I pretend to be master of." See *The Letters of Daniel Defoe*, ed. George Healey (Oxford: The Clarendon Press, 1955), Letters No. 9 and 109.

21. Classical accounting assumes that the world can be represented in an equilibrated text. Thus it assumes that what is in inventory (and reflected in one's books under a perpetual inventory) will really be on one's shelves—not pilfered by staff, eaten by mice, spoiled, out of fashion or fallen in value. Accounting is paradoxical

in that while one's accounts may be maintained with up-to-the-minute accuracy, time itself can erode their accuracy.

22. See Alexander Macghie, *Principles of Book-keeping, explain'd* (Edinburgh: 1718), 9-10.

23. Robert Colinson, *Idea Rationaria, or the perfect accomptant* (London: 1683), Preface.

24. North acknowledges that some businesses not dependent on credit do not employ double-entry. However, he does not teach any other method, and "absolutely require[s], that whatever is wrote, be a Part of, and approach in some degree towards the ultimate Perfection of Form, that Accompts can possibly receive" (56). Other accounting texts disparage methods not compliant with double-entry. In Debtor and Creditor Made Easy (1708), Stephen Monteage asks of tradesmen using such methods: "[W]hat ballance can they bring these Books to? None at all" (Preface).

25. On *The Compleat English Tradesman* as a species of Protestant guide book, and on the didactic genres of the period, see J. Paul Hunter, Before Novels, Chapters 9-11.

26. Michael Shinagel suggests that Defoe fled the production of fiction after Roxana, on grounds that his Puritan sensibility could not tolerate the pressure of sustained imaginative excess. See *Daniel Defoe and Middle Class Gentility* (Cambridge: Harvard University Press, 1968), 193-96. For a thoughtful response to Shinagel, see David Marshall, Chapter 6, esp. n. 15.

27. Following such logic, the author of *The Compleat English Tradesman* may himself be exculpated from creating a text which, though didactic in form, escapes into a rationale excusing the author of fictions.

8

Inevitable Politics: Rulership and Identity in Robinson Crusoe

—Frank Donoghue

During his stay on the island, Robinson Crusoe resorts to several politically expedient though still perplexing impersonations. Although he is in reality a plantation owner and part-time slave trader, he spends his first solitary years indulging in half-joking fantasies that he is a king. He continues this pose even after the native he names Friday, Friday's father, and a Spanish sailor arrive on the island. Once a group of English mutineers and their deposed captain appear, however, Crusoe is suddenly transformed into the island's "governour." And when, in the process of restoring the captain to power, the dishevelled Crusoe must address the imprisoned mutineers, he does so as the governor's jailor, threatening them with the awful wrath of his fictional superior. This odd series of transmutations, as I hope to show, is compounded by Crusoe's conflicted sense of his public self. Though he dearly wishes to be idealistically (and Puritanically) self-sufficient, he is repeatedly confronted with the unsettling sense that he is connected to the European world. The first of these self images has intrigued those who find in Crusoe's isolation an attractive myth of the self-sufficient man. But the rapid escalation of political and economic engagement between Europe and the Americas made the world of the seventeenth century an increasingly inclusive place, one that left less and less room for the kind of autonomy about which Crusoe fantasizes. I hope to rectify what I see as an imbalance in the critical history of Robinson Crusoe by making the case that Crusoe is never so solitary as he imagines himself, and moreover that the individual identity that he does possess is in a sense produced by the mercantilist world that he denies. That identity no sooner appears than it is immediately regularized and incorporated into an all but universal political network that erases earlier notions of privacy.[1]

By the end of his adventures, Crusoe is not only forced to acknowledge political authority and to compromise his behavior accordingly, but he is also forced to impersonate the figure of that authority on the island (by becoming "governour") in order to survive. In other words, Crusoe participates alternately on both sides of the political-economic forces that polarized the world during the second half of the seventeenth century: the egoistic impulse towards commerce on a global scale (along with the renegade absolutism that Crusoe finds so appealing), and the corresponding desire to consolidate the state power to which that commerce posed a threat. Crusoe's identity, then, hovers in a kind of political limbo. He is not the king of the island, nor is he the island's governor, or the governor's jailor; his readiness to abandon each of these offices suggests that he never really inhabited any of them in the first place. His efforts to define himself privately are thwarted, while his attempts to define himself politically- the playful as well as the desperate- are necessarily multiple and inauthentic.

The history of mythic interpretations of Crusoe originates with Defoe himself, who, in Serious Reflections (1720), the third installment of the series of books he wrote about Crusoe, presents his hero's adventures as allegorical. To treat Crusoe as an allegorical figure is to perceive him as a free-standing gloss on civilization rather than as an individual embedded in it and answerable to all its customs and conventions. The danger in treating Crusoe as a type, in other words, is that one can be led into the mistaken assumptions that he exists independently of the European civilization that he attempts to reproduce and that the island comes for the duration of his stay simply to replace the world. Such a view authorizes the idealized terms in which Crusoe creates his own political fantasy. During the first third of the novel, when he most frequently represents himself as king, the issue of rivalry figures as the chief threat; Crusoe is virtually obsessed with reassuring himself that everything in his political world is his property, and that everyone is properly subjected and completely under his control. Before the island is populated, he states:

> I was Lord of the whole Mannor; or if I pleas'd, I might call my self King, or Emperor over the whole Country which I had Possession of. There were no Rivals. I had no Competitor, none to dispute Sovereignty or Command with Me.[2]

And after the rescue of the Spaniard and Friday's father he reiterates his claim:

> My Island was now peopled, and I thought myself very rich in Subjects; and it was a merry Reflection which I frequently made, How like a King I look'd. First of all, the whole Country was my own meer Property; so that I had an undoubted Right of Dominion. 2ndly, My People were perfectly subjected: I was absolute Lord and Law-giver; they all owed their Lives to me, and were ready to lay down their Lives, if there had been Occasion of it, for me. (p. 241)

Crusoe's vaunting is an attempt to reaffirm the status that so many of his readers all too readily grant him: that of being singular, independent, and self-determined. But I would suggest instead that he makes his assertions in response to a well-founded and politically pragmatic set of fears. For the island is not Crusoe's and its inhabitants are not his subjects. The island is located not far from the mouth of the Oroonoko River, and East-Southeast of Trinidad (p. 215), and is therefore almost certainly in the domain of either Spain or Portugal.[3] As Peter Hulme points out, "the only uninhabited land in America [in the mid-seventeenth century] tended to be uninhabitable . . . the Amerindians would certainly not have ignored Crusoe's remarkably fertile island unless they had been driven off by the European competition for Caribbean land which was in full swing by 1659."[4] Thus Crusoe's possessiveness of the island is an expression of his fantasy of isolation and an attempt to suppress his more plausible suspicions that someone else owns it. His full awareness of the identities of his potential rivals becomes clear as soon as a European lands on the island. During his ambush of the savages who have brought three victims to feast upon, Crusoe shrewdly addresses the white man among the prisoners in Portuguese and shows no surprise when the man turns out to be Spanish (p. 235). Later, Crusoe attempts to establish legitimate authority over the English mutineers who land on the island by addressing them in Spanish, that is, in one of the most likely languages of a colonial government in that area (p. 254). These choices suggest that Crusoe harbors specific suspicions that his real situation differs fundamentally from the absolutist reverie in which he so often indulges. Moreover, they establish the pattern of compromise which characterizes the last part of the narrative, in which Crusoe consistently trades imaginary sovereignty for real political leverage.

Crusoe seems least aware of his status as a member of the imperialist European economic community, from which he is never for a moment excluded. Even during his twenty-eight year exile on the island, his estate in the Brasils, entrusted to a far-reaching, benevolent, conscientious mercantile network, continues to make money. Upon his return, Crusoe is astounded by the remarkable capacity of the economic system to include him as a member even while he has been physically absent from his own property:

> I was now Master, all on a Sudden, of above 5,000 [pounds]. Sterling in Money, and had an Estate, as I might well call it, in the Brasils, of above a thousand Pounds a year, as sure as an Estate of Lands in England: And in a Word, I was in a Condition which I scarce knew how to understand, or how to compose my self, for the Enjoyment of it. (p. 285)

The transitivity of capital insures that Crusoe's estate is interchangeable with any of comparable value in England, and that its value increases at a stable rate independently of his active management of it. Crusoe's astonishment at worldly economics leads Hulme to conceive of him as two characters rather than one: the benevolent ruler of a simple, moral economy on the island and, at the same time, an enterprising slave owner in the world market. These divided selves, Hulme argues, are "a technique for negating the inseparable- and eventually uncloseable- gap between the violence of slavery and the notion of a moral economy." This constitutes what he calls the "colonial alibi," which serves to vindicate imperialism into the nineteenth century.[5]

But if we acknowledge that Robinson Crusoe functions as a denial of the reality of global economy, I think it is equally important to notice Crusoe's liminal understanding of the political conflicts implicit in his precarious situation on the island. The ever expanding boundaries of imperialist

Europe repeatedly impinge upon and complicate Crusoe's naive dreams, frequently forcing him to adjust his political self-image. He willingly abandons the office of benevolent sovereign when circumstances require it late in his stay. That is, Crusoe readily revises the "simple and moral" government that parallels the island's utopian economy—he appears at least on the verge of admitting that he is implicated in the global politics that are inevitably in force on the island. Robinson Crusoe is hardly anxious to excuse its hero through recourse to a "colonial alibi"; rather it seems eager to justify Crusoe's crimes as expedient police actions. Crusoe is forced, by the arrival of fellow Englishmen, to negotiate the closure of the gap that separates his "divided selves" and to reinsert himself into a universal imperialist narrative.

Or, perhaps more accurately, Crusoe is inserted into that narrative. His political status is destabilized from the moment he and Friday rescue Friday's father and the Spaniard from the band of savages that has taken them to the island. First he is mistaken for a god. After the rescue, made possible by the use of firearms, Crusoe polls his "two new Subjects" for their assessment of the surviving natives' reactions (p. 242). Friday's father's opinion is that they will thereafter consider Crusoe and Friday "Heavenly Spirits or Furies," a guess borne out by the fact that "the Savages never attempted to go over to the Island afterwards; they were so terrified . . . that they believ'd whoever went to that enchanted Island would be destroy'd with Fire from the Gods" (p . 243).

Though the notion that Crusoe transcends politics by being a god is short-lived, it is nevertheless the first impression that he evokes among the English captain and his two mates, victims of a mutiny, who are the next to arrive on the island. Crusoe dwells on his appearance as he approaches them:

> my Figure indeed was very fierce; I had my formidable Goat-Skin Coat on, with the great Cap I have mention'd, a naked Sword by my side, two Pistols in my Belt, and a Gun upon each Shoulder. (p. 253)

In a bizarre combination of political self-consciousness and outright fantasy, Crusoe, enjoying the thought of his other-worldly "Spectre-like Figure," nevertheless demonstrates once again a surprisingly shrewd awareness of his place in this world: he addresses the men in Spanish, and speaks English only when they begin to flee. At this moment of greatest confusion, Crusoe does admit the fragility and insubstantiality of his "kingdom." When the captain, bewildered by Crusoe's wild appearance, asks, "Am I talking to God, or Man! Is it a real Man or an Angel!" Crusoe responds with uncharacteristic candor, "I am a Man, an English-man, and dispos'd to assist you, you see; I have one Servant only; we have Arms and Ammunition; tell us freely, Can we serve you?" (pp. 254-55). But in the military maneuvers that ensue, during which Crusoe, Friday, and the captain and his two mates are joined by three "Prisoners of War" who have come over to the captain's side, Crusoe assumes the quasi-official position of "Generalissimo" (p. 267).[6] As they surrender, one of the mutineers raises a mild objection, to which the captain replies by decisively placing Crusoe in a preexisting. readily available imperial hierarchy:

> the Captain told him he must lay down his Arms at Discretion, and trust to the Governour's Mercy, by which he meant me; for they all call'd me Governour. (p. 268)

Crusoe readily acquiesces to the role of governor that the Englishmen assign him, even though it represents a demotion from his previous rank of king. He soon demotes himself even further when he actually comes to deal with two of the mutineers who have surrendered to him:

> When I shew'd my self to the two Hostages, it was with the Captain, who told them, I was the Person the Governour had order'd to look after them, and that it was the Governour's Pleasure they should not stir any where, but by my Direction; that if they did, they should be fetched into the Castle, and be lay'd in Irons; so that as we never suffered them to see me as Governour, so I now appear'd as another Person, and spoke of the Governour, the Garrison, the Castle, and the like, upon all Occasions. (p. 271)

These improvisations are made seamlessly, without hesitation, as moves that require no explanation. Indeed, all that is left unsaid leaves the impression that Crusoe has never forgotten a cosmopolitanism borne of years of instantiation in the global political culture.

How can we account for the fluctuation in Crusoe's political self-representation once other people begin arriving on the island? My contention has been that we must keep in mind that the island, remote as it is, is nevertheless in and of the civilized world and not simply a replica of it. Crusoe demonstrates his awareness of this fact when he addresses the first refugee, the Spaniard, in Portuguese. During the brief interlude in which Crusoe has only three "Subjects"—Friday, Friday's father, and the Spaniard—he continues to think of himself as king. Only when Englishmen appear is Crusoe jolted from his utopian monarchism. Since both Crusoe and the ship's captain owe allegiance to the king of England, Crusoe is forced to occupy a different role.[7]

But this does not completely solve the problem. There is considerable ideological over-determination associated with this transfer of power from the fantasy king, Crusoe, to the real king of England. As "Governour," Crusoe take s on the task of restoring the captain to his rightful place as ruler of the ship, an echo, perhaps, of the Restoration of Charles II in 1660. But Crusoe brings about the captain's restoration by means of a treacherous bluff. He has himself no legitimate authority over the mutineers and can get them to surrender only by lying about his military strength (saying he has fifty men armed and ready). That lie is relayed to the seamen by an ex-mutineer who shares Crusoe's name, Robinson (p. 267).

Crusoe's political allegiances are also highly ambiguous. As Michael Seidel observes, at the time of his shipwreck (September 30, 1659), the Protectorate was being reformed through one constitution after another, and the Restoration was imminent.[8] At the time of Crusoe's dealings with the mutineers James II was king but he was about to be deposed and replaced by William III, who would become England's ruler a year after Crusoe's return home on June 11, 1687. Given his place on the time-line of the late seventeenth century, it is very hard indeed to imagine what Crusoe's ideological position might be. He simply missed thirty of the most turbulent years in British political history, a period during which the proper relationship between king and subject was twice redefined, and during which the open secret of the king's divided loyalties (Charles' and James' Catholicism) was a constant subject of criticism.

Moreover, the chief instrument by which Crusoe negotiates his place in the political world outside the island- the contract- is always highly unstable. From the start, Crusoe's understanding of the nature of contracts is irrational. The contractual relationships into which he enters are absurdly lopsided, and all of them leave Crusoe himself undefined and his behavior unregulated. In the first of these arrangements, Crusoe enlists the help of

Xury, a Moslem youth, in his escape from the Captain of the Turkish rover. With a loaded rifle in his hands, Crusoe says to the boy,

> "Xury, if you will be faithful to me I'll make you a great Man, but if you will not stroak your Face to be true to me, that is, swear by Mahomet and his Father's Beard, I must throw you into the Sea too." (p. 23)

In an astonishing display of naive faith in the conventions of oath-taking, Crusoe firmly believes the boy's promise, even though it is a heathen oath sworn under palpable duress. He reveals an almost desperate hope that the contract will in effect define the boy, But Crusoe's own intentions and behavior are nowhere to be found in this bond or in the subsequent developments in this episode. He places no restrictions on his own behavior except for a vague promise, and he breaks even that promise almost immediately, selling Xury into slavery as soon as he is rescued. His relationship with Xury anticipates all the ensuing social contracts that assume, with little or no warrant, Crusoe's unregulated dominance over other people. Friday is so named to remind the native of the day on which Crusoe saved his life, and Friday's first instructions are to call Crusoe "Master" (p. 206). Once the titles and hierarchy are established, Crusoe proceeds to reshape much of Friday's identity, a process that begins in earnest with instruction in Christianity and extends even to a meticulous concern with the native's new (non-cannibalistic) diet (p. 212). As more people arrive, Crusoe demands more and more oaths to assure himself that he is still in power and can control his chances for survival and rescue. The Spanish sailor, if he hopes to get off the island, must swear allegiance to Crusoe over his own countrymen (p. 245); the sixteen Spaniards shipwrecked on the mainland would, if there had been pen and ink available, have had to sign written promises of obedience to him (p. 248). Crusoe extracts a variety of commitments from the English prisoners, and when he decides to leave them on the island- over the captain's protests- he asserts:

> Upon this I seem'd a little angry with the Captain, and told him, That they were my Prisoners, not his; and that seeing I had offered them so much Favour, I would be as good as my Word. (p. 276)

Crusoe's "word," of course, in no way affects his behavior and actions except in the proper disposal of the prisoners who have, in his mind, come to be exclusively his own property. Moreover, the curious phrase, "I seem'd a little angry" reminds us that we are in the dark not only about how Crusoe will act, but also about how he really feels. Seidel argues that Crusoe is willing to step down from his fantasy of kingship and become an ordinary national subject "once certain conditions are met, certain contracts arranged, certain powers displayed."[9] But in fact, while Crusoe is obsessed with contracts, conditions, and arrangements, he uses these instruments to guarantee a degree of reliable behavior, indeed stable identity, which he is (with the one exception) never willing to manifest himself. Even part of Crusoe's presentation of himself to the English captain, namely his admission that he too is an Englishman, is far more ambiguous than it may first appear. Defoe had long ago exploded the notion that the term "Englishman" signifies a self-evident, homogenous national identity. He writes in A True-Born Englishman (1700):

> A true-born Englishman's a contradiction, In speech an irony, in fact a fiction
>
> A metaphor invented to express A man akin to all the universe.[10]

Crusoe's status as an Englishman can almost be seen to warrant the multiplicity of political stances he takes during his adventures. If there is no such thing as essential

Englishness, then Crusoe's claim to his countryman is simply one more fiction that he employs to regulate, and possibly dominate his relationship with yet another kind of visitor to the island.

The fictionality of Crusoe the Englishman is compounded in his encounters with the mutineers. In every situation, he seems intuitively to gauge the credulity of his audience and then to assume the very political office they would expect him to occupy. These theatricalizations by which Crusoe consolidates his power are all, paradoxically, displacements of power—assertions that the real authority on the island lies elsewhere, outside himself. Crusoe convinces the mutineers that he, as governor (the representative of the king), commands a militia of fifty men, and thereby persuades them to surrender. Once they are his prisoners, Crusoe persuades them that he is the governor's jailor and has been put in charge of them. In each case, the ultimate authority- the king, whose office Crusoe had once playfully assumed- is placed at one farther remove.

Crusoe's decision to take the captain into his confidence and admit his weakness paradoxically leads to his political success: he luckily (or providentially) chooses the right confessor. Given Crusoe's habitual practice, however, the choice seems to make no sense at all; and as an anomaly, it leads us to reconsider the issues of identity and self-presentation that have long been central puzzles in Defoe's fiction. I have argued thus far that a host of political pressures combine first to bring the autobiographical subject into existence in Defoe's narrative, and then to make it vanish. Nowhere is this process more lucidly illustrated than in the encounter with the English captain. The arrival of the captain tests the capacity of the political dreamworld that Crusoe has constructed for himself and that has until that point defined him as king. The crisis marked by their conversation, in effect, produces the conditions of sincerity that we associate with the notion of a private self. In other words, the collision of the two political contexts in which Crusoe had heretofore defined himself (the island on which he is king, and, before that, the England in which he was a subject) force him to describe himself to the captain in yet another way, one that we would characterize as honest, candid, sincere. Though it includes features of public self-definition- the claim to be an Englishman (however ambiguous that may be), and the offer of service- the scene generates the impression that Crusoe has laid himself bare. He admits his "real" self and situation in a moment of panic when any exclusively political identity is suddenly unavailable to him.

But that self exists only for a moment, since Crusoe no sooner confesses it than he is denominated "governour." That is, he is absorbed into a new political fantasy, which, while it is different from the one he has hitherto rehearsed, is also fictional. The conditions of Crusoe's existence, even on the remote island, are so completely entrenched in civilized European society that "sincerity" is no sooner required of him than it is annihilated.

Defoe seemed at least partially aware that the boundaries of an older social and political order were being stretched thin during his age by an assortment of modernizing forces, and he represents perhaps the most powerful of those forces in Robinson Crusoe. Specifically, England's expanding empire, defined by an emergent mercantilist ideology, forced Defoe to furnish Crusoe with more complex answers to questions about his political identity than would have been required of an Englishman in an earlier age.[11] For, in a mercantilist view of world economy, directive political authority is constantly pitted against individual or corporate commercial speculation.[12] Ideally, commerce is subordinated to politics, and all individuals and institutions are rendered secondary to state power. But as Joyce Appleby observes:

> Despite the unchallenged assumption that the English government had the right and the responsibility to regulate economic activities in the interest of the common good, the ambit of private initiative widened considerably during the middle decades of the seventeenth century. Circumstances—usually in the form of a political crisis—permitted men to pursue their private profit with little official interference.[13]

Ultimately this dichotomy raises disturbing questions about the proper relationship between the individual and the state because it implies that individual agency is disorganized and potentially subversive, and stands in constant need of justification and correction. Crusoe's attempts to define himself thus can be seen as a series of experiments (none of them completely successful) to get that relationship right.

NOTES

1. Since its publication in 1719, Defoe's narrative has typically been characterized as a paradigm of the political and economic dimension of human nature, and early readings tended to alter Defoe's narrative in a way that enhances rather than questions this image of its hero. Rousseau claims that his imaginary pupil, Emile, will benefit from his study of Robinson Crusoe "beginning with Robinson's shipwreck near his island, and ending with the arrival of the ship which comes to take him from it" (Emile, trans. Allan Bloom [New York: Basic Books; 1979], p. 185). But of course these points are not the beginning and end of Crusoe's adventures: Rousseau abridges the narrative in a way that disentangles its hero from all his associations with civilization, deleting among other things his disobedience to his father, his brief stint as a slave, and his triumphant return from the island as a wealthy plantation owner. Marx makes the somewhat misleading claim that "the relations between Robinson and the objects that form the wealth

of his own creation . . . contain all that is essential to the determination of value" (*Capital*, trans. Samuel Moore and Edward Aveling [Chicago: Charles H. Kerr & Co., 1921], 1:88). In fact, though, virtually all the "wealth of his own creation" would have been unattainable if Crusoe had not salvaged so much from the shipwreck, including an assortment of tools and weapons. The ship is Crusoe's umbilical cord to European civilization; Marx omits it in order to reinforce an image of Crusoe as isolated individual. Even the most powerful psychological readings of Robinson Crusoe tend to take Crusoe's fantasy of isolation at face value. See Leo Braudy, "Daniel Defoe and the Anxieties of Autobiography," *Genre* 6 (1973): 97, and Homer O. Brown, "The Displaced Self in the Novels of Daniel Defoe," *ELH* 38 (1971): 562-90.

Only recently have there appeared alternatives to uncritical acceptance of Crusoe's singularity. Peter Hulme largely succeeds in his attempt to "return Robinson Crusoe to the Caribbean," correctly calling attention to all the points at which Crusoe's fantasy collides with the realities of imperialism (Colonial Encounters [London: Methuen, 1986], p. 176. See also Manuel Schonhorn, *Defoe's Politics* (Cambridge: Cambridge Univ. Press, 1991), especially pp. 141-64; Michael Seidel, *Robinson Crusoe: Island Myths and the Novel* (Boston: Twayne Publishers, 1991), and Seidel's earlier, "Crusoe in Exile," *PMLA* 96 (1981): 363-74; and Carol Kay, *Political Constructions: Defoe, Richardson, and Sterne in Relation to Hobbes, Hume, and Burke* (Ithaca, NY: Cornell Univ. Press, 1988), pp. 75-91. These studies establish precedent in Defoe's canon for the political stances that Crusoe takes while on the island. An important source of my thinking in this essay is Philippe Aries' conclusion that public and private life were radically redefined by the development of centralized state authority in the late Renaissance. As a result, by the eighteenth century, "what mattered was no longer what an individual was but what he appeared to be, or, rather, what he could successfully pass himself off as being" (*Arthur Goldhammer*, trans., and Roger Chartier, ed., *A History of Private Life* [Cambridge, MA: The Bellknap Press of Harvard Univ. Press, 1989], 3:2-3).

2. Daniel Defoe, *The Life and Adventures of Robinson Crusoe* (New York: Oxford Classics, 1973), p. 128. All further references are included parenthetically. Schonhorn connects Crusoe's thoughts about kingship to his conversion, asserting that after the conversion "Crusoe appears to be a king by God's immediate design, his reign certified by the deity" (p. 155).

3. For a brief useful survey of the balance of power in the West Indies at the time of Crusoe's shipwreck, see Pat Rogers, *Robinson Crusoe* (London: Allen & Unwin, 1978), pp. 39-40.

4. Hulme, *Colonial Encounters*, p. 186. See also, John H. Parry, "A Secular Sense of Responsibility," in F. Chiapelli, ed., *First Images of the New World: The Impact of the New World on the Old* (Berkeley: Univ. of California Press, 1976), 1:289.

5. *Ibid.*, p. 222.

6. According to Schonhorn, Prince William of Orange was given the title "generalissimo by sea and land" by James II (p. 152, n. 51), though it is uncertain that Defoe, writing some two generations later, would have intended the title as an allusion.

7. These distinctions are somewhat obscured by the fact that Woodes Rogers, in his account of Alexander Selkirk's island exile, reports that Selkirk's rescuers called him "governour"; Rogers himself calls him the "absolute monarch" of the island. See Michael McKeon, *The Origins of the English Novel* (Baltimore: Johns Hopkins Univ. Press, 1987), p. 492, n. 28.

8. Seidel, *Robinson Crusoe: Island Myths and the Novel*, p. 46.

9. Seidel, *Exile and the Narrative Imagination* (New Haven: Yale Univ. Press, 1986), p. 42. Schonhorn argues that "the political component of Crusoe's condition-making activity, comprised of a sovereign monarch and a grateful and dependent community, resembles that of a constitutional monarch" (p. 152).

10. George de Forest Lord, ed., *Anthology of Poems on Affairs of State: Augustan Satirical Verse 1660-1714* (New Haven: Yale Univ. Press, 1975), pp. 633-34, lines 372-73, 375-76. Though it may seem dubious to draw conclusions about Defoe's political opinions in 1719 from a polemic poem written nineteen years earlier, I am persuaded by Schonhorn that "Defoe the novelist evolved out of Defoe the journalist." A constant component of Defoe's belief in the ideal of the warrior-king, epitomized by William III, is that "the sword-bearing sovereign was made necessary by England's variegated society" (p. 4). That variegation, largely a function of trade, is precisely what makes the true-born Englishman a contradiction. Crusoe himself is divided between the model of the warrior-king, which for a while he is able to emulate, and the variegated English society of which he has always been a representative part.

11. I have chiefly followed the lead of James H. Bunn, "The Aesthetics of British Mercantilism," *New Literary History* 11 (1980): 305-06, though it is important to note that "mercantilism" was not a term in circulation in Defoe's time but rather a scholarly concept first systematically explicated in Adam Smith's *The Wealth of Nations* (1776). After receiving its most encyclopedic treatment in Eli Heckscher, *Mercantilism* (1931), it has undergone serious revaluation; the most recent responses range from skepticism in D.C. Coleman, "Mercantilism Revisited," *Historical Journal* 23 (1980): 774-85, to outright dismissal in John Brewer, *The Sinews of Power: War, Money and the English State, 1688-1788* (New York: Alfred A. Knopf, 1989) pp. 168-70. I believe that the term, loosely employed, can help make sense of what is clearly an ideological crisis.

12. Bunn describes the esthetic developments that this opposition produced, and explores the questions that must be asked about the many objects—"bric-a-brac"—that were removed from their point of origin and reconstructed in another culture.

13. Joyce Oldham Appleby, *Economic Thought and Ideology in Seventeenth-Century England* (Princeton: Princeton Univ. Press, 1978), p. 99.

9

Arguments to the Self in Defoe's 'Roxana'

—Malinda Snow

Readers of Defoe's Roxana tend to see it as different, in degree if not in kind, from the author's other works of prose fiction. "Roxana," says David Blewett, "is Defoe's darkest novel. . . . Roxana is Defoe's only protagonist who is passive in the face of disaster." John Richetti calls Roxana "the most conventional and the most disturbing of Defoe's major narratives." Maximillian Novak and G.A. Start conclude that Defoe's heroine is damned. A related theme of retribution is also pointed out by various readers. In Roxana, James Sutherland notes, "there are more links than usual between the past and the present."[1] Roxana does not break free of a past marked by sin, error, and crime to achieve repentance and peace. Thus, unlike Crusoe, Moll, and Colonel Jack, she does not narrate her past misdeeds from a position of physical and spiritual safety?[2] The careful reader, having heard Roxana's voice for more than three hundred pages, will not be surprised at her concluding words: "I was brought so low again, that my Repentance seem'd to be only the Consequence of my Misery, as my Misery was of my Crime".[3]

Traditionally, repentance results from grace, not misery: true penitents can admit wrongdoing and stop judging themselves. Roxana, however, cannot. Intensely self-aware, she reasons with herself, judges herself, and ultimately cannot forgive herself. I would argue that the darkness and hints of damnation noted in Roxana arise from the narrator's self-awareness: her tendency to argue with herself, and her inclination, as narrator and finally as character, to judge herself.[4]

Roxana's particular kind of self-awareness accounts not only for the novel's somber mood, however, but also for a rhetorical complexity not found in Defoe's other fiction. Roxana opens with a preface by a "Relator," who claims to be acquainted with Roxana's first husband. The relator assures us that the events of the narrative will be diverting, and that "the most diverting Parts of it" are "adapted to the Instruction and Improvement of the Reader". Much of the narrative does reflect this aim. Roxana presents herself to us as an example and expends substantial rhetorical effort in arguing for the wickedness of her life. Although these arguments appear prominently in the narration, however, they are not the only arguments developed. In the "narrative present," the old Roxana recounts her past life. The narrative present—a fixed point in time—becomes the means for us to see the 'narrative past," which is not fixed but evolving. The narrator's argument is synchronic with the narrating. From her vantage point in the narrative present, Roxana combines an anamnesis-a remembering-and a warning: she recounts the events of her life as an argument to her reader, urging that the reader not do as Roxana herself has done. Because of the anamnesis, however, the reader's position is not precisely what Roxana as narrator implies; embedded in the narrative past are arguments that tend to undercut or contradict what she says as narrator. Those embedded arguments are the ones.Roxana posed to herself in the course of her life, arguments justifying choices she would later advise her reader to reject. Thus, in reading Roxana, one hears the narrator's argument and overhears Roxana's ongoing arguments to herself. Janet Aikins has said that Roxana is "listening to her tale."[5] Actually, Roxana listens to her arguments at least twice: once while she is at a moment of deciding and again when she recalls the decision for the reader. Often the reader may find that the younger Roxana's arguments to herself have sufficient merit to undercut the old narrator's counterarguments.

Analysis of the argumentative structure of Defoe's narrative will complement earlier, essentially theological, analyses of Roxana and help readers understand the rhetorical complexity that makes Roxana an intriguing narrator and character. Such an approach requires an analytic method that can address the chronological overlaying of Roxana's arguments. I propose to use a paradigm from Aristotle's Rhetoric. By choosing Aristotle here I do not wish to imply any Aristotelian agenda on Defoe's part. Nor do I mean to suggest any particular Aristotelian influence on Defoe. Rather I have chosen to analyze Roxana according to Aristotelian principles because those principles contain a precise way to describe what Defoe's heroine does as rhetor. On a more basic level, I would argue that such a method of reading a work of fiction offers the opportunity to perceive the heroine and other characters as rhetors advocating argumentative propositions. This perception of Roxana accords well with the fictional circumstances Defoe establishes, beginning with his introduction of the "Relator."

Aristotle's Rhetoric offers convenient terms for the two kinds of argument in Roxana. According to Aristotle, argument provides a means to examine the past, the present, or the future. Argument about the past he calls forensic; speakers examine previous actions and attempt to make judgments about them, as in a law court. Argument about the present he calls epideictic; speakers celebrate (or decry) contemporary events, as in Pericles' funeral oration. Argument about the future Aristotle calls deliberative; speakers examine what is to be done, attempting to persuade the audience that such-and-such is the best course (1358b7-21). In Aristotelian terms, then, Roxana uses forensic rhetoric in the narrative present, while looking back on her life and condemning it. The reader is the audience addressed. As in a court, the rhetor urges that a particular judgment be reached. In the narrative past, Roxana the heroine argued deliberatively to herself about what she was going to do, weighing alternatives and choosing one of several paths.

The narrator's forensic rhetoric advances traditional propositions of clear social and religious orthodoxy. These propositions are familiar: Roxana herself originated none of them, and like all statements of general principle, they sometimes fit uneasily with the specific events of life.[6] Roxana may be said to "invent" most of the deliberative arguments that develop in the course of her life, however.[7] In rhetorical terms, the two strains of argument in Roxana represent two inventional theories: Sharon Crowley explains that "ancient inventional theory" is based on the premise that knowledge is "possessed in common by all members of a community" whereas modern theory assumes "that knowledge result[s] from the actions of individual minds on the things of the world."[8] The dialectic between the individual and the tradition, between the deliberative and the forensic, establishes a sustained polyvocal narrative.

This narrative complexity sets Roxana apart from Defoe's other fiction, notably from Moll Flanders. Although Moll, like Roxana, tells the reader about a life of "continued variety," including abandoned children, adultery, and so on, she does not see herself as capable of deliberating or advising herself. She tells the reader that "to be Friendless is the worst Condition, next to being in want, that a Woman can be reduc'd to: I say a Woman, because 'tis evident Men can be their own advisors".[9] Because Moll acts with less self-scrutiny and deliberation, Moll Flanders lacks the sort of polyvocal rhetorical structure that Roxana exhibits.[10] This polyvocal rhetoric, with its frequent tensions and contradictions, generates and sustains the somber mood noted by Roxana's readers. Moreover, just as Roxana's arguments to herself often clash with the forensic arguments to the reader and prevent the narrative from reaching the conventional moral/rhetorical closure, those deliberative arguments create in Roxana a self-definition that effectively prevents the kind of repentance attained by Defoe's other narrators. Moll Flanders punctuates her narrative—especially the story of her criminal exploits—with "little closures" that allow her to pack away experiences so that they no longer need be considered. After telling of robbing Lady Betty in Pall Mall, for example, she closes that adventure and announces the next: "I made another Adventure after this, of a Nature different from all I had been concern'd in yet, and this was at a Gaming-House near Covent-Garden". Roxana does not make these "little closures" any more than she attains final closure and repose.

That Roxana argues privately to herself rather than publicly to an audience sitting as legislature distinguishes her, of course, from the sort of deliberative rhetor Aristotle imagines in the Rhetoric. One might object to the use of the rhetorical schema for internal debate.[11] But for rhetors to address themselves, however, is quite possible. Not only is the internal debate possible, it is central to the novelistic portrayal of human experience. A major contribution of the novel to our literary/rhetorical awareness is its capacity to demonstrate the dialectical quality of our inner discourse. The depth of such narratives as Huckleberry Finn, for instance, arises largely from the complex rhetoric of the narrative voice. Moreover, in Roxana's case, the very fact that her deliberations are private rather than public, as the Aristotelian rhetor's would have been, reminds us of her position as a woman. Being a woman, Roxana occupies no public position and engages in no deliberation about "significant" affairs. Her legislative sphere of influence extends no farther than her own individual experience, just as her judicial influence extends only into the private realm of the audience's experience. And, as Paula Backscheider has demonstrated, the old narrator's audience is essentially female.[12]

Deliberative rhetoric of the sort Roxana engages in stimulates the development of the individual. Reading Roxana, we see the heroine develop and change. We also see that arguments to the self stimulate and guide these changes more particularly than raw circumstance does.

The deliberative arguments in Roxana are not necessarily addressed to the self at the time we hear them; occasionally they are addressed to other characters, notably to Roxana's maid and confidante Amy—her "other self," to the Dutch merchant who courts Roxana, and to the Quaker woman who befriends her. No matter whom they are literally addressed to, though, these arguments address the question "What should I do, and why?"

Roxana's first occasion to answer this question comes when her fool of a husband deserts her and their children. Aristotle notes that deliberative rhetoric concerns itself with goods and evils, and not all goods and evils, but only those likely to come to pass (Rhetoric, 1359a33-5).[13] The probable evil that young Roxana as the deserted wife faces is her own and her children's starvation. To save her children, she decides to give them up to her husband's relatives. In debating what to do, she recalls arguing to herself in the following vein:

> But the Misery of my own Circumstances hardned my Heart against my own Flesh and Blood; and

> when I consider'd they must inevitably be Starv'd, and I too, if I continued to keep them about me, I began to be reconcil'd to parting with them all, any how, and any where, that I might be freed from the dreadful Necessity of seeing them all perish, and perishing with them myself.

We may ascribe the theological terminology (and implied judgment) in the phrase "hardned my Heart against my own Flesh and Blood" to the older narrator. The remainder of the passage, however, represents the young Roxana's deliberation. Her reasoning is more practical than tender-hearted, but it follows generally accepted morality and wisdom. So far, Roxana's deliberative arguments to herself do not vary from social convention and from the morality that guides the forensic rhetoric of the older narrator.

At the next exigency, however, we notice a variance. Impoverished and threatened with eviction, Roxana and Amy consider what to do. When Amy suggests that the landlord would take Roxana as his mistress, Roxana's initial response is shocked virtue: "I tell you again, I'd die before I would consent". Despite its impracticality, this statement accords with conventional wisdom. In the scenes that follow, however, Roxana, with promptings from Amy, convinces herself to yield. The retrospective voice puts in "I shou'd have . . . I shou'd have", but young Roxana reasons her way clearly enough: "If I had ventur'd to disoblige this Gentleman, I had no Friend in the World to have Recourse to; I had no Prospect, no, not of a Bit of Bread; I had nothing before me, but to fall back into the same Misery that I had been in before". Thus Roxana counsels herself to become the landlord's mistress. The retrospective narrator adds, "So with my Eyes open, and with my Conscience, as I may say, awake, I sinn'd, knowing it to be a Sin, but having no Power to resist".

We should note that young Roxana does not resort to the easy conclusion that she, as a deserted wife, and her landlord, as an abandoned husband, are free to live as spouses. She flatly calls herself whore, adding, "The Conviction . . . was from the beginning, upon me, that I was a Whore, not a Wife; nor cou'd I ever frame my Mouth to call him Husband". The scene that follows, in which Roxana puts Amy to bed with her landlord-lover, has excited much critical speculation. Novak calls it Roxana's one actively evil deed. Richetti describes it as an assertion of power over the landlord and Amy.[14] Richetti is correct, I think, in concluding that the action is a means of asserting something, but I believe that the chief audience is Roxana herself. Viewed in terms of rhetoric, the scene is a terrifying argument to the self. It is as if Roxana must convince herself that she is a whore. "Had I look'd upon myself as a Wife, you cannot suppose I would have been willing to let my Husband lye with my Maid". By putting Amy and the landlord in bed together, then standing by to watch, Roxana breaks away from the conventional position of wife. She and Amy enter into a long spell of genteel prostitution, and her deliberative arguments likewise diverge from traditional moral reasoning as represented by the forensic rhetoric of the older narrator.

The narrator does not always simply ascribe the younger Roxana's nonconventional arguments to personal initiative. On several occasions she suggests diabolic interference, implying that the unconventional deliberative persuasion comes from the devil.[15] For instance, of Roxana's reasoning about her next affair, that with the prince, the narrator tells us: "The Devil had play'd a new Game with me, and prevail'd with me to satisfie myself with this Amour, as a lawful Thing".

The reasoning here is young Roxana's. To identify such reasoning with diabolic power, as the narrator does, is, in fact, one of society's ready explanations of arguments supporting actions that diverge from what society accepts.

If deliberative arguments running counter to popular teaching are associated with the devil, those supporting such teaching are just as readily associated with Providence, as the voice of conscience. During Roxana's first affair, her mind becomes the scene of a debate between the diabolic and the providential. And during the second affair the diabolic wins out as Roxana settles in with her princely lover, effectively silencing conscience. "That Centinel," she tells us, "once doz'd, sleeps fast, not to be awaken'd while the Tide of Pleasure continues to flow, or till something dark and dreadful brings us to ourselves again". Recalling Aristotle's terms, we note that Roxana in her deliberation has persuaded herself to take the immediate good, the lover's attention and gifts, rather than the more distant good of peace and clear conscience at the close of life. Although her conscience troubles her enough to make her consider confessing to a priest, Roxana tells us that she had felt its pangs more sharply when she was with the landlord-jeweler, and that as the prince's mistress she enjoys "the most profound Tranquility".

The fact is that Roxana is not thinking much of the future and the goods or ills it might bring. In her deliberations, she is using experience with the brewer as the ultimate evil and arguing to herself for choices that will not only insure her immediate happiness and prosperity but prevent her from repeating that calamity. Through her arguments, she has begun to invent a self more to her liking than the naive wife who could be ruined by a fool. That old self surfaces occasionally, as in a long passage of introspection in which she describes herself as one knowing "what this Carcass . . . had been but a few Years before; how overwhelm'd with Grief, drown'd in Tears, frighted with the Prospect of Beggary, and surrounded with Rags, and Fatherless Children; that was pawning and selling the Rags that cover'd me, for a Dinner, and sat on the Ground, despairing of Help". Acting on her own initiative and guided by her deliberations, Roxana has raised herself from great misfortune. But she has raised herself, in her own terms, from a wronged wife to a "Whore for Bread", and thence to the "Queen of Whores". Ever since flinging Amy into bed with her own lover, Roxana has defined herself as a whore. That was an immediate judgment upon herself, not a piece of moralizing inserted by the old narrator. Even in France, when she says her conscience dozed, Roxana identified herself as whore. She laments the fate of her child by the prince, and yet she and her lover decide "to SIN ON".

Roxana's fear of poverty never entirely fades, but it no longer haunts her as the only evil to be avoided. A related fear emerges, that of losing her now substantial fortune: "Thinking of it sometimes, almost distracted me, for want of knowing how to dispose of it, and for fear of losing it all again by some Cheat or Trick". At the end of her affair with the prince, she defines herself as wealthy and deliberates her future actions as if loss of wealth were the ultimate evil.

The aged narrator thinks occasionally of Job and his troubles as she tells her story. Job lost both his fortune and his children, leaving him in a state similar to that of Roxana early in her life.[16] However Roxana, unlike Job, grows to see herself, the deliberative woman, as the chief cause of her good fortune. The narrator observes: "Had I had any Religion, or any Sence of a Supreme Power managing, directing, and governing in both Causes and Events in this World, such a Case as this wou'd have given anybody room to have been very thankful". But she has no such sense of a "fortunate" cause outside her own self. Her arguments to herself have persuaded her of her power to control, and they result in a kind of pride never reached by Job. Neither the close call with her fortune nor the subsequent close call with her life, during the storm, moves Roxana to acknowledge a beneficent cause outside herself.

Roxana's sense of self is, nevertheless, subtly changing once again, and with this change Roxana makes some of her most articulate and forceful deliberative arguments. She has come to recognize the freedom gained by choosing against matrimony: "I had no Inclination to be a Wife again . . . a Wife is treated with Indifference, a Mistress with a strong Passion; a Wife is look'd upon, as but an Upper-Servant, a Mistress is a Sovereign". Her sense of herself as free and her desire to preserve this freedom lead her to refuse the Dutch merchant's proposal. She means to live like a man and keep control of her money. She tells the merchant, "While a Woman was single, she was a Masculine in her politick Capacity . . . she had then the full Command of what she had, and the full Direction of what she did".

Independence, the freedom to manage her own wealth and direct her life according to her own aims and views, is the good (in the Aristotelian sense) that Roxana chooses at this stage in her life. The old narrator argues for the folly of refusing the Dutchman's offer. But the facts are that conscience recommended starvation, and marriage is not always a safe haven, despite the narrator's words. The reader can see the sense of Roxana's arguments against marriage and understand some of the complexity of her dilemma. Many a reader will cheer for Roxana not only for her courage but for her articulate justification of her actions. As rhetor she makes her strongest arguments against the prevailing standard of wifely rectitude. The narrator's condemnation of her earlier behavior—"I am a Memorial to all that shall read my Story; a standing Monument of the Madness and Distraction which Pride and Infatuations from Hell runs us into"—plunges us as readers into the conflict and leaves us unsure which course we should have liked Roxana to follow. The younger Roxana forcefully argues for the unconventional choice, while the older Roxana defends the conventions in a voice that reveals the loneliness of one outside the pale.

A result of Roxana's deciding against the conventionally accepted choice is, ironically, a loss—or at least a burial—of part of herself, which she reserves and does not reveal. This reserve, this resistance to showing herself fully, guides Roxana's deliberations in the concluding sections of the narrative, and it results in an estrangement from herself, an inward and spiritual estrangement.[17] What she will not reveal, she cannot repent of. Her oldest selves, the wronged wife and the "whore for bread," still lie buried within her, and now she sees the revealing of either as evils to deliberate how to avoid.

When she decides to seek out her five children (by the fool husband), she sends Amy rather than show herself to them. Even when Susan pursues her mother, Roxana will not acknowledge her daughter and her self. Just as she often has before, she deliberates and decides that the greatest good will be gained, and the greatest evil avoided, by keeping people in the dark about her previous life. At about the same time she concludes that she should change her life: "It came so very strong upon my Mind one Morning, when I had been lying awake some time in my Bed, as if somebody had ask'd me the Question, What was I a Whore for now?".[18] Moreover, she finds in her children strong arguments for deploring her past: "I cou'd not find in my Heart to let my Son know what a Mother he had, and what a Life she liv'd". Only when her children appear as potential judges does she think ill of her life. "Thus it was with me; and this, no doubt, considering Parents always find it, that their own Children are a Restraint to them in their worst Courses, when the Sence of a Superiour Power has not the same Influence". At this point, when Roxana begins to concern herself with her children and their opinion of her, the reader will find that the character's deliberative arguments to herself grow more conventional: she no longer chooses pleasure or convenience or freedom or wealth as her chief goods. But she cannot be rid of the person, the complex self, she created as the result of her earlier deliberations.[19] "Amy, says I, what will my Children say to themselves, and to one another, when they find their Mother, however rich she may be, is at best but a Whore, a common Whore?". The immediate solution she chooses, renting rooms from the Quaker woman and assuming the guise of a Quaker herself, serves to remove her from her old haunts. But she cannot change who she is and what she has done, and although she will not reveal her past actions, she regrets them bitterly. Not only does she regret her profligate life, she regrets her refusal of the Dutch merchant and sets out to find him. But Roxana's fear of her past thwarts a conventional happy ending with the heroine married, rich, and repentant, with her children rising up to call her blessed.

What happens instead is that Roxana is married and rich, but not happy, not satisfied in her repentance, and convinced that her children, or at least her daughter Susan, will be the damnation of her. During this portion of the narrative, the deliberative and forensic rhetoric are less at odds with each other because, Roxana having passed judgment on herself, the narrator need not do so as relentlessly as in earlier scenes. Roxana's condemnation of herself becomes the most significant matter she considers as she deliberates her course of action. Not only does she mean to keep her past a secret from her children, she also means to keep it hidden from the merchant: "Sometimes I was terrify'd with Apprehensions, lest if I shou'd come into a close Correspondence with him, he shou'd any-way come to hear what kind of Life I had led at Pall-Mall, and in other Places". She can enjoy no true happiness for fear of retribution: "I repented of the Crime, but it was of another and lower kind of Repentance, and rather mov'd by my Fears of Vengeance, than from a Sense of being spar'd from being punish'd, and landed safe after a Storm". And her daughter's pursuit of her appears to be the retribution she dreads.

Unwilling to reveal herself to her daughter, or to anyone, Roxana cuts herself off from the chance of happiness. Rather than face her daughter, she allows the girl to hound her, and she ultimately wishes her daughter dead. When both Susan and Amy disappear, Roxana concludes the worst, that Amy has murdered her, and that she—Roxana—shares in the guilt. For this guilt, she cannot forgive herself, and whatever calamities befall her she perceives as retribution.

Readers may argue over whether Defoe viewed Roxana as a damned soul? Whatever Defoe's views, Roxana gives every appearance of believing herself damned. Her harsh judgment against herself, her fear of revealing her past to her husband and children, her fear of retribution, and the profound dread in her voice at the narrative's end all point to that supposition but do not resolve the question. The narrative's conclusion lacks closure of the sort found in Moll Flanders and thus lacks certain clues about how to read the narrative. In the case of Moll Flanders the conclusion prompts the reader to read Moll's narrative as a convert's tale (whether the reader chooses to do so is another issue).

How to read Roxana becomes a significant hermeneutical question. What does the narrative mean? Does it deconstruct itself by presenting contrary arguments—deliberative and forensic? I suggest that the answer lies in the unconventional ending. In a conversion narrative, of course, the speaker might overwhelm the old deliberations with exhortation to the contrary. That Roxana is not a conversion narrative, however, the conclusion makes clear. Roxana is not converted and the rhetoric of the novel is not that of the convert's tale.[21] She is profoundly affected, but she cannot say, as the convert does, "I once was lost but now am found." In the now of Roxana, the narrative present, the narrator has not found the means, spiritual or rhetorical, to put aside her past. Roxana's narrative is an anamnesis, not an amnesis—remembering, not forgetting.

As to the question of whether the narrative deconstructs itself, I would argue that it does not. The key to its meaning lies in the anamnesis, the remembering of the past and its deliberations. For both reader and narrator, the past exerts a strong influence upon the present moment. In telling her tale Roxana tells how, through deliberation, she created the self that speaks at the narrative's end. What Roxana means involves the way "the past" remains present and formative within the individual. Lacking the "little closures" of Moll Flanders, Roxana prevents both reader and heroine from putting away the deliberations of the past.

A constant in Roxana's character is her tendency to respond rhetorically to every exigency. And her response is appropriate: rhetoric by its very nature allows us to consider more than one proposition at once, to examine difficult questions and weigh alternatives when no certain answer presents itself. As we saw, however, Roxana deliberates within herself and not within the external forum that Aristotle and most rhetoricians assume. What that external forum provides is a means of resolution; Aristotle is right to spend at least half the Rhetoric discussing audience. Issues that require rhetorical deliberation by their very nature resist resolving. Unlike, say, mathematics, where the means of resolution lies within the question itself, rhetorical closure and resolution of the question(s) under discussion originate in the audience's response. Roxana's solipsistic deliberation isolates her from the audience—the part of the rhetorical paradigm that generates the closure. Though she may win the sympathy of her overhearing reader, who is willing to conclude that she acted for the best with the landlord or with the Dutch merchant, Roxana has not finally convinced herself. In Roxana the active, deliberative self finally merges with the forensic, judging self rather than breaking free from it, as Roxana carries her past choices with her, unforgetting and unforgiving. Roxana is Defoe's most somber narrative; in the end it offers not closure but silence. The silence of the broken-off conclusion leaves the reader reflecting on the profound dilemmas that Roxana faced and on the ultimate failure of rhetoric to serve her ends. In a sense, of course, the heroine/narrator's deliberations undercut the forensic proposition implied throughout the book. But the ultimate meaning of the book may be found at this same point. Formation and destruction of the self arise not in circumstance but in our linguistic-rhetorical response to circumstance. Defoe's narrative method encourages us to seek a "right way" to talk (to ourselves and others) about our choices rather than seeking a "right choice."[22]

NOTES

1. David Blewett, *Defoe's Art of Fiction: Robinson Crusoe, Moll Flanders, Colonel Jack, and Roxana* (Toronto: Univ. of Toronto Press, 1979), p. 116; John J. Richetti, *Defoe's Narratives: Situations and Structures* (Oxford: Clarendon Press, 1975), p. 192; Maximillian E. Novak, *Realism, Myth, and History in Defoe's Fiction* (Lincoln and London: Univ. of Nebraska Press, 1983), pp. 100, 110-12; G.A. Starr, *Defoe and Spiritual Autobiography* (Princeton: Princeton Univ. Press, 1965), pp. 163-65; Starr, *Defoe and Casuistry* (Princeton: Princeton Univ. Press, 1971), p. 165; James Sutherland, *Daniel Defoe: A Critical Study* (Cambridge, MA: Harvard Univ. Press, 1971), p. 205; see also Novak, pp. 108-109; and Everett Zimmerman, *Defoe and the Novel* (Berkeley and Los Angeles: Univ. of California Press, 1975), p. 155.
2. Michael McKeon describes the conventional pattern revealed in seventeenth-century Protestant narratives.

There is "a structural interplay between the sinful present of the Character and the repentant retrospection of the Narrator, who, incorporating God's omniscience, knows how the story will end. This interplay lends itself, of course, to a very traditional sort of Christian pedagogy. As the plot unfolds horizontally, the dangerous gap between Character and Narrator gradually diminishes through vertical narrative intrusions, until the two finally are one, the latter consciousness having subsumed the former in what might be seen as the narrative equivalent of atonement" (*The Origins of the English Novel, 1600-1740* [Baltimore and London: Johns Hopkins Univ. Press, 1987], p. 95).

3. Parenthetical references are to *Roxana: The Fortunate Mistress*, ed. Jane Jack (London: Oxford Univ. Press, 1969).

4. The concept of self evident in eighteenth-century narrative has been the subject of extensive study. Still provocative is Homer O. Brown's "The Displaced Self in the Novels of Daniel Defoe," *ELH* 38, 4 (December 1971): 562-90. Among the most interesting general studies have been those comparing the concept of self in (auto)biography and in fiction, with Patricia Meyer Spacks's *Imagining a Self: Autobiography and Novel in Eighteenth-Century England* (Cambridge, MA and London: Harvard Univ. Press, 1976), acting as a forerunner. Feminist critics examining the fictional and biographical self offer still further material for students of Defoe's heroine. An especially stimulating examination of gender and self in biographical narrative is Felicity A. Nussbaum's *The Autobiographical Subject: Gender and Ideology in Eighteenth-Century England* (Baltimore and London: Johns Hopkins Univ. Press, 1989). Readers of Roxana will find other pertinent commentary in the following: Paula R. Backscheider, *A Being More Intense: A Study of the Prose Works of Bunyan, Swift, and Defoe*, AMS Studies in the Eighteenth Century 7 (New York: AMS Press, 1984); Virginia Ogden Birdsall, *Defoe's Perpetual Seekers: A Study of the Major Fiction* (Lewisburg, PA: Bucknell Univ. Press, 1985); and Leopold Damrosch, Jr., *God's Plot and Man's Stories: Studies in the Fictional*

Imagination from Milton to Fielding (Chicago and London: Univ. of Chicago Press, 1985).

5. Janet Aikins, "Roxana: The Unfortunate Mistress of Conversation," *SEL* 25, 3 (Summer 1985): 529-56, 531.

6. See Backscheider, *A Being More Intense*, pp. xvii-xix, for a general discussion of the crisis of "epistemological uncertainties and their consequences" in the late seventeenth and early eighteenth centuries.

7. As G.A. Starr established in Defoe and Casuistry, Defoe himself did not invent many of the casuistical circumstances his characters encounter but instead appropriated interesting cases, notably those dealing with marriage, from theological literature.

8. Sharon Crowley, *The Methodical Memory: Invention in Current-Traditional Rhetoric* (Carbondale and Edwardsville: Southern Illinois Univ. Press, 1990), p. 4. Speaking in terms theological rather than rhetorical, Nussbaum describes the conflict: "The crisis of the eighteenth-century self reflects, in large part, the attempt to render secular experience in the terms of paradigmatic biblical models" (p. 21). The dialectic between individual experience and tradition, both as a source of religious angst and a crucible of rhetorical invention, drives the reflective person to self-examination and self-definition.

9. Parenthetical references are to *Moll Flanders*, ed. Edward Kelly (New York: W.W. Norton, 1973).

10. Aikins comments that "unlike Moll Flanders, Roxana might have been better off not telling her story at all" (p. 538). Ian A. Bell contrasts Roxana not only with Moll Flanders but also with Robinson Crusoe. "What makes [Roxana] idiosyncratic . . . is the stress on the narrator's reconstruction and disillusioned reinterpretation of her past life, which makes the whole narrative operate on two levels. Roxana looks back over her adventures with a sustained abhorrence that contrasts remarkably with Crusoe's lack of commentary and Moll's breeziness" ("Narrators and Narrative in Defoe," *Novel: A Forum on Fiction* 18, 2 [Winter 1985]: 154-72, 165-66).

11. Barbara Warnick argues the inappropriateness of "an assimilation of rhetoric to internal reasoning and dialogue" ("Judgment, Probability, and Aristotle's Rhetoric," *Quarterly Journal of Speech* 75, 3 [August 1989]: 299-311, 301).

12. Paula R. Backscheider, "The Genesis of Roxana," *The Eighteenth Century: Theory and Interpretation* 27, 3 (Fall 1986): 211-29.

13. For more on deliberation, see Aristotle's *Nichomachean Ethics*, Book iii (111165).

14. Novak, p. 110; Richetti, pp. 208-209; see also Zimmerman, p. 158, and Bell, p. 171.

16. For more on the diabolic, see my "Diabolic Intervention in Defoe's Roxana," *Essays in Literature* 3, 1 (Spring 1976): 52-60.

    On her return to England after nearly losing her lately acquired fortune at the hands of the scheming moneylender, she observes, "Thus I took my Leave of France, and got clear of an ugly Business, which, had it gone on, might have ruin'd me, and sent me back as Naked to England, as I was a little before I left it" (p. 121). Job responds to the news of his losses with "Naked came I out of my mother's womb, and naked shall I return thither: the Lord gave, and the Lord hath taken away; blessed be the name of the Lord" (Job 1:21 KJV). Colonel Jack likewise compares himself to Job, although with notably different effect from Roxana: "I had . . . leisure to reflect, and to repent, to call to mind things pass'd, and with a just Detestation, learn as Job says, to abhor my self in Dust and Ashes" (*The History and Remarkable Life of . . . Col. Jacque*, ed. Samuel Holt Monk, Oxford English Novels [London: Oxford Univ. Press, 1965], p. 308).

17. G.A. Starr argues that Roxana becomes estranged from her readers (*Defoe and Casuistry*, p. 189). The estrangement seems to me more an inner separation than a distancing between the character and the reader.

18. Whereas Roxana asks the deliberative question "What was I a Whore for now?" Moll, at the midwife's lying-in establishment, lets the question of her identity (and her future action) pass: "I found presently, that whether I was a Whore or a Wife, I was to pass for a Whore here, so I let that go" (p. 127).

19. David Durant, in "Roxana's Fictions," *Studies in the Novel* 13, 3 (Fall 1981): 225-36, argues that Roxana's life is a fiction of her own making.

20. In contrast to the opinions noted earlier, see Sutherland, pp. 212-13.

21. As Charles J.G. Griffin notes, the convert is challenged "to create myths of self that account plausibly for the dramatic shifts in attitude and behavior that follow from an authentic conversion experience" ("The Rhetoric of Form in Conversion Narratives," *Quarterly Journal of Speech* 76, 2 [May 1990]: 152-63, 152).

22. "I wish to acknowledge the many ideas and insights gained from discussion with my students in English Novel I, especially Delia Konzett.

10

Reading and Righting Moll Flanders

—Thomas Grant Olsen

> Kinship laws, which govern the system of combinations in mating, correspond to linguistic laws governing the combinations of words in a sentence or letters in a word . . . [I]ncest is bad grammar.
>
> —Maud Ellmann

The connection between the rules that govern kinship and grammar offers a critical reader of Moll Flanders a tool to understand the connection between the troubling presence of incest and the renowned problem of language in the novel.[1] Kinship and language are most tangled in the preface, a part of the text that, with few significant exceptions, has been treated as little more than an interesting addendum to the body of the novel. However, within the preface the character of the editor attempts to situate the novel's characters, readers, and text itself in a recuperative family dynamic that undoes the familial and linguistic "bad grammar" that appears throughout the novel. By exploring these efforts and failures, I extend and re-craft the traditional critical problems and arguments regarding irony and voice; the force of my argument coincides with the assertion that incest informs the (mis)use of language and that language constructs incest.

The character of the editor is rife with ambiguity. The gender of the editor is never clearly stated; almost every critic assumes that the editor is male, and most make the distinction between Defoe and this character. I argue that it is the recuperative function the editor performs that must be understood loosely as male and specifically as paternalistic. These qualities are consistently revealed by the editor's rhetoric: he rewrites Moll's "own memorandums" (p. 1) and has "had no little difficulty to put it into a Dress fit to be seen, and to make it speak Language fit to be read" (p. 3). The "moral laundering"[2] Moll's story undergoes through a process of censorship and "finishing" (p. 3) is clear in the preface, but what is not so clear is the editor's motive in performing this "laundering. "While he emphasizes the reader's "Instruction" (p. 5), not every episode neatly fits this purpose. The notorious ironies of the preface are irresolvable conundrums unless read together with the rest of the narrative and vice versa.[3] When read together, the editor's act of making Moll "tell her own Tale in modester Words than she told it at first" (p. 3) obliterates the notion that the narrative is Moll's at all; instead, the narrative reveals itself as a tale of figurative and recuperative paternalism over an unruly narrative child.

The editor positions himself as the figurative father who "dresses up" his narrative daughter, but he is no single parent: his rhetorically savvy construction of his reader as figurative mother shackles both the reader and Moll to a recuperative fiction of bourgeois family norms intended to rework the original and disruptive "amorous Chain of Story" (p. 4). What is at stake in this creation of a normative family structure is only revealed during the narrative's descriptions of figurative and literal incest. For the critical reader—distinguishable from the editor's constructed reader—who finishes the novel and then turns back to the beginning, the discovery of incest by Moll is arguably the most pivotal revelation in the text.[4] The passages about incest allow the critical reader to return to the preface and detect the paternalistic intent of the editor. The practice of incest threatens social structures and, by extension, the very practice of narrative that contributes to the cultural work of this society. Because Moll discovers maternal and economic fecundity through incest without punishment, and because she "was not so extraordinary a Penitent as she was" (p. 6) at the time she wrote her memorandums, the editor demonstrates the necessity of recouping her narrative for a purpose vastly different from what Moll's "original" narrative teaches: the reconstruction of the bourgeois family structure in order to perpetuate it.

The editor's paternal role in Moll's narrative is established progressively over the course of the novel, but the groundwork is set as early as the title page: Moll was "five times a Wife (whereof once to her own Brother)" (p. 1). As a parenthetical statement, the act of incest is subordinate because it appears as an aside to the information that she was married five times and, at the same time, the parenthetical holds the privileged position as the most noteworthy of her marriages, deserving its own clause. The aside acts as a lure for the yet-to-be-constructed reader: it tantalizes because it announces transgression and begs for explication, but no further explanation is found in the preface. Instead, what the critical reader finds is the editor's construction of an ideal reader who "know[s] how to read" the text "and how to make the good Uses of it" (p. 4). Without specifically naming them, the editor appeals to his assumed readers' awareness of, and agreement with, dominant fictions regarding morality, t he law, and normative family structures. The absence of any discussion of incest in a preface that explicitly addresses many of Moll's other crimes and misadventures marks the incest as an ideological battlefield because it, more than anything else, threatens the dominant fictions that rely upon stable familial relationships and, thus, of gender as well: a male "Author [is] hard put to it to wrap it up so clean" when a "Woman debauch'd . . . comes to give an Account of all her vicious Practises" (p. 3). Both the explicit and implicit lines drawn in the preface pit male against female and, more specifically, figurative father against daughter and editor/husband against reader/wife.

The editor's pen fathers the narrative, but destruction is the prerequisite for his (re)production. The editor kills off the real Moll of the original memorandums in order to create a reconfigured representation of her, and the preface attempts to authorize this transformation. Ironically, Moll's transformation does not cancel the threat the story of her life poses. Her otherness persists in the potential for even her altered "autobiography" to be misread, and so the editor must enlist his ideal, feminized reader. Referring to himself as "[t]he Pen," the editor explains that the motivation for changing the language results from his assumptions about his reading audience; he fears that "vicious Readers" will "turn it to his Disadvantage" (p. 3) if the language were to remain genuine. The editor's construction of his reader is a simultaneously ambivalent, ambiguous, gendered, and deft rhetorical manipulation.

The preface consistently stresses the moral instruction the narrative provides, yet the censorship that the editor commits reveals a contradiction. While the editor appears to grant the "moral" rather than "vicious" reader the freedom to interpret, he does not grant either reader the freedom to hear the unexpurgated story, thus betraying the editor's "true and overriding fear that the reader is no more to be trusted than Moll."[5] The threat that the publication of Moll's memorandums poses is that her attitudes and behaviors will influence the readers; as a result, the reader "comes under the editor's critical scrutiny and becomes the source of his greatest suspicions and anxieties."[6] The editor's concerns about Moll's unruly femininity are transferred to the reader. The editor needs his ideal readers to complete the recuperative, figurative family triangle, but because they are positioned as female—in spite of his use of the male personal pronoun—they are as suspect of straying from the moral path as Moll. As a way to control readers, the editor rhetorically constructs them as partners in an interpretive "marriage" contract intended for the correction and correct use of Moll's narrative. The responsibility for "moral" reading—the "righting" of Moll's narrative—shifts between "the Pen's" writing to the reader's readings "even where the Story might incline him to be otherwise" (p. 3).

The invitation to do otherwise suggests desire, seduction, and rhetorical mastery. Whenever the content of the narrative appears to transgress the bounds of the "chastest Reader or the modestest Hearer" (p. 3), "the Pen," in the guise of Moll, will insert himself into the text and directly address the readers to inform them that only they can turn the content to the right moral purpose. The mastery present in the phallic overwriting of Moll's narrative by the editor and, coercively, by the fictional reader operates as a recuperative device for familial desire gone awry. Part of this mastery is found in the models of narration and reading that various characters provide. Moll and, in turn, the editor and reader learn narrative techniques through observation, and models of good and bad reading are produced as a result of these observations. When a character performs a "bad reading" of an event, certain terrible circumstances follow that provide moral directives and models of interpretation. At the same time, t he ambiguous statement of moral purpose that undergirds everything represented in the work is unsettling because not every adversity Moll encounters is conscious: what moral is to be gained from those events of Moll's life that seem accidental? The editor makes a lengthy promise to his readers that every aspect of the story carries with it a moral lesson (p. 5), but the editor does not explicitly mention the episodes of incest, nor does he deliver on his promise where incest is concerned. This absence shows the critical reader that incest is an act in excess of the power and mastery of language and interpretation that either the editor or his reader have to contain. The excess of incest explains the editor's extreme recuperative measures and their inevitable failure.

WHAT DOES A READER WANT?

The claims that I have made about the editor's rhetorical mastery apply only to his approach to his constructed reader in the preface and the claims he makes about Moll. In fact, his relationship to the original memorandums is much more complex than simple dominance. It must be remembered that at one point the editor himself played the role of reader to Moll's rhetorical authority and much of the ambiguity and irony of the text is the result of the inability of the critical reader to determine where one voice is separate from another, where the lines of influence begin and end, or where control can be unquestioningly identified.[7] Ultimately, whose words are whose is an irresolvable conundrum, but the state of confusion that results does explain why the editor chooses not to censor the narrative of incest: the incestuous desires and their implications master him.

The editor adopts a variety of narrative techniques from the memorandums that he employs against Moll and, in turn, the reader. Moll's early experience of language, the process of storytelling, and sexuality are important because what happens early in her life forms a template for her later experiences, especially in regard to incest.

When a quasi-incestuous relationship forms with the two brothers, the narrative that represents this relationship is threatened: what is at stake is—in the language of the novel—being "undone," an action akin to narrative death. Because of the threat, it is necessary to explore how Moll learns to understand the value of language and the narratives of others. During her midteens she learns to tell a persuasive story by example, the same kind of story that she and the editor will eventually tell in the memorandums. A parallel relationship develops between how Moll understands the story she is told by the elder brother regarding marriage and how readers are to understand their position as coerced co-author of the editor's version of Moll's story. Moll remarks that "Never poor vain Creature was so wrapt up with every part of the Story, as I was, not Considering what was before me, and how near my Ruin was at the Door; indeed I think, I rather wish'd for that Ruin, than studyed to avoid it" (p. 22). This passage serves as a warning to those readers of the novel who are, at this point, so wrapped up in the story that they are not able to see the ruin that awaits them if they are seduced by the narrative. In another way, this passage is a signal to those "vicious Readers" that the editor fears Moll is about to be seduced: the moment they have been waiting for has arrived. Moll is not able to discern the good from the bad, and so she believes "every part" that she hears without discriminating. The elder brother is aware of his listener's innocence-just as the editor plays upon his constructed reader's assumed innocence-and he manipulates the elements of his narrative to produce the desired effect. The editor learns from Moll this important narrative technique that Moll learned from the elder brother, and both will use it in turn on the readers of their stories.

This method of seduction by a story is similar both to Moll's and to the editor's writing of the narrative. Moll admits the elder brother makes his job of seduction harder than it actually has to be: "he made more Circumlocution... The Work appearing Difficult to him, he really made it so" (p. 22). The elder brother's sexual desire and enjoyment lie in delay, and both the editor and Moll seduce the reader by delaying her actual seduction: the act of telling about the elder brother telling stories is a repetition that in effect delays the telling of Moll's seduction even longer. In this sense, the elder brother's delay serves as a kind of synecdoche for the reworked narrative itself. The same kind of circumlocution the elder brother employs is used by the editor in his preface; the editor delays and extends the story of his intentions before revealing what many critics have taken as the crux of the preface, if not the entire novel: that Moll does not remain as penitent as she appears. In the body of the text, circumlocution postpones the death of narrative threatened by incest by evading and delaying its revelation.

The "long Stor(ies)" (p. 22) the elder brother tells are always ones of deception, concealment, and sexuality in the sense that it is necessary to tell a tale in order to perform the act: he "made a thousand more Preambles than he need to have done" (p. 23). The elder brother's prolongation is countered by Moll's ambiguous silences: "But- and there I stopp'd as if I left him to Guess the rest" (p. 24, emphasis mine). The elder brother fills in the gap in Moll's speech with 100 guineas now, and to be paid every year into perpetuity if she gets pregnant. The "as if" in the passage is as pregnant as her silence, and Moll never reveals what it is that she was pausing for, so the reader is left to guess along with the elder brother. The reader is invited again into the position of being interested in the process of Moll's seduction, but also into the position of being seduced by the editor's narrative of Moll's seduction. The "gap" left to be filled in the narrative by the reader is perhaps meant to be filled with a question: is the deception being performed on Moll being performed on the reader even as the deception is revealed for what it is? Moll's ambiguously empty pause is like the absence that occurs between the parenthetical acknowledgement of incest in the title page and the end of the preface, as if the editor expects the reader to fill this gap.

After Moll has sold her virtue to the elder brother, the younger brother begins to tell "a Story of the same Kind to me" (p. 24). That "kin" is the root word of "kind," and that the two words were, for a period of time, intertwined, is significant because the quasi-incestuous "same kind" mirrors Moll's quasi-incestuous relationship to the brothers.[8] The characters not only share kin, they share the same kinds of stories. Moll, in turn, begins to tell the younger brother a story structurally similar to the elder brother's seduction narrative about the various reasons why a match between them would be unacceptable (p. 25). How Moll tells the elder brother about the younger's desires is, in many ways, a duplicate of the pattern of telling stories that the elder brother has used to seduce her and, of course, the editor's reader, too. This quasi-incestuous "amorous Chain of Story" is "begun at a Distance" (p. 27), and it reveals the links in the chain of storytelling that appear in the following order: the elder brother to Moll; Moll to the younger brother; Moll to the editor through her memorandums; and the editor to the reader in his rewriting. The frames of reference created by these retellings are structurally similar to the familial ordering of generations, where each successive generation repeats, in part, the previous generation. However, the confusion that results from the frames of reference in the novel is like the confusion that incest causes in families. The method of storytelling, the links on the narrative chain, and the figurative chain itself are circuitous. They all turn back on one another, leading to the repetition without difference that is akin to incest. That the reader is implicated in the construction of the text in the ways suggested so far indicts the reader in the same system that forces Moll to act as she does; it implicates the reader in the passages about incest that are inextricably bound up with the issues of language because the prohibition of incest ensures the continuation of the paternalistic system. The reader is put into the position of reincorporating the seemingly anomalous events and situations of Moll's life—just as the editor has attempted recuperation prior to the fictional reader's consumption of the text—so that Moll's narrative appeals to the "Palate" (p. 4) of the "moral" reading public.

Because the burden of authorship is constantly and simultaneously being evaded and asserted by the editor, a complex conflation of roles eerily similar to the incestuous conflation of the hierarchical family structure occurs. If authorship is figurative fatherhood, then who is responsible for incest becomes an alarming question to pose.[9] The combined voices of Moll and the editor defer responsibility, at least rhetorically, leaving the reader in the uncomfortable position of complicity with an incestuous act (accidental or not): the absence of a patronym wreaks havoc throughout Moll's story, leaving the reader to sort out the pieces.[10]

The strange conflation of the family structure poses problems for the continuation of Moll's life with the family. Moll says that the family of the two brothers "used me with so much Tenderness, as if I had been one of their own Children" (p. 27). To have a relationship with the elder brother is a kind of incest because of her figurative family position, and to have a relationship with the younger brother is—in Moll's terms—to commit "Adultery and Incest" (p. 47). This figural familiarity, although not recognized by the elder brother, fills Moll with a kind of loathing and aversion toward the younger brother that is similar to the biological incest that occurs later in the novel.[11] Just as the elder brother suggests that Moll marry the younger brother, her brother/husband suggests that they stay married and that they continue to deceive the rest of the world about their incestuous act. Moll is unable to speak after the elder brother makes the suggestion that everything "we have done may be wrapt up in an eternal Silence" (p. 31). This silence prefigures her biological brother's muteness, her mother's advice, and the potential end of the narrative that the consanguine incest threatens. The horror of even the figural act puts an end to speech and, therefore, threatens the end of the storytelling.

By conceding to the elder brother's proposal for a kind of platonic incest and adultery, Moll is treated very well by the younger brother, and is loved by him as much "as any Woman could desire," but the elder brother "being so always in my sight, at least, while we were in the Country, was a continual Snare to me; and I never was in Bed with my Husband, but I wish'd my self in the Arms of his Brother; and tho' his Brother never offer'd me the least Kindness that way, after our Marriage, but carried it just as a Brother ought to do; yet, it was impossible for me to do so to him: In short, I committed Adultery and Incest with him every Day in my Desires, which without doubt, was as effectually Criminal in the Nature of the Guilt, as if I had actually done it" (p. 47). The conflation of family relations in this passage reveals desire's power to usurp, to "snare," language and narrative, especially when the desire is for a taboo object. Moll directs her "kindness" toward an incestuous and adulterous object here (a now obscure definition of kindness is "kinship"), but when consanguine incest happens later in her life, she claims she is repulsed by it.[12] The irony is that her biological brother is more of a stranger to her than the elder brother because she spent many years living with them as "one of their own children." She never has a similar experience with her biological brother. Moll effectually feels like a family member, and her attitude is enough to produce incestuous feelings. Whereas the episode with the elder and younger brother seems like incest to Moll, what she confronts during her stay in the colony has much more serious emotional consequences, and these episodes reveal what is at stake for narrative, language, and the relationship between editor, reader, and Moll.

THE NARRATIVE SNARE OF INCEST

After Moll Flanders hears the narrative of her mother's life, but before her mother realizes the ramifications of her narrative, Moll laments: "O had the Story never been told me, all had been well; it had been no Crime to have lain with my Husband, since as to his being my Relation, I had known nothing of it" (p. 70). The most tragic moment in Moll's life occurs because Moll's mother assumes that she has nothing to fear from telling her story. Moll's mother's story produces the crux of Moll's; its ramifications ripple outward, affecting what has come before and after its telling, including the editor's approach to Moll's narrative and to his reader. The narrative of incest in Moll's original memorandums operates as a series of events that are in excess of the editor's power to explain and contain Moll's life story. As a result, the figural relationships that the editor creates are an attempt to reverse the genesis and chronology of the story so that it conforms to the bourgeois family norm rather than the structural disarray of incest. Opposed to the original order of telling (Moll's mother-Moll-editor—reader), the preface attempts to reverse the temporal order to introduce a patronymic grammar to the form of the narrative. The editor tries to reframe for readers a story they may wish they were never told because, as Moll's mother reveals, the stakes are quite high: the life and death of the narrative itself.

After Moll's mother learns the significance of her own narration, she warns Moll to "bury the whole thing entirely," to "lie as we [Moll and her brother] us'd to do," and to "let the whole matter remain a secret as close as Death; for Child, says she, we are both undone if it comes out" (p. 77). Incest threatens symbolic death for the characters and the narrative, but to remain silent about it also equals death. The very structural ordering of the family will be "undone" if the story is told. At the same time, the exact opposite of this principle is present: the telling and, especially, the retelling, of incest engenders much of the narrative and counters its undoing. Moll wants to speak "that [she] might be prevail'd with to bring out that which indeed it was like Death to [her] to conceal" (p. 80). Keeping "a secret as close as death" and a secret that is "like death . . . to conceal" is not as diametrically opposed a proposition as it may seem. The passages fit together because they suggest that narrative is co-extensive with life and death: there is no life or death without narrative.

The tension between these narrative desires both undergirds and undermines dominant fictions about the stability of family structures. Moll thwarts her mother's attempt to get involved in the married couple's dispute by stating "that the Reason and Mystery of the whole matter lay in herself [the mother]" (p. 75): the maternal body breeds social riddles in the form of children. How each member of a culture is or is not related to one another is important to the stories that the culture tells itself and to the continuation of the systems that support the social structure. At this historical moment, children understand who their family is through proximity and by being told; without this closeness and family narrative they would all be, in a manner of speaking, strangers, riddled by and with "bad grammar." The presence of the patronym is what ought to solve maternal riddles, but "confusion in the generational code (incest) is parallel to confusion in the linguistic code."[13] Because of the missing father, mot her, and, scheme of "correct" patronymic relations when Moll is young, her blood relationships are unsolved riddles until, to her horror, she hears the story—a linguistic and generational code—she wishes she had never been told.

Moll's mother begins to show symptoms that signify the impact that incest has on the telling of stories. Moll's mother "was not inclin'd to believe the Story, or to remember the Particulars, for she immediately foresaw the Confusions that must follow in the Family upon it" (pp. 75—6). The potential destruction of the family narrative affects how the mother "reads" Moll's narrative. Almost in proportion to what Moll reveals, the mother symptomatically attempts to conceal. If the story cannot be proven, then the fiction can continue. And yet the nature of the relationship is so disturbing to the characters that even the mother's denial cannot completely overcome her horror: "why we are all undone! . . . Confusion and Destraction forever! miserable Family! what will become of us? what is to be said? what is to be done?" (p. 76). The "undoing" that is the revelation of incest has brought a state of confused "decay" and "ruin" that has "destroyed" the family narrative by undoing (through overdoing) the family relationships.

Because incest produces the inability to properly distinguish relations, the resulting confusion disrupts traditional systems of order and signification, making them unreadable. In other words, the relationships of kinship and, ostensibly, of love between brother, sister, mother, and children are in direct conflict with the relationships of feeling between husband, wife, mother-in-law, and children. What the attempts to separate relationships underscore is that when Moll conceals most personal names throughout the novel, both Moll and the reader are forced to refer to the characters by their personal relationships to one another, which in the case of her marriage to her brother/husband are always already present in the wrong combinations; when referred to as mother, the mother is always also a mother-in-law, and the brother is simultaneously always a brother, a husband, and a son, each overdone in its own way. When Moil discusses the risks in revealing the incest, she states that what she risks is the loss o f her brother: "who would have been neither a Husband or a Brother" (p. 71), an impossible proposition. Incest suggests the undoing of the family narrative because the family no longer descends in the "natural" way.

The mother attempts to keep the story by retelling the stories of her life "with Alterations and Omissions" (p. 76). The mother's symptoms remarkably resemble the editor's tactics in the preface. Yet the repetition of the incest story preserves the life of the narrative even as the collapsing content of the narrative threatens its own demise. The reason she retells a story she wishes she had never been told is to keep the narrative alive in the face of its impending death. This contradictory movement informs Moil's entire story. The editor's and reader's roles as co-authors not only make them complicit, but allow the entire narrative process itself to exist. The discursive presence of incest puts the social function of narrative at cross-purposes to itself, which in turn reveals a paradox inherent in incest. Narratives are based on the (re)telling of information; the secret of incest threatens the narrative if it is kept a secret, but it also threatens the narrative if it is told, because what traditionally drives narrative is the conventional family structure of heterosexuality, marriage, and reproduction, and these narratives of structure are jeopardized when incest is present.[14] Her participation in the incestuous relationship causes Moll to hover between mutually exclusive categories. Her attempts to reconcile the two states of being are made possible by incest's ability to confuse taboo and transgression and narrative life and death. Prolonging this resolution, Moll waits three years to tell her brother/husband about the incest. She reveals a little bit at a time, which has the now familiar characteristic of circuitously and seductively delaying the narrative that must come to an end. Moil's refusal to speak serves to underscore her ambivalent desire for, and in, the incestuous relationship.

For Moll, the desire and erotics of narrating the story are present in her ambivalence about ending the narrative of her marriage to her brother/husband (p. 79). The delay operates both as an extension of the "decaying" family narrative and as a kind of expression of the ambivalent desire that Moll has for the brother/husband and newfound mother: "could I have satisfied my self to have gone on with it, I believe it might have continued as long as we had continued alive together" (p. 79). The "kindest thing that I could do" is to "keep him in the dark about it" (p. 80). Acts of kindness are always loaded in this novel; in Moll's case, they are a smokescreen that conceals her feelings for kin. The moral question for Moll is the one about concealing or revealing the story more than it is about the act of incest itself. Moll is ambivalent partially because she makes the attempt to keep the family categories separate in her own mind, and she attempts to hate her brother/husband discretely as a husband as well as for being her brother; she claims that it is not the incest that causes the aversion, but the incest is only something that adds to it. This attempt at separating—of occupying the grammatical space of the conjunction between two (ir)reconcilable terms—further illustrates Moll's ambivalence toward the brother/husband: "I had no great concern about it [the incest] in point of Conscience" (p. 78). This statement reveals that the distinctions in Moll's mind are often arbitrary and fluctuating. But at the same time, "every thing added to make Cohabiting with him the most nauseous thing to me in the World" (p. 78). Every time Moll suggests that her feelings are ambivalent, she immediately reasserts a stable relationship that attempts to eliminate the possibility for ambivalence.

The editor's ambivalence about his paternity of the story is revealed through his adoption of Moll's narrative means even as he castigates the behavior that created these techniques. The confusion that results is similar to the confusion of the linguistic code that leads to incest.

The editor both denies and asserts his paternity over his narrative "child," leaving the constructed reader in the uncomfortable position of recuperating the unruly narrative. The ambiguity, indeterminacy, and undifferentiatability produced throughout the narrative because of its complex frames of reference, incestuous relationships, and moral obligations leave the reader without the option of disavowal. There is no one left to shift responsibility to, so the reader is left to reassert the patronym, which will reorder the bad grammar of this "amorous Chain of Story."

The "moral purpose" of this story is an attempt to rewrite the narrative so that the obvious pitfalls to order and narrative that the prospect of incest threatens are once again subsumed into a traditional confessional narrative, causing fear and teaching the already known moral lesson. Moll's memorandums are co-opted in the sense that "the Pen" has the last word: he has attempted to re-configure and rewrite her dangerous narrative to be more acceptable to his constructed audience. Yet Moll warns the reader that it is "very seldom that some Snare or other is not in their way" (p. 210). The reference is to thievery in London, but these snares also have relevance to the reading of the narrative itself. The reading of the direct address as symptom reveals that this technique is the product of ambivalence, or of the moral confusion resulting from incest. A snare is a textual moment that binds the reader in a variety of ways to the "amorous Chain of Story." The content of the novel is disruptive because of its representations of taboo acts, of which incest is the most central and extreme: incest ensnares more securely because the links between relations bind themselves too tightly. The reader is forced to participate vicariously in those same acts; incest is, in this sense, an amorous snare that inscribes and encircles the reader within the tenuousness of familial structures and the desire they produce.

Whereas Moll's narrative recounts her passage from ignorance to knowledge, from being constructed by to constructing through language, it is presupposed by the editor that the fictional reader ought to have already successfully traversed these dichotomies: "this Work is chiefly recommended to those who know how to Read it" (p. 4). The reader is either "vicious" or "Moral" according to the editor, but not in the naive way that Moll is either a gentlewoman or a madam. As Moll's memorandums illustrate, the world that is exemplified and made possible by paternalistic fictions is, at the same time, made untenable by incest, and this untenable proposition is present throughout the novel. For Moll, it is present in the "continual Snare" (p. 47) that is her felt incest with the brothers, and it is continually present in the conjunction that binds brother and husband together in her incestuous relationship. To what end are these untenable propositions present? Why does the editor reveal a story so potentially damaging? "The Pen" functions as a recuperative force throughout the novel. The censorship the memorandums undergo prior to publication, the preface, the direct addresses to the reader, and the models of reading that the novel contains all operate to order and reorder the "amorous Chain of Story." They shackle the reader not to the potentially destructive act of incest, but to the always recuperative act of (re)ordering incest. But the editor is aware that the fictive reader may be as unruly and unpredictable as Moll herself, and perhaps not so penitent in the end. His desire for readers is as ambivalent as his desire for Moll. The readers—"moral" or "vicious"—are closer akin to Moll than not: they amorously (un)do for one another.

NOTES

1. The epigraph comes from Maud Ellmann, *Psychoanalytic Literary Criticism* (New York: Longman, 1994), p. 16 (emphasis mine). Daniel Defoe, *Moll Flanders*, ed. Edward H. Kelly (New York: W.W. Norton, 1973). All citations of

this work will be from this edition and will appear parenthetically within the text according to page number.

2. Larry L. Langford, "Retelling Moll's Story: The Editor's Preface to Mall Flanders," *JNT* 22, 3 (Fall 1992): 164—79, 165. Langford is the one critic who foregrounds the preface and the role of the editor. My analysis differs from Langford's in my emphasis upon incest and understanding of the editor's and reader's figurative roles.

3. I am not the first to suggest irresolvability in Moll Flanders. See Homer 0. Brown, "The Displaced Self in the Novels of Daniel Defoe," *ELH* 38, 4 (Winter 1971): 562—90, 584, who calls Defoe's novels books "whose ambiguity is deep, thorough, and finally unresolvable." See Michael M. Boardman, *Defoe and the Uses of Narrative* (New Brunswick NJ: Rutgers Univ. Press, 1983): and Ian Watt, "Defoe as Novelist," in *Moll Flanders*, pp. 351—61 for grammatical explanations of this irresolvability. Also, see Maximillian E. Novak, "Defoe's 'Indifferent Monitor': The Complexity of Moll Flanders," *ECS* 3, 3 (Spring 1970): 351—65: and G.A. Starr, *Defoe and Casuistry* (Princeton: Princeton Univ. Press, 1971) for diction.

4. There is a short list of critics who share the view that the incest in the novel is an important episode. See Douglas Brooks, "Moll Flanders: An Interpretation," *EIC* 19, 1 (Winter 1969): 46—59: Ellen Pollak, "Mall Flanders, Incest, and the Structure of Exchange," *ECent* 30, 1 (Spring 1989): 3—22: and Ann Louise Kibbie, "Monstrous Generation: The Birth of Capital in Defoe's Mall Flanders and Roxana," *PMLA* 110, 5 (October 1995): 1023—34.

5. Langford, p. 170.

6. Langford, p. 171.

7. Nearly every critic discusses Moll's unique voice. See Starr and Watt for overviews of the issue.

8. OED, 2d edn., s.v. "Kind," I, la.

9. Edward W. Said, *Beginnings: Intention and Method* (New York: Columbia Univ. Press, 1975).

10. Although beyond the scope of this essay, Starr argues compellingly for casuistry's influence upon Issues of responsibility in the novel.

11. A number of critics see the episode with the elder and younger brother as prefiguring the episode with Mall's biological brother. See the studies by Brooks, p.48; Starr, p. 121; and David Blewett, *Defoe's Art of Fiction "Robinson Crusoe," "Mall Flanders," "Colonel Jack" and "Roxana"* (Toronto: Univ. of Toronto Press, 1979), p. 61.

12. See W. Daniel Wilson, "Science, Natural Law, and Unwitting Sibling Incest in Eighteenth-Century Literature," *SECC* 13 (1984): 249—70.

13. Charles Segal, *Interpreting Greek Tragedy: Myth. Poetry, Text* (Ithaca: Cornell Univ. Press. 1986), p. 68.

14. Teresa de Lauretis, *Alice Doesn't: Feminism, Semiotics, Cinema* (Bloomington: Indiana Univ. Press, 1984).

Index

□□□